Additional praise for *The Islamic Jesus*

"In this highly readable and provocative book, Mustafa Akyol establishes the unique role played by Jesus within the Islamic tradition. Most importantly, Akyol turns radical revisionist arguments on their head to make the compelling case that Jesus' life, when properly understood, confirms the Islamic belief that there is no inherent contradiction between the Biblical and Qur'anic worldviews. From this vantage point, Jesus does not divide the Abrahamic religions but reconciles them, a message much needed in our divisive times."

—Asma Afsaruddin, Professor of Islamic Studies,
Indiana University

"Anyone interested in the deeper relationship between Judaism, Christianity, and Islam will learn much from Mustafa Akyol's thoughtful, clearly written, and well researched analysis of how Jewish beliefs and practices carried over into Christianity. Christian themes were preserved by some Jewish groups, and both, but especially Christianity, were received in Islam. Drawing upon accepted Christian scriptures as well as lesser known apocryphal writings and related sources, Akyol makes a compelling case for recognizing more common ground among the three faiths than has been heretofore acknowledged. His compelling book is a must read for friends and foes of the Children of Abraham theme."

—Charles Butterworth, Emeritus Professor,
Department of Government and Politics, University of Maryland

"*The Islamic Jesus* is a learned and thought-provoking exploration of the figure of Jesus in Islam. Mustafa Akyol develops a measured and distinctive argument of how the Islamic understanding of Jesus is connected to Judaism and Christianity. At the same time, he challenges readers to consider how earlier religious controversies, and the figure of Jesus himself, might offer guidance for Islam today."

—Gabriel Said Reynolds, Professor of Islamic Studies and
Theology, University of Notre Dame

"*The Islamic Jesus* is a read worth the consideration of those from both the Biblically based faith tradition and the Qur'anic based faith tradition who are serious about their faith. Akyol's focus on the message of the Christ rather than on the nature of the Christ is a helpful focus towards interaction which can benefit all."

—Jerald Whitehouse, former Director,
Global Center for Adventist Muslim Relations of the
General Conference of Seventh-day Adventists

THE
ISLAMIC JESUS

---◆---

How the King of the Jews Became

a Prophet of the Muslims

MUSTAFA AKYOL

St. Martin's Press

New York

THE ISLAMIC JESUS. Copyright © 2017 by Mustafa Akyol. All rights reserved. Printed in
the United States of America. For information, address St. Martin's Press, 175 Fifth Ave-
nue, New York, N.Y. 10010.

www.stmartins.com

Library of Congress Cataloging-in-Publication Data

Names: Akyol, Mustafa, 1972- author.
Title: The Islamic Jesus : how the king of the Jews became a prophet of the
    Muslims / Mustafa Akyol.
Description: First [edition]. | New York : St. Martins Press, 2017. | Includes
    bibliographical references and index.
Identifiers: LCCN 2016038747| ISBN 9781250088697 (hardcover) |
    ISBN 9781250088703 (e-book)
Subjects: LCSH: Jesus Christ—Islamic interpretations. | Islam—History. | Islam—
    Relations—Christianity. | Islam—Relations—Judaism. | Christianity and other
    religions—Islam. | Judaism—Relations—Islam.
Classification: LCC BP172 .A436 2017 | DDC 297.2/465—dc23
LC record available at https://lccn.loc.gov/2016038747

Our books may be purchased in bulk for promotional, educational, or business use. Please
contact your local bookseller or the Macmillan Corporate and Premium Sales Department
at 1-800-221-7945, extension 5442, or by e-mail at MacmillanSpecialMarkets@macmillan
.com.

First Edition: February 2017

10 9 8 7 6 5 4 3 2 1

For Riada, the love of my life

What Mahometans believe concerning Christ and his doctrine were [not] the inventions of Mahomet . . . but they were as old as the time of the Apostles, having been the sentiments of whole Sects or Churches.

—John Toland, *Nazarenus: Or Jewish, Gentile, and Mahometan Christianity*, London, 1718

CONTENTS

THE
ISLAMIC JESUS

MEETING JAMES

James can serve as a desperately needed "missing link" between the children of Abraham.

—Jeffrey J. Bütz, scholar of religion, Lutheran minister[1]

IT WAS ONE OF THE EARLY DAYS OF THE THIRD MILLENNIUM after Christ. I was walking on the busiest street of my home city, Istanbul—also known as Constantinople—to meet an old friend at an ever-busy cafe. As usual, the street, named İstiklal, which means "Independence," was swarmed by not only thousands of urbanites and tourists but also various political activists.

First, I saw the communists. They were wearing red shirts on which large yellow letters spelled the acronyms of the specific brand of the "people's party" that they supported. One of them handed me a flyer about the glory of the impending proletarian revolution. I took it politely, only to put it in my pocket intending to keep it until I saw the next recycling bin. Then I saw a group of Kurdish mothers sitting on the street mourning for their sons who, most probably, had been victims of Turkey's then two-decades-old and infamously draconian campaign of "counterterrorism."

Walking a little farther, I saw another group that looked less familiar to my eyes. One of them, a notably smiling young man, approached me politely and asked:

"Hello, sir, have you ever read the Good News?"

While I was still in the "Well, er" moment, he deftly handed me a small book entitled *İncil*, which is the Turkish word for gospel.

"Hmm, I see," I silently said to myself. These were the Christian missionaries, in flesh and blood, that Turkey's ultranationalists and Islamists were obsessing about. There were a lot of rumors in the press at that time about a secret decision in the West to "Christian-ize" the Turks and then somehow conquer their homeland. Some newspapers had even written that the missionaries were funded by the CIA and were distributing hundred-dollar bills inside every Bible that they passed out.

I checked the copy in my hand. Unfortunately, there was no hundred-dollar bill. Yet still it was a valuable gift that I decided to keep. I thanked the young missionary, whose name I had then learned but would never be able to recall, and moved on for the rest of the day.

At night, before I went to sleep, I opened my copy of the Good News and began reading it. It really sucked me in. I think I finished the Gospel of Matthew that very night. In the next couple of weeks, I read the whole New Testament, gospel after gospel, epistle after epistle, with great attention. Most of the teachings, especially those of Jesus, struck me with their admirable passion, devotion, sincer-ity, and godliness. As a faithful Muslim—and thus a believer in the all-compassionate God, the God of Abraham—I found much of the Christian scripture quite appealing and inspiring.

The only passages not to my liking were those that emphasized the divinity of Jesus—a belief that Islam's strict monotheism can never accept and, no wonder, the Qur'an explicitly condemns. To my Muslim mind, Jesus as a messenger of God was a very familiar, appealing theme. But Jesus *as* God was anathema.

That is why, at some point during my reading, I decided to use a method: I began underlining the passages of the New Testament that I liked the most with a blue pen while underlining the passages that I found objectionable with a red pen. It soon turned out that I had more blue lines in the gospels, especially in the first three, whereas the epistles of Paul got filled with many red lines. Paul's "christology"—a term I would learn later—was just not working for me.

Then, toward the end of the New Testament, I came to an epistle that rekindled my ambiguous affection for this book. This particular document was both full of teachings that deeply resonated with my faith and, more importantly, contained nothing that contradicted my faith. My underlining turned out to be all blue, in other words, and no red.

There were even passages in this epistle that I found strikingly similar to my own scripture, the Qur'an. I was awestruck, for example, when I read the passage below in this canonical epistle:

Come now, you who say, "Today or tomorrow let's go into this city, and spend a year there, trade, and make a profit." Whereas you don't know what your life will be like tomorrow . . . You ought to say, "If the Lord wills, we will both live, and do this or that."[2]

I was astonished because this was so similar to a Qur'anic verse that I knew well: "Never say about anything, 'I am doing that tomorrow,' without adding 'If God wills.'"[3]

I loved this epistle so much that I decided to share it with my informal Qur'anic study group—a circle of friends which, for many years, has met once every week or two to read and discuss Islam's scripture and its exegeses. As believing yet questioning Muslims, my friends were happy to listen when I said I wanted to read them a passage from the Christian Bible. They listened carefully and, as I expected, they liked what they heard.

"This is very similar to the Qur'an," one of my friends said. "And there is nothing in it which says that Jesus is the Son of God," another one noted. "Are you sure it is from the Christian Bible?"

"Yes, yes, of course," I replied. "It is from the New Testament, and it is called the Epistle of James."

"James? Who is James?" one of them asked.

In return, I asked myself: Yes, really, who was James?

A THEOLOGICAL AHA

Over the next few months, I did some research to understand who the James was whose letter I admired so much. I learned that he was known in Christian history as James the Just and that he had a very special relationship with Jesus: he was, as suggested by a plain reading of the New Testament, his very brother. For after the virgin birth, Jesus' mother, Mary, had married a man named Joseph and they apparently had other children, James being the eldest.[4]

I also learned that, despite James's striking connection to Jesus, his letter, a short, three-page document buried toward the final pages of the New Testament, has not been a popular text in Christian history. I read that when early Christians decided on the canon of their scripture in the fourth century, the Epistle of James was regarded as a "disputed book," one that was accepted by church fathers only reluctantly.[5] In later centuries, some prominent Christian figures continued to cast doubt on the letter, prominent among them Martin Luther, who openly wrote against it, calling it a "straw-epistle."

I realized then that I was onto something by noticing these oddities about the Epistle of James—its implicit divergence from mainstream Christianity and its curious resonance with my Muslim faith. But I had no time to dig deeper. I was trying to finish a master's thesis on something totally different—Turkey's Kurdish question—and I would be kept busy by other political and religious writings that followed in the years ahead. Yet, in the meantime, I kept reading about early Christianity. And I kept James, and his elder brother Jesus, in mind.

It was about a decade after my first encounter with the New Testament that I decided to put more thought and effort into this curious matter. I acquired and read dozens of academic books on early Christianity and the historical Jesus. All these works suffered the strokes of my blue and red pens, but probably no passage captured my attention—and made up my aha moment—more than one by James D. Tabor, a scholar of Christian origins and ancient Judaism:

> There are two completely separate and distinct Christianities embedded in the New Testament. One is quite familiar and became the version of the Christian faith known to billions over the past two millennia. Its main proponent was the apostle Paul. The other has been largely forgotten and by the turn of the first century A.D. had been effectively marginalized and suppressed by the other . . . Its champion was none other than James the brother of Jesus.[6]

Of course, as I also noticed in my research, not every expert on early Christianity agrees with this provocative thesis. Traditional Christian scholars have long offered a more reconciliatory take on James and Paul, suggesting that the two apostles espoused not different doctrines, but only different emphases. On the other hand, since the late 1970s, some scholars have developed a "new perspective" on Paul, arguing that Paul's interpretations and reformations were not as radically different from those of James as some Christians later assumed.[7]

Yet still, to me, the divergence between the teachings of James and Paul were unmistakable. Even more telling was the historical fact that the two men had become the orginators of two different branches of Christianity. James, who assumed the leadership of the Jesus movement in Jerusalem right after Jesus' crucifixion, was the pillar of "Jewish Christianity." This was quite different from the Pauline Christianity that spread mainly among Gentiles in the Greco-Roman world, and gradually became the globe's most popular religion, which we all know today. While Paul's line had amazing success, its Jewish counterpart vanished in history, only finding a place for itself as one of the many "heresies" of the faith.

Jewish Christians, despite being devoted followers of Jesus, were still Jews—in practice, doctrine, and mind-set. In other words, they still observed the Jewish Law, sought their salvation in the Jewish way, and believed in concepts such as God and Messiah in the Jewish sense. Especially in three aspects of their faith, they were quite different from the other Christians:

- For them, God was strictly "one," and not triune.
- Jesus was the promised Messiah of the Jews, but not divine.
- Men could be saved only by two things: faith in God *and* good deeds.

When I became aware of these aspects of the Jewish Christian faith, once again, the parallelism with Islam left me bewildered. The Qur'an, proclaimed by Prophet Muhammad almost six centuries after James, also taught that:

- God is strictly "one," and not triune.
- Jesus is the promised Messiah of the Jews, but not divine.
- Men can be saved only by two things: faith in God *and* good deeds.

Hence I kept asking myself: Is all this mere coincidence? Or is it rather too much coincidence?

CURIOUS CONNECTIONS

At this point, it might surprise some readers that the scripture of Islam says anything about Jesus. (Well, no one can blame them, for the content of the Qur'an is often misreported in our day and age. It does *not* decree, for example, that suicide bombers will get "seventy-two virgins" in heaven, or adulteresses should be stoned to death, or apostates from Islam should be killed.[8])

But, yes, the Qur'an says a lot of things about Jesus—and his mother, Mary. Its sura, or chapter, 19, a pretty long one, is even named "Mary," and gives a detailed account of the virgin birth. In various chapters of the Qur'an, the teachings and the miracles of Jesus are narrated, and Muslims are even advised to imitate the apostles.[9] Most of these Qur'anic accounts are very similar to, or at least not in contradiction to, the gospels. However, there is one key point that the Qur'an repeatedly emphasizes, presenting a clear rejection of mainstream Christianity: Jesus, like Abraham, Moses, and Muhammad himself, was a human prophet of God—but certainly not himself God. He deserves to be praised, admired, and followed, but not worshiped as though he were divine.

Tabor, whom I quoted above, is one of the experts who noted this curious parallelism between the two seemingly unrelated faiths. "There are some rather striking connections between the research I have presented [on Jewish Christianity] . . . and the traditional beliefs of Islam," he notes at the very end of his popular book, *The Jesus Dynasty*. "The Muslim emphasis on Jesus as messianic prophet and teacher is quite parallel to . . . the book of James."[10]

Robert Eisenman, a prominent biblical scholar, historian, and archeologist, also finds it "very curious" that "the key ideology of faith and works together, associated with James in New Testament Scripture, fairly shines through the Koran."[11] Furthermore, he argues, "Muslim dietary law is also based on James' directives to overseas communities as delineated in the Book of Acts."[12]

But how is that possible? How could there be such striking connections between the theology of the Jewish followers of Jesus and the Arab followers of Muhammad? If Jewish Christians lived in and around Jerusalem during the first century AD and then vanished from history by the end of the fifth century as historians believe, how could they be linked to Islam, which appeared in early seventh-century Arabia with a new call for faith, repentance, and salvation?

In this book, I will seek to answer these questions, while also introducing the Islamic view of Jesus. What makes my work relatively easy is that both Jewish Christianity and Islam's view of Christ have been studied thoroughly by expert scholars—but often independently and as unrelated subjects. A handful of academics—most of them notably European, especially German—have noticed the connection between these seemingly unrelated stories and examined their intersection in academic books and articles as well. However, the issue has not yet been explored as comprehensively as it should be and remains largely unknown to the general public. Hence with this book, I will probe deeply into the matter, which I believe is one of the key puzzles, if not mysteries, in the history of religion.

To start to collect the pieces of the puzzle, I will first go back to the first century AD, to Palestine, to get a sense of Jesus the Jew and his earliest followers—the small community of Jewish Christians. Then I will move forward in time, to the seventh century AD, to Arabia, to see the emergence of Islam. Then I will show how these two separate stories match.

I will also look more carefully into what the Qur'an teaches about Jesus, and about his mother Mary, and how these Islamic narratives resonate with Christian sources, including not just the Bible but also the Apocrypha. I will also discuss whether, according to Islamic sources, Jesus will come back to the world for the second time and what Muslims can understand today from such prophecy.

In the meantime, deep down, I will explore how the three great Abrahamic religions of our battered world, despite all the past and present tensions between them, come together at the story of this most amazing man—this Jesus of Nazareth. Whether we are Jews, Christians, or Muslims, we share either a faith followed by him, or a faith built on him, or a faith that venerates him.

CHAPTER ONE

THE KING OF THE JEWS

The first Christian preachers did not draw the conclusion that [Jesus] was himself God, but that he was a man chosen by God for a special role.

—John Hick, prominent theologian[1]

ON APRIL 3, AD 33—OR PERHAPS THREE YEARS BEFORE THAT—a quite dramatic event took place in the holy city of Jerusalem.[2] The colossal Roman Empire, which then dominated large parts of what we call Europe and the Middle East today, executed an unusual Jewish preacher from Galilee, a region to the north of Jerusalem. This thirty-something-year-old man's name was Yeshua, which was thought to mean "savior" in his own Aramaic language (the Hebrew form is *Yeshua* or *Yehoshua*). He must have been a troublemaker, at least in the eyes of the authorities, for he was arrested, tried, and then given the cruel punishment that the Romans decreed for the enemies of the state: crucifixion.

The cruelty in fact began with Roman soldiers flogging Yeshua and then making him carry his own cross uphill. Then the victim was nailed by his hands and feet and left to die in agonizing pain. Once all these technicalities were over, the soldiers also put an inscription over his head:

"Yeshua of Nazareth, the King of the Jews."

Some prominent Jews who happened to be witnessing the execution objected to this title. To the Roman governor who decided upon the inscription, they said: "Do not write, 'The King of the Jews,' but, 'This man said, "I am King of the Jews." ' " The governor, with little interest in that nuance, replied: "What I have written I have written."[3]

This is, at the very least, what the collection of writings commonly known as the New Testament tells us about Yeshua—or Jesus, as his name is translated into English and as we will keep calling him. They also tell us that Jesus was not an ordinary human being, but the divine "Son of God," who existed before time and who came down to earth to "become flesh" and dwell among men. His crucifixion, we are also told, was an event with a cosmic theological meaning: Jesus died for our sins, as God offered salvation to all humankind through his sacrifice. We human beings can be saved forever only by following Jesus, for he is "the way, and the truth, and the life."[4]

Today, about 2.2 billion people on earth believe in more or less what I summarized in the paragraph above. They are called Christians. I am not one of them, but I see many things about their faith that deserve respect. Even when one does not share the theology of Christianity, one can appreciate its moral teachings on modesty, compassion, and forgiveness. Moreover, quite a few Christians put these values into practice by an abundance of acts and institutions of charity, from soup kitchens to medical missions. For sure, Christianity has had its dark episodes throughout history as well, especially when it allied with self-righteousness and brute power. But that is true for almost all religions, as we see in the dark episodes of my religion, Islam, today.

This book is not meant to be a critique of, let alone an attack on, Christianity. It is just an effort to highlight a view of Jesus that is somewhat different from the one that lies at the heart of Christians' faith—and that can have its own claim to be "historical."

By the latter term, I refer to the historical Jesus, a concept developed by Western scholars who have been engaged in the "higher criticism" of the Bible since the nineteenth century. Their idea has been to read the Old and New Testaments independent of church dogma and in the light of textual, linguistic, historical, and archeological data. Thanks to them, we now have a much more detailed knowledge about the life and times of Jesus, his early followers, and the evolution of Christianity.

This does not mean that scholars of the "historical Jesus" have been able to map out the real Jesus with pure factuality and without any subjectivity of their own. Such an objective grasp of historical truth is probably impossible—at least for us, mortal humans. No wonder the seekers of "historical Jesus" have diverged from each other, based less on different findings than on different perspectives.

So, admittedly, this chapter will present you a reading of the historical Jesus from my perspective—a Muslim one. Yet the same perspective also necessitates a self-limitation that traditional Islamic scholars turned into an intellectual custom that I happily follow: share your view, but admit, "God knows the best."

THE OPPRESSOR

The beginning of wisdom about the historical Jesus, as with any other historical figure, is to understand the world to which he was born. It was, in a nutshell, a troubled world, defined by a very unequal dichotomy: the mighty Roman Empire versus the tiny Jewish people.

Rome's occupation of the Land of Israel—Jerusalem and its surroundings, broadly called Judaea by the Romans[5]—had begun some six decades before the birth of Jesus, in 63 BC. In that year, Roman armies first crushed the Kingdom of Pontus, which was then a significant power based in central Anatolia, and took control of Syria as well. For the glorious Roman commander, Pompey, it did not take much time to move from Syria farther south, to conquer the Jews—these strange people who believed in only one God. After three months of siege, the superior Roman army took Jerusalem, with very few casualties of their own, but some twelve thousand losses on the Jewish side.

The victorious Pompey wasted no time in visiting the magnificent Temple that lay at the heart of the city, including the most sacred interior part of the Temple, the Holy of Holies. This was the chamber in which the Ark of the Covenant, which preserved the Ten Commandments given by God to Moses, was once kept, before it was lost during earlier invasions. It was so sacred that only the Jewish high priest could enter once a year, on the day of Yom Kippur, humbly barefoot and only after intense ritual purification. Yet the pagan Pompey, enacting one of the famous crosscultural encounters in world history, walked into the Holy of Holies heedlessly, only to experience one of his life's major astonishments: there was no god there! For the pagan Pompey, the idea of a god was synonymous with the image of an idol. But the God of the Jews, quite perplexingly, was totally invisible.

To his credit, Pompey actually meant no disrespect to Jews with his visit to the Temple. He, in fact, was careful not to touch the treasures in it, including the golden table, the holy candlestick, and various spices. The first-century Jewish historian Flavius Josephus, our key source for this era, noted this appreciatively in his chronicles, *Antiquities of the Jews.* "Pompey touch[ed] nothing of all this, on account of his regard to religion," he recorded, "in a manner that was worthy of his virtue."[6]

Yet for other Jews, Pompey had still defiled the Temple, putting his filthy sandals on sacred ground. In fact, the very subjugation of God's chosen people by a pagan empire was enough of an affront. There was already the memory of a worse pagan onslaught, when Judaea was invaded a century earlier by the Seleucid Empire, which "abolished" the Jewish religion and blasphemously put up an image of Zeus in the Temple. Now the even more powerful Romans had come, to rule and tax the Jews, and also to bring with them their hedonist, seductive, sinful culture.

THE OPPRESSED

The Romans soon went for the easy way of imperial rule: setting up a client king—or, more precisely, a collaborating tyrant—known in history as Herod the Great. The man was "great" for his colossal building projects, including the reconstruction of the Temple, but he was also a brutal despot. He had several members of his own family and many rabbis executed, while overtaxing his own people. For many Jews, he was a decadent sellout to the despicable Romans. (The Gospel of Matthew tells us that Herod the Great also ordered the massacre of the innocents, intending to kill the baby Jesus in order to prevent any political challenge he might pose; yet there is no other historical record of this awful incident.)

Many other peoples in Europe and around the Mediterranean had succumbed to Roman rule before. But the Jews were different. Their uncompromising monotheism was not much satisfied by the relative religious freedom the Romans offered, which basically assumed that all "gods," including the emperor himself, were equally worthy of worship. Moreover, the very belief of Jews that they were the chosen people of the one true God made it hard for them to accept being ruled by the heathen. That is why most Jews detested Roman rule and why some tried to overthrow it with a series of revolts—the last of which ended disastrously in AD 135, when Rome turned Jerusalem into a pagan city named *Aelia Capitolina* and banned the Jews from living there, initiating a centuries-long era of exile.

However, throughout the centuries the Jews spent under Roman rule, their response to that rule was not uniform. As in most other similar colonial episodes in world history, some among the subjugated people decided to accept the political reality and work with it. Others despised foreign rule, but withdrew to a more spiritual realm. And still others decided to resist the occupation, with methods that modern governments would probably call insurgency or even terrorism.

We know about this Jewish diversity under Roman rule again thanks to the writings of the historian Josephus. In his chronicles, he listed three main parties. The first comprised the aristocratic, worldly Sadducees who presided at the Temple rituals and collaborated with the Romans to preserve their wealth and power. The second party was the Torah-focused Pharisees, who disliked Roman rule and focused on legalism, or the meticulous effort to live according to the smallest points of the Jewish law. The third party was the mystical Essenes, who withdrew from the world to live an ascetic life of piety and poverty in isolated communities—one of which probably left us the famous Dead Sea Scrolls, accidentally found in the Qumran caves in the Judaean Desert in 1947.

A fourth Jewish party was born after the year AD 6, when Romans abolished the divided remnants of Herod's client kingdom and established direct Roman rule in Judaea. Among the Pharisees, a more nationalist and fervent faction openly condemned this foreign rule, declaring, "God is to be [our] only Ruler and Lord."[7] Called Zealots, they emerged as the most radical faction among first-century Jews. They even had a terrorist offshoot called *Sicarii*, or "dagger men," who carried out assassinations of both Roman officials and the "apostate" Jews who dared to collaborate with them.

Such differences among Jews were probably even more complex than what we have learned from Josephus and the New Testament. Some scholars now believe, for example, that neither the Sadducees nor the Pharisees had a uniform stance vis-à-vis Rome: there were rather collaborationist Sadducees versus opposition Sadducees, as well as collaborationist Pharisees versus opposition Pharisees. Similarly, the Pharisees who opposed Jesus and his message were probably not the totality of this party, as one could assume while reading the canonical gospels.[8] No wonder even the Book of Acts speaks of "the believers who belonged to the party of the Pharisees."[9]

THE AWAITED

Among the Jews who resented Roman rule, there was not only discontent but also hope. God's chosen people had been persecuted before, but the Lord did not leave them alone. He sent Moses to liberate them from Pharaoh's cruel reign, as He raised David to establish a Jewish kingdom in the face of hostile pagans. Now, many Jews believed, God would save them again by sending a savior from the bloodline of David—someone called the Messiah.

The term literally meant "the anointed one," for it was custom in ancient Israel to bless kings or the high priests of the Temple by anointing their heads with holy oil. The Jewish scripture did not explicitly promise the Messiah, but it included some implicit references to him, and the idea had become quite established among first-century Jews. According to this belief, at the Jews' darkest hour, the Messiah, a son of David, would appear, to unite Jews and save them from foreign bondage, give them a glorious kingdom, and initiate a global era of peace and justice.

No wonder several messiah-wannabes appeared during the Roman rule over Judaea. One was Judas of Galilee, the very founder of the party of Zealots, who led an armed rebellion against the Romans in the year AD 6. He had proclaimed "a republic recognizing God alone as king and ruler," or a perfect theocracy, as our modern political science would call it.[10] But the Romans easily crushed the revolt and Judas perished. Two of his sons, Jacob and Simon, were crucified by the Roman authorities some four decades later for their ongoing sedition. Judas's grandson, Menahem, continued the resistance as a leader of the *Sicarii*, and even ostentatiously marched on Jerusalem as the Messiah in AD 66—only to be killed by another Zealot leader in an intraparty struggle. Simon of Perea, another rebel leader who plundered Herod's palace in Jericho, was captured by Romans and beheaded in 4 BC. His contemporary Athronges, who was a shepherd just like King David, also led an attack against

Roman and Herodian armies, only to be devastated. The First Jewish-Roman War of AD 66–73 also had its messianic pretender, named Simon bar Giora, or Simon, son of Giora, who was defeated, taken to the city of Rome, and executed by being thrown from a rock near the Temple of Jupiter. Finally, the most famous Jewish rebel of all, Simon bar Kokhba, who launched the final Jewish rebellion against Rome in AD 132 and established an independent state that lasted three years, was also hailed as the Messiah.

Jesus of Nazareth was born into such an agitated world. He, too, was hailed by his followers as the Messiah—and later as *Christós*, the Greek word for the same term. Moreover, Jesus ended up being crucified, which was a punishment the Romans deemed fit for rebels. These two simple facts have led some scholars of the historical Jesus to suggest that he was nothing more than yet another failed militant rebel against Roman rule. Jesus of Nazareth, in this view, was just another Judas of Galilee or Simon bar Kokhba, who aspired to become "the king of the Jews" through an armed campaign against the oppressors of the Jews.

This view, however, is not persuasive to me nor is it what the Islamic tradition suggests about Jesus.[11] For one thing, imagining Jesus as just a militant Jewish rebel—say, a Zealot—leaves us with a major question: Why did all other messiah-wannabes of first-century Judaism fade in history, while Jesus' followers persisted as a religious community and ultimately formed the world's largest religion? Why do billions of believers in churches across the world today pray not in the name of Judas of Galilee or Simon bar Kokhba, but in the name of Jesus of Nazareth?

The New Testament, which is the basic source that gives us a detailed narrative of who Jesus was, suggests an answer to this key question. Even if Jesus' mission did include a political stance against Rome, and even if such a stance was played down by writers of the gospels in order to present their creed to Roman authorities as docile and harmless, as some argued, that political stance could not be the only definitive aspect of this peculiar Nazarene. All four gospels in the New Testament—and the "sayings" gospel that preceded them, which we will examine later—indicate that Jesus was intensely interested in something that is not directly political: reviving and reforming the faith of his people. The same sources also tell us that he was a wonder-worker, who healed the sick, raised the dead, and turned water into wine. Although our modern minds may be prone to reinterpret such miracles in less literal, and more naturalistic, terms, they still indicate that Jesus' contemporaries saw him as something more than an armed insurgent. All that powerful teaching and extraordinary work must be why Jesus "made a lasting impact on his disciples," and the impact "resonated down through history."[12]

In other words, even if Jesus' mission included a political aspect as well, it was also intensely religious—even miraculous. Notably, a notion of such a spiritual Messiah, who would conquer Israel's enemies through "the word of his mouth," already existed among Jews, as we see in the *Psalms of Solomon*, a nonbiblical Jewish text dating from the first century BC. Here, the "Lord Messiah" was defined as "the son of David," who would save Jews from the Gentile yoke without a military conquest, for he would be "powerful in the holy spirit" and strengthened by "wisdom and understanding." This Messiah would especially revive the piety of Jews themselves, because the Roman occupation was nothing but a punishment for the unrighteousness of the rulers and people of Israel. He would "faithfully and righteously shepherd the Lord's flock," and would make sure that "there will be no arrogance among them."[13]

Yet there was still something distinct about this spiritual Messiah, which needs to be contrasted with the later Christian notions, a point we will soon investigate more deeply: he was "sinless and powerful," as a Christian study of the New Testament notes, but still "a human rather than a supernatural figure, God's agent but not a divine being."[14]

Who wrote the *Psalms of Solomon* and who followed it? Scholars are divided on the answer, as some point to the legalist Pharisees and others to the mystical Essenes.[15] Moreover, some of the same scholars jump to a conclusion from this precedent and argue that since Jesus arguably fit into the expectations of such communities— a spiritual and eschatological Messiah—he must have been one of them.[16] A. N. Wilson, a British writer and a Christian turned skeptic, was wise to reject such tempting simplifications in his beautifully written 1992 biography of Jesus. "For the last hundred years, there has been no shortage of books attempting to show," he wrote, "[that Jesus] might have chosen to ally himself to one of the existent causes, sects or groups available to him in his day." Hence, he added:

> We have read of Jesus the revolutionary, Jesus the Zealot, Jesus the Essene, Jesus of the supporter of the Pharisees. All these ideas have the vice of simplicity. They "make sense" of Jesus, and the only evidence which we possess in the Gospels would suggest that his contemporaries found it impossible to make sense of him; which is why they accused him of being mad, or possessed by the Devil.[17]

Indeed, the reason why Jesus' Way—as it was called by his earliest followers—outlived and overshadowed all other parties and movements of his time must have been something other than mere luck. Most probably, while this Way had a place and purpose within the drama of the Jews of the first century, it also had a message that went well beyond its historical context and appealed to the timeless aspirations of humanity.

To discover that message, we have to seriously read the Good News, or the gospels, about Jesus. Not at face value, necessarily, but still seriously.

READING THE GOSPELS

When you begin to read the New Testament, you begin with the Gospel of Matthew. And it begins by giving us a long genealogy of "Jesus Christ, the son of David, the son of Abraham." Jesus' connection to David is highlighted, and for an obvious reason: the Messiah was supposed to come from the bloodline of King David.

Yet King David was born in Bethlehem, a town just a few miles south of Jerusalem. Jesus, on the other hand, was from Nazareth: a small hill village in the rural and agricultural district of Galilee, some ninety miles north of Jerusalem. Could this have presented a challenge to his connection with David? It probably would have. Indeed the fourth gospel in the New Testament, John, informs us that Jesus' messianic claim was ridiculed precisely because he was not from Bethlehem. Accordingly, Philip, who had just become a disciple of Jesus, tried to convince another one, Nathanael, telling him: "We have found him of whom Moses in the law and also the prophets wrote." In return, Nathanael suspiciously asked: "Can anything good come from Nazareth?"[18]

No wonder that two of the four gospels in the New Testament, Matthew and Luke, offer a solution to this problem by arguing that, although Jesus was from Nazareth, he was actually born in Bethlehem. However, the stories they offer are quite different from each other and really hard to reconcile.[19] Moreover, the one that Luke offers is a bit incredible itself.

Here is why. Luke's explanation of how Jesus was born in Bethlehem is centered around a Roman census held at that time and a compulsory road trip. "In those days a decree went out from Caesar Augustus that all the world should be enrolled," Luke explains, "and all went to be enrolled, each to his own city."[20] Then Luke tells us that Jesus' family, at the time when Mary was pregnant, traveled from Nazareth to Bethlehem just to be registered in the latter town. Then, "in case his readers may have missed the point," as Reza Aslan rightly emphasized, Luke tells us why Jesus' connection to Bethlehem, the town of David, is so important: Jesus "belonged to the house and the lineage of David."[21]

However, historical facts are a bit more complicated than this religious truth. In fact, we learn from Roman records that there was indeed a census in the year 6 BC. Yet it was held not in "all the world," but only in Roman-controlled Judaea, which did include Je-rusalem and Bethlehem, but not Galilee, where Nazareth was. Second, in Roman records there is no mention of people going to their birthplaces to be registered, for the census was about taxes and what mattered was where people lived. Third, it is really incredible to believe that hundreds of thousands of people would take road trips from one city to another with all their family and wait there until some Roman official appeared to register them on paper. That would be unthinkable even in our highly organized and wildly mo-bile modern world. That is why Luke's story of Jesus traveling in his mother's womb from Nazareth to Bethlehem, just to be born there, is seen by most historians as mythical—if not even "pre-posterous."[22]

In more practical terms, does this mean that Luke—or the au-thor who is known to us as Luke—was lying to us? Not necessarily. He was perhaps rather seeing facts, and interpreting them, through the eyes of faith. For people of the ancient world, facts and faith were not clearly separated as in our modern categories, as neither were history and prophecy. The author of Luke, who is believed to be a companion of Apostle Paul, whom we shall properly meet later, wrote his gospel some eight or nine decades after the birth of Jesus. Looking back, he possibly interpreted historical facts according to his powerful beliefs about Jesus. As Messiah, Jesus should have been born in Bethlehem, but he was from Nazareth. But, wait, there was an unusual Roman census right around the time he was born. So, the Lord's plan must have worked through that scheme to bring the unborn Messiah to where he was supposed to be born.

When reading the gospels, we should keep in mind the im-pact of such faith-based reporting by the authors. (The same thing should be kept in mind when studying other reported traditions, such as the hadiths, or sayings, attributed to the Prophet Muhammad as well.) In that way, we can both learn a lot from the gospels and also avoid looking at history from only within the subjective lens of their particular theology.

THE NAZARENE

Wherever he was really born, Jesus was born of Mary, a Galilean Jewish woman whose name would be Mariam or Maryam in her native tongue. Jesus was Mary's first child, which she conceived while she was a virgin—miraculously, as we are told in the gospels, and also in the Qur'an, as we shall see later. Yet when Mary became pregnant, she was already betrothed to a man named Joseph, whom she married later. After Jesus, the couple seems to have had four other sons. The eldest was James, whom we met in the Introduction, and to whom we will return again. The others were Joseph, Judas, and Simon. The gospels also mention the daughters of the family, but not by name. Sadly, at that time, as in most of human history, males were more worthy of being named and honored than females.

We know very little about these siblings of Jesus and their overall family life, mainly because the gospels show no interest in them. In fact, there is even a tradition within Catholic Christianity—shared by some Orthodox and Protestant churches as well—that trivializes these siblings of Jesus by recasting them as his "cousins." Yet to be forced to make this interpretation, one has to believe in the "perpetual virginity of Mary," a late Christian doctrine which itself has no clear basis in the gospels.[23]

The gospels also tell us very little about Jesus' childhood. We are rather fully introduced to him when he, probably around the age of thirty, leaves Nazareth and heads to the Jordan River to be baptized by another notable figure of his time, John the Baptist. Then Jesus, after forty days in the Judaean Desert, where he averts the temptations of the devil, begins his public mission, which goes on for about two to three years. During this time, Jesus visits town after town and preaches to audience after audience. His basic message is summarized for us in the Gospel of Matthew: "Repent, for the kingdom of heaven is at hand."[24] In other words, the glorious time for which the Jews have been waiting has finally come. And what they need to do is to face their sins, soften their hearts, and reconnect with their God.

Besides his call to repentance and piety, Jesus also performs miracles. He heals demoniacs, epileptics, and paralytics, with a mere touch of his hand. He makes the blind to see and the lame to walk again. He turns water into wine and feeds thousands with just five loaves of bread and two fish. He even brings the dead back to life. No matter how literally we take these stories today, at least some people at the time of Jesus witnessed them literally, or at least they believed so.

Some of these miracles are accompanied by a notable reminder from Jesus. After making a blind man see, for example, he says, "Go; your faith has made you well."[25] Or after healing a woman who suffered from a hemorrhage for twenty years, Jesus says, "Take heart, daughter; your faith has made you well."[26] It is really worth deliberating on what this "faith" exactly was. It could not be Catholicism, Lutheranism, or, say, Southern Baptism, since such categories did not exist at time. It could not be the Nicene Creed, or any other Christian dogma, since neither a religion called "Christianity" nor its formal doctrines existed yet. For both Jesus and his people, there was only one valid faith, the faith of their father Abraham, which we commonly know today as Judaism. Jesus was a prophetic voice within this Judaic tradition, not outside of it.

Notably similar Jewish prophets had appeared before, such as Amos, Jeremiah, Hosea, and Elijah, who, at similar times of crises, warned their people about their excess of sin and inadequacy of faith. No wonder, as we read in the gospels, that the people who heard Jesus believed that he must be "Elijah, Jeremiah . . . or one of the prophets."[27] Notably, some of those former Jewish prophets had also performed stunning miracles—Moses parted the sea and Elijah even raised the dead. If one had to summarize the message of all these prophets in three simple words, it would read: "Be better Jews."[28] Jesus, who throughout his mission preached to fellow Jews and no one else, also gave the same message: Be more godly, more faithful, more virtuous Jews.

Did Jesus think that he initiated a new religion which would part ways with Judaism? A mere reading of the gospels, especially of the first three, the Synoptics (so called because Matthew, Mark, and Luke show many similarities in content and wording), do not give that impression. "Do not think that I have come to abolish the Law or the Prophets," Jesus rather tells us, "I have not come to abolish them, but to fulfill them."[29]

In *A Marginal Jew: Rethinking the Historical Jesus*, one of the most comprehensive works ever written on the topic, the American Roman Catholic priest and biblical scholar John P. Meier emphatically underlines this much-overlooked Jewishness of Jesus. "The historical Jesus is the halakic Jesus," he simply asserts, referring to the Halakha, or the body of Jewish law that derives from the Torah and oral tradition. Then he adds:

> Many American books on the historical Jesus may be dismissed out of hand: their presentation of 1st-century Judaism and especially of Jewish Law is either missing in action or so hopelessly skewed that it renders any portrait of Jesus the Jew distorted from the start. It is odd that it has taken American scholarship so long to absorb this basic insight: either one takes Jewish Law seriously and "gets it right" or one should abandon the quest for the historical Jesus entirely.[30]

However, would getting Jewish law, and Jesus' loyalty to it, right be enough to get Jesus right? If that were the only thing about him, besides his miracles, then Jesus would have been just a wondrous Pharisee. But the gospels show us that he had some serious criticisms of the Pharisees, and precisely on the matter of law. They reflect a Jesus who was both loyal to the law but also very much inclined to reinterpret it.

THE REFORMER

When I read the New Testament for the first time, as I noted in the Introduction, I was struck by the passion, devotion, and sincerity

I found in it. Particularly striking were Jesus' attitude to the Pharisees—although modern scholarship has suggested that Jesus targeted not *all* Pharisees, whose negative image in the Christian tradition might be a caricature, but only a group among them who took advantage of their authority to exploit the Jewish masses.[31] Jesus was blaming these self-righteous pietists for their obsession with the minute details of the Halakha, while neglecting moral teachings that relate to the spirit. This sounded extremely similar to attitudes I see among some contemporary self-righteous Muslim pietists, who admonish fellow believers for not fully observing the minute details of the Shariah, or Islamic law, but neglect the moral teachings that relate to the spirit.

Everything Jesus said in the passage below, for example, sounded very relevant to me and my own world of Muslim legalists:

> "But woe to you Pharisees! for you tithe mint and rue and every herb, and neglect justice and the love of God; these you ought to have done, without neglecting the others. Woe to you Pharisees! for you love the best seat in the synagogues and salutations in the market places. Woe to you! for you are like graves which are not seen, and men walk over them without knowing it." One of the lawyers answered him, "Teacher, in saying this you reproach us also." And he said, "Woe to you lawyers also! for you load men with burdens hard to bear, and you yourselves do not touch the burdens with one of your fingers."[32]

Such criticisms did not mean that Jesus was telling his fellow Jews to do away with the law. Note that, in the passage above, he lists the laws about the tithe and adds: "These you ought to have done." What Jesus opposes is not the observance of law, but stripping that observance from its spiritual meaning and, far worse, turning it into a basis for self-importance. "While claiming not to infringe or curtail the Law," the *Jewish Encyclopedia* thus rightly observes, "Jesus directed his followers to pay more attention to the intention and motive with which any act was done than to the deed itself."[33]

Was this a totally new idea in Judaism? No, not really. But Jesus emphasized this key matter probably more than another Jewish rabbi, or teacher, a term repeatedly used for him in the gospels, to the extent of calling for "a revolution in spiritual life."[34] That is probably the reason why, while his teaching was grounded in Judaism, it also offered a spiritual vision that transcended religious boundaries, to inspire souls among other God-fearers, or Gentile monotheists. Moreover, Jesus himself was probably aware that his message would transcend Judaism, as he opened the minds of his disciples toward non-Jewish people such as the Samaritans—who were actually despised by the Jews.[35]

F. E. Peters, a prominent scholar of the history of religion, also thinks that Jesus initiated a spiritual revolution leading toward "a more individual, more internal, conscience-driven morality." This means that "Jesus was grounded in the Torah, but he took spiritual wing above it."[36] However, this nuance was soon lost in a move to another extreme, just a little after Jesus' death:

> The figure is a gentle one, but to "rise above" can with remarkable ease become to "fly away from," to transcend. It is difficult to say if Jesus understood his—and others'—relationship to God as transcending the Torah, but in less than a generation, some of his followers, most notoriously Paul, when attempting to transfer Jesus' teachings to non-Jews (for whom the teachings came associated with, but different from, the Torah), were forced to concede that it did.[37]

In fact, during the transfer of Jesus' teachings to non-Jews, some other key nuances would be lost, as new meanings would be made. That is how a distinctively Jewish teaching—reformist, even revolutionary, yet still Jewish—would become the foundation of a whole new religion. In this new religion, what got reinterpreted would be not only the teaching of Jesus, but also his very self.

WHO DO PEOPLE SAY I AM?

One of the striking passages in Mark—the earliest of the four gospels, according to most experts—is the one in which Jesus asks his disciples what people think of him. It reads:

> Jesus and his disciples went on to the villages around Caesarea Philippi. On the way he asked them, "Who do people say I am?"
> They replied, "Some say John the Baptist; others say Elijah; and still others, one of the prophets."
> "But what about you?" he asked. "Who do you say I am?"
> Peter answered, "You are the Christ."
> Jesus warned them not to tell anyone about him.[38]

The first remarkable point here is that the people who heard Jesus had begun to think of him as "one of the prophets"—a very Jewish interpretation of what he was. The second point is Peter's insight: that Jesus was "the Christ"—or the Messiah, as Peter would have said in his own language. The third point is that Jesus tells Peter and others to be silent about this insight, for it must have been a dangerous thing to say out loud.

We know that it was dangerous indeed. As we have seen, in first-century Judaea, the claim to be the Messiah—the awaited King of the Jews—had strong political implications that could get one into serious trouble. No matter how "spiritual" this claim to kingship could be, the Roman authorities could take it as an expression of rebellion. Moreover, among the Jews, there could be hypocritical *dunatoi*, or powerful elites, who could betray this Messiah contender to the Romans, pretentiously insisting, "We have no king but the Caesar."[39]

Yet besides such obvious political risks, what did it exactly mean to be the Messiah? What exactly did Peter think of Jesus, when he professed him to be the awaited one? Well, Peter and the other disciples were all Jews living in a fully Jewish culture and they must have been thinking in Jewish terms. Hence, they must have understood the Messiah in the Jewish sense: the awaited redeemer of Israel. Surely, there were differences between various Jewish groups in the exact definition of the Messiah, but none of them perceived him as a divine being. In the words of the late Geza Vermes, one of the towering scholars of the historical Jesus:

> If a pollster had interrogated the men in the street in Palestine two millennia ago, asking for a definition of "Messiah," he would have heard people mumbling about the greatest Jewish king, who would defeat the Romans. The more religiously minded would have added that the Messiah would also be just and holy, and would subject all the nations to Israel and to God. In more peripheral circles, such as the Dead Sea sect, several Messiahs were expected, one royal, one priestly and possibly one prophetic.[40]

None of these Jews, however, thought of the Messiah as a divine being—a God, or God the Son, as Christianity would later define its notion of Christ. Because as a basic Jewish source emphatically notes: "The notion of an innocent, divine or semi-divine being who will sacrifice himself to save us from the consequences of our own sins is a purely Christian concept that has no basis in Jewish thought."[41]

No wonder that when Jesus entered Jerusalem triumphantly, coming down from the Mount of Olives and on the back of an ass, fulfilling an ancient Jewish prophesy about the Messiah, the disciples rejoiced and said: "Blessed is the King who comes in the name of the Lord!"[42] The King of the Jews, in other words, was not the Lord. He was the one who came in the name of the Lord.

THE END

Jesus' triumphal entry into Jerusalem, which probably took place on April 6, AD 32, was also the beginning of his end. Some in the city welcomed him, crying, "Blessed is the coming kingdom of our father David!"[43] But others were not happy with this strange Messiah who poked his finger at the whole Jewish establishment, created a turbulence at the Temple by chasing the merchants and the money-changers, and probably alarmed the Roman authorities as well given the rumor that he was really the coming King of the Jews.

Hence Jesus soon got arrested, was put on trial, and was sentenced to death. The course of events in these final days of Jesus is narrated in the gospels in detail, albeit with some confusing inconsistencies. What is most curious for our quest, though, is for what "crime" Jesus was convicted. The Synoptic Gospels tell us that after his arrest at the Garden of Gethsemane, Jesus in fact faced two stages of trial: first by the council of Jewish elders called the Sanhedrin, and then by the Roman governor Pontius Pilate. The same gospels also tell that the Sanhedrin found Jesus guilty of "blasphemy," whereas Pilate simply gave in to the demand that came from the Jews: "Crucify him!"

One wonders, however, how Jesus could really be sentenced for "blasphemy" at a Jewish court. In fact, the Gospel of Mark initially tells us, "they sought testimony against Jesus to put him to death; but they found none." Then it elaborates:

> And the high priest asked him, "Are you the Christ, the Son of the Blessed?" And Jesus said, "I am; and you will see the Son of Man seated at the right hand of Power, and coming with the clouds of heaven." And the high priest tore his garments, and said, "Why do we still need witnesses? You have heard his blasphemy."[44]

Yet there is something strange about this passage, and it is centered on the meaning of being the Christ—or the Messiah, in Jewish terms. This claim could be seen by the Sanhedrin as dangerous, arrogant, or crazy, but it could not be taken as blasphemy. Jews did expect a Messiah, and the assertion to be that person could be condemned as haughtiness, but not as an affront to God.

What about being "the Son of the Blessed," the term that we read as the definition of the Messiah in the Markan passage above? Well, if this were the way the high priest defined what it means to be the Messiah, then claiming to be that person would again not be heretical. Or, alternatively, if being "the Son of the Blessed" was a heretical claim for Jews, then the high priest would pose the question quite differently: "Are you the Christ, and do you even really dare to present yourself as the 'son' of the Blessed?"

What is also strange is that the Sanhedrin did not sentence Jesus to the punishment that the Torah decrees for blasphemers: "The one who blasphemes the name of the Lord shall surely be put to death: the congregation shall stone him to death."[45] Could that be because the Roman rule over Judaea deprived Jewish priests of the right to carry out such punishments? Well, not really, because we learn from the New Testament itself that this was not the case at all: just a few years after Jesus' crucifixion, Stephen, commonly known as the first Christian martyr, was sentenced by the same Sanhedrin for blasphemy and summarily executed by stoning.[46]

None of this means that the Sanhedrin, or at least certain members of it, would not have reasons to want to get rid of Jesus—a bold reformer who challenged the status quo, including the Jewish establishment and its vested interests.[47] But it is hard to see how they could sentence Jesus to death on the basis of Jewish law. No wonder the sentence came not from the Sanhedrin but from Pilate. Jesus was not stoned to death in the Jewish fashion, but nailed to a cross in the Roman fashion. This may not be a proof in itself that he was nothing more than a rebel against Rome. But it may be a proof that he was not a blasphemer against the Jewish God.

The gospels also tell us that three days after his crucifixion, Jesus rose from the dead, appeared to some of his disciples, and finally ascended to heaven. It is naturally a matter of faith to believe in these supernatural narratives. For the historian and the impartial observer, though, what may be more remarkable is the only non-Christian source that mentions Jesus, the Jewish historian Josephus, whom we met earlier. In his *Antiquities of the Jews*, book 18, chapter 3, he includes a paragraph that speaks of Jesus and his movement; it became famous in Christian tradition as the *Testimonium Flavianum*. However, many modern scholars think that this "testimony" has been partly "edited," and extended with interpolations, by later Christian authors. But a simpler version of the testimony was discovered in the 1970s in the works of a tenth-century Arab Christian bishop from Syria. The passage lacks the suspected "Christianizing elements" in the *Testimonium* and is thus widely considered as authentic. In it, Josephus writes:

> At this time there was a wise man who was called Jesus. And his conduct was good, and [he] was known to be virtuous. And many people from among the Jews and the other nations became his disciples. Pilate condemned him to be crucified and to die. And those who had become his disciples did not desert his discipleship. They reported that he had appeared to them three days after his crucifixion and that he was alive; accordingly, he was perhaps the Messiah concerning whom the prophets have recounted wonders.[48]

Indeed, those who became Jesus' disciples did not desert his discipleship. Moreover, others joined them, hearing the Good News and stepping into the spiritual "Kingdom of Heaven." But soon a major split would occur between these believers on the question of whether they were reformed Jews or members of a whole new religion. The first line was held by the original Jewish disciples of Jesus, whereas the latter one was held by the Gentiles who joined the movement much later. Yet, in an amazing irony of history, the first would become the last and the last would become the first.

CHAPTER TWO

THE JEWISH CHRISTIAN "HERESY"

Since they want to be both Jews and Christians, they are
neither Jews nor Christians.

—Jerome, fourth-century church father [1]

THE PASSING OF THE CHARISMATIC LEADER IS A SERIOUS CHAL-lenge to every religious movement. After the crucifixion of Jesus, his followers must have faced this challenge as well. The man who inspired them, who showed them the way, who foretold the future was now gone. What were they supposed to do? Was the mission over? Would they just go back to normal life?

Apparently, some of the closest disciples of Jesus thought so—that the mission was over and life had to go on. We learn this, incidentally, from the last chapter of the Fourth Gospel, John, which tells us that after the crucifixion of Jesus, one of the most prominent disciples, Peter, decided to return to his home district of Galilee, back to his fishing nets. We also learn that others joined him, saying, "We will go with you."[2]

Yet this is not the way the Jesus movement ended up—if it did, we would not have known about it. Rather, the followers of the crucified Messiah continued the mission, by first establishing a tight-knit community devoted to practicing and spreading the faith. This community is known in the Christian tradition as the "Jerusalem Church," which is in fact an anachronistic term, given that this community was still a Jewish movement that would probably have gathered at a "synagogue."[3]

At the center of the movement, there were the twelve key disciples of Jesus, often simply called "the Twelve." Other members were called "believers." All together, they constituted a group noted for its exemplary piety. They shared their meals, and even their money and property. They spent much of their time in prayer, in the Temple and elsewhere, and also in preaching to other Jews about the Good News. They were seeing God's miracles everywhere, whereas others jokingly suggested that they must have drunk too much wine. In the beginning, their total number was about a hundred and twenty. There were others who admired them, though. In one instance, three thousand new believers joined them, by accepting to be baptized in the name of Jesus.

We know all of these things from the document called the Acts of the Apostles, the New Testament book that comes right after the four gospels. The author of this document is widely accepted as Luke, who is also the author of the third gospel. He was a Gentile who accepted Jesus' message thanks to Paul, whose companion he had become. Had he not written the book of Acts, our knowledge of early Christianity would be much more limited.

Yet there is something strange about Luke's work. Although he gives lots of details about the post-Jesus phase of the movement, he does not tells us who assumed the leadership of the community and saved it from dissolution. Yes, the Twelve were influential, but even key members of this circle, such as Peter, had felt lost after the passing of Jesus. Someone must have taken the lead and shown the way. Someone must have become the leader.

In fact, Luke does reveal who this leader was: James, the brother of Jesus. But oddly, Luke tells almost nothing about James's life, his leadership of the community, or his teaching. In fact, James appears almost inadvertently, in relation to the real hero of the book of Acts, Paul. Once he appears in this history of the nascent Jesus movement, Paul dominates the scene so unilaterally that the Acts of the Apostles could have been rather named, some argued, the Acts of Paul.[4]

James must have been a very important figure though, for two reasons. First, after Jesus, he was the eldest male of the messianic house, in a culture where bloodline really mattered, as we know from genealogies of Jesus presented by the gospels of Matthew and Luke.[5] Second, as Acts confirms, again inadvertently, James was the ultimate authority on matters of doctrine.[6] "If we were to call any Apostle 'pope' in a primitive [Christian] hierarchy," a scholar hence rightly notes, "it would be James."[7]

Why, then, is the image of James so blurred in the book of Acts—and in fact in the whole Christian tradition?

JAMES'S WAY

James, whose original Hebrew name was Ya'akov, is also known in history as James the Just. Some of the things we know about him come from Saint Hegesippus, a Christian chronicler who lived in the second century and, notably, a Jewish convert. "James, the brother of the Lord succeeded to the government of the Church in conjunction with the apostles," Hegesippus first informed us. Then he explained why James, not someone else, was leader of the Jesus movement:

> He was called "Just" by all men from the Lord's time to ours, since many are called James, but he was holy from his mother's womb. He drank no wine or strong drink, nor did he eat flesh. No razor went upon his head; he did not anoint himself with oil, nor did he go to the baths. He alone was allowed to enter into the Place of Holiness, for he did not wear wool, but linen, and he used to enter the Temple alone, and was often found upon his bended knees, interceding for the forgiveness of the people, so that his knees

became as callused as a camel's, because of the constant impor-
tuning he did and kneeling before God and asking forgiveness for
the people.[8]

As we can see from this description, the place for prayer for
James was the Jewish Temple centered on the Holy of Holies—not a
"church" centered on the cross. For he and his followers were still
observant Jews following the Mosaic Law. They diverged from other
Jews only by accepting Jesus as the awaited Messiah. Meanwhile the
note that James did not "go to the baths" probably implied not that
he disliked hygeine, but that he abstained from Roman baths, which
had a negative image as centers of promiscuity.[9]

We know more about James thanks to his epistle, which is
considered by some scholars as the earliest document in the
whole New Testament.[10] Whether it was really written by him or
attributed to him by one of his followers has been debated, as is
the case for many other canonical books. Yet the epistle still tells
us a lot about the faith of James and the "Jerusalem Church" that
he led.[11]

The epistle begins by identifying the author: "James, a servant
of God and of the Lord Jesus Christ." But it never gets into the te-
nets of the Christian faith, as we know them today, such as the nature of Jesus, his crucifixion as atonement for humankind, or his
resurrection as a testimony to his divinity. The focus of the Epistle
of James is rather an age-old Jewish idea: devotion to God, and
steadfastness and sincerity in obeying His Law. No wonder a modern evangelical writer finds the Epistle of James, somewhat disap-
provingly, "a bit like the Old Testament book of Proverbs dressed
up in New Testament clothes."[12] A few scholars had even suggested
that it was merely a Jewish document into which "a clever redactor
added the words 'Jesus Christ.'"[13]

In the letter, Jesus is mentioned only once more after the opening line—and to remind fellow believers of the essence of "the faith
of our Lord Jesus Christ":

My brothers and sisters, believers in our glorious Lord Jesus Christ must not show favoritism. Suppose a man comes into your meeting wearing a gold ring and fine clothes, and a poor man in filthy old clothes also comes in. If you show special attention to the man wearing fine clothes and say, "Here's a good seat for you," but say to the poor man, "You stand there" or "Sit on the floor by my feet," have you not discriminated among yourselves and become judges with evil thoughts?[14]

This passage, along with others in the letter, sounds very much like the moral teachings of Jesus in the gospels, in which he preaches against the arrogance of the rich and the privileged while praising the poor and the downtrodden. Hence it can be easily argued that James was indeed promoting the faith *of* Jesus—which was not, necessarily, a faith *about* Jesus.

This Way, as James and his fellow believers called it, was opened and defined by Jesus not as a new religion but as an update of Judaism. "[James's] religious beliefs were primarily those of the orthodox Jew of the first century," an American Christian scholar put it, "modified little save by the conviction that [Jesus] was the Messiah."[15] And for both James and his fellow believers at the "Jerusalem Church," this Messiah was not God incarnate, but "the last great Jewish prophet."[16]

PAUL'S WAY

Had the message of Jesus reached us only via the Way of James, it would not be the Christianity that we know. No wonder the Christianity that we know came from a different way—the Way of Paul.

I have alluded to Paul before, but now is the time to meet him properly. Born in Tarsus, a coastal town in today's southern Turkey, his original name was Saul. As introduced in his own writings and also those of his protégé, Luke, Saul was a Roman citizen and a Hellenized Jew, but also the son of a Pharisee who was raised as a

Pharisee. At a young age he was sent to Jerusalem to be educated "at the feet of Gamaliel," one of the authoritative rabbis of the era. He initially opposed the Jesus movement and even took an active part in the stoning of Stephen, commonly known as the first Christian martyr.

Yet something dramatic happened to Saul a few years after Jesus' crucifixion, sometime between the years AD 33 and 36. He was on his way from Jerusalem to Damascus, reportedly to arrest the followers of Jesus. Yet the journey was cut short when Saul saw a blinding light from the sky that struck him down. Then a heavenly voice called out to him, and asked: "Saul, Saul, why do you persecute me?"

"Who are you, Lord?" Saul asked. "I am Jesus, whom you are persecuting," the voice replied. "Now get up and go into the city, and you will be told what you must do."

This incident, which we learn from both his own letters and the book of Acts, not only changed Saul's life, but also world history. In the next three decades, with his new name Paul, the devoted convert worked relentlessly to spread the Good News about Jesus to the Greco-Roman world, establishing not only churches but also many of the key documents of the new faith. Of the twenty-seven books of the New Testament, thirteen are letters written by Paul—or at least attributed to him. The four canonical gospels also carry his mark: one of the writers, Luke, was clearly his protégé, whereas the Fourth Gospel adopted his theology and took it to a higher level. That is why some historians who studied early Christianity came to define Paul as the real founder of the religion. He was even called "the first Christian."[17]

Yet there is something mind-boggling about this most influential apostle of Jesus: he had never seen Jesus with his own eyes or heard him speak with his own ears. He was not a member of the Twelve who followed Jesus throughout his ministry. He was not even a member of the "Jerusalem Church" that was led by James and others who knew Jesus in person.

Could this have been a problem for Paul's claim to be an apostle? It could well have been, for we read in the book of Acts that when the original apostles were electing a new member to the Twelve, after the treason and death of Judas Iscariot, Peter said: "It is necessary to choose one of the men who have been with us the whole time the Lord Jesus was living among us, beginning from John's baptism to the time when Jesus was taken up from us."[18]

Yet Paul believed that he did not need such a natural acquaintance with Jesus at all. He rather had a supernatural acquaintance, which was far superior. "I want you to know, brothers and sisters, that the gospel I preached is not of human origin," hence he wrote in his Epistle to the Galatians. "I did not receive it from any man, nor was I taught it; rather, I received it by revelation from Jesus Christ."[19]

With such a powerful conviction, Paul developed his own theology independently of the "Jerusalem Church" led by James. After his miraculous conversion on the way to Damascus, he spent three years in "Arabia," an imprecise location which probably corresponds to modern-day Jordan.[20] Here, his Christian faith began to be formed—all by himself, for he had decided "not to consult any human being."[21] Only after that did Paul visit Jerusalem for two weeks, there to meet only Peter and, much more briefly, James. Paul writes that these original followers of Jesus were initially suspicious of him, but were finally convinced of his faith and "praised God because of me." He also ensured his readers: "I assure you before God that what I am writing you is no lie."[22]

Then, in the next decades, Paul made his legendary journeys, to Asia Minor, Greece, and ultimately Rome, to establish the roots of Gentile Christianity, which is the only one we have today. He went back to Jerusalem twice more, again to meet James and other apostles, and for a curious reason: his preaching to the Gentiles had created some serious questions among his fellow Jews.

A WAR OF IDEAS

Sometime in the year AD 50, some fourteen years after his first reported acceptance by James, Paul returned to Jerusalem to attend
what is known in history as the Jerusalem Council. The meeting
was held mainly because Paul's preaching to the Gentiles had given
rise to a controversy within the early Jesus movement. Paul was telling Gentiles that Jewish law was not valid for them and all they had
to do was to merely accept Jesus as "the Christ." But some men who
"came down from Judaea" were preaching something very different. "Unless you have yourselves circumcised in the tradition of
Moses," these Jewish followers of Jesus were warning Gentiles, "you
cannot be saved."[23]

We learn about these events from the book of Acts. We also
learn that it was up to James to decide about this crucial controversy
over doctrine. After hearing both Paul and his opponents at the
Jerusalem Council, we are told, James decided that Gentiles need to
observe not the whole Mosaic Law, but only four rules: "abstain[ing]
from things sacrificed to idols, and from blood, and from things
strangled, and from sexual immorality."[24] Then the Jerusalem Council ended happily and Paul continued his preaching.

Yet the issue would come up soon again, as new "rumors"
reached Jerusalem suggesting that Paul was telling not only Gentiles but also fellow Jews to abandon the Mosaic Law. Hence Paul
had to come to Jerusalem again, seven years after the Jerusalem
Council. James and the elders of the community warned Paul that
he was in trouble. "You teach all the Jews living among the Gentiles
to forsake Moses," as people heard, "and that you tell them not to
circumcise their children or observe the customs."[25] This was no
minor matter, as it amounted to nothing less than apostasy from
Judaism. Hence James suggested that Paul convince every other Jew
in Jerusalem that this rumor was false and that he in fact lived in
full observance of the Torah. Paul apparently agreed and took a
"purification" ritual to reestablish his Jewish credentials.

Yet some Jews remained unconvinced. They seized Paul and tried to get him killed. Paul was only saved because he was a Roman citizen. He was taken into custody by Roman soldiers, spent about two years in prison, and was ultimately transferred to Rome, where he spent the rest of his life. He is believed to have been executed there sometime in the mid-60s, during the persecution of Christians under the mad and cruel emperor Nero.[26]

This is the summary of what we learn from the book of Acts about Paul's tension with the "Judaizers"—Jews who believed in Jesus as the Messiah but also honored the Mosaic Law. Acts also gives us the impression that the latter group were a bunch of fanatic legalists separate from the "Jerusalem Church" led by James. James rather is presented as someone who checked the Judaizers' excesses and approved and even blessed Paul's mission to the Gentiles.

However, since the nineteenth century, some critical scholars have questioned the accuracy of this picture of harmony. First, the liberal Protestant theologian Ferdinand Christian Baur, the pioneer of the German school that studied the historical Jesus, suggested that the Judaizers with whom Paul struggled were in fact none other than James and the "Jerusalem Church." Once the subjective narrative of the Acts—and the traditional Christian imagination that was built upon it—was left aside, and Paul's own letters were read carefully, Baur argued, the real tension showed up—an argument that, to date, has been admittedly controversial.[27]

One key passage that gives a glimpse of that tension is what Paul wrote about the famous "incident at Antioch," which took place right before the Jerusalem Council. According to his account in Galatians, Paul had established a small community at Antioch, where both Jewish and Gentile followers of Jesus would meet and eat together. The apostle Peter, also called Cephas, who had come to Antioch, had also adapted to this practice. However, things changed when "certain men from James" came to Antioch, to bring Peter and others back to their Jewish senses. Paul narrates the story from his vantage point:

> But when Cephas came to Antioch I opposed him to his face, because he stood condemned. For before certain men came from James, he ate with the Gentiles; but when they came he drew back and separated himself, fearing the circumcision party. And with him the rest of the Jews acted insincerely, so that even Barnabas was carried away by their insincerity.[28]

This remarkable passage tells us a lot. First, it tells us about James's ultimate authority over all other disciples, including Peter. It also tells us that it was James, not someone else, who sent emissaries from Jerusalem to diaspora Jews to correct what they saw as Paul's misguided teaching. Then it shows us that Paul despised this "party of the circumcision," and blamed them—including Peter and Barnabas, his own companion—for "hypocrisy."

Paul's letters include several denunciations of these "hypocrites" who "[come] and [preach] another Jesus than the one we preached" and of those who dare to teach "a different Gospel." They are "false apostles, deceitful workers, masquerading as apostles of Christ." He takes their offense very personally and asks:

> Are they Hebrews? So am I. Are they Israelites? So am I. Are they descendants of Abraham? So am I. Are they servants of Christ?— I speak as if insane—I more so; in far more labors, in far more imprisonments, beaten times without number, often in danger of death.[29]

The reason why Paul needed to justify himself so insistently, not just in this passage but also elsewhere in his letters, was probably because his "gospel" was in some conflict with the one upheld by the original Jesus movement in Jerusalem.[30] As time went by, Paul's rhetoric got even more strident against these "Judaizers," as seen in his latest work, the Letter to the Philippians. Here he had quite harsh things to say against "those who mutilate the flesh," or those who keep the Jewish custom of circumcision. He called

them, "dogs ... evil workers," and claimed, "we are the true circumcision."[31]

From the Acts and other books of the New Testament, this whole
tension between Paul and the "Judaizers" first seems to be only
about the application of Mosaic Law. But there might well be another major issue: theology, including christology, or the views
about the nature and meaning of Christ. Perhaps the difference between Paul and the "Judaizers" was less detectable than a focus on
law, for one can instantly see whether Jewish Law is applied or not,
whereas theology is a more abstract matter, boiling down to the
semantics of concepts such as "Christ," or "Son of God." It is possible
that Paul used these terms without creating any scandal for Jewish
ears, although giving them very un-Jewish meanings.[32]

Yet a difference in theology is visible as well, in the divergent
contents of Paul's and James's writings. James's canonical epistle is
unmistakably "theocentric [rather] than Christocentric."[33] In return,
christocentricity is the very thing that defines Paul's letters.[34] Moreover, James's strong emphasis on works, instead of mere faith, as the
basis of justification in the sight of God is not only different from Paul's
doctrine, but it also seems to be set consciously against it. The following passage from the Epistle of James, for example, is quite explicit:

> Do you want to be shown, you senseless person, that faith apart
> from works is barren? Was not our ancestor Abraham justified by
> works when he offered his son Isaac on the altar? You see that
> faith was active along with works, and faith was brought to
> completion by the works. Thus the scripture was fulfilled that
> says, "Abraham had faith in God, and it was reckoned to him as
> righteousness" [Gen 15:6], and he was called the friend of God.[35]

In case we don't get the point from the example of Abraham,
James further explains it for us: "You see that a person is justified
by works and not by faith alone ... For just as the body without
the spirit is dead, so faith without works is also dead."[36] With such

emphatic remarks, the Epistle of James "does not merely repudiate, but actually satirizes Paul's doctrine of Justification by Faith."[37] It also shows, implicitly, that there was indeed a major war of ideas in the early Jesus movement—a war between not just the personalities but also the visions of James and Paul.

This war of ideas would ultimately breed the most extreme Paulinist position, a century after Paul, in the preaching of Marcion (d. 160), a theologian from Sinope, a coastal town on the Black Sea. Marcion declared that the teachings of Jesus were in fact totally incompatible with the Old Testament, whose God, YHWH, he saw as a rival and cruel deity. Not too surprisingly, among the apostles of Jesus he respected only Paul, whom he saw as the only one who rightly understood the mission of Christ, while condemning all other apostles as "Judaizers." Marcion would be branded as a heretic by church fathers, as he probably did exaggerate the gap between the "Judaizers" and Paul. But the gap itself was not his fiction.

THE FALL OF JERUSALEM

While the Pauline teaching was flourishing among Gentiles, James and the "Jerusalem Church" were active among Jews, trying to bring them to the conviction that the Messiah they were promised was none other than Jesus of Nazareth. He was obviously not the military Messiah that the Zealots expected—for Jesus was clearly no victor against Rome. He was rather the eschatological Messiah, who was miraculously raised from the dead and who would soon come back, "in clouds, with great power and glory."[38]

So far, I have referred to these earliest Jewish followers of Jesus as the "Jerusalem Church," in quotation marks, in line with the Christian tradition. But their contemporaries called them something else: "the sect of the Nazarenes." We know this, again, from the book of Acts, which reports that Paul was confronted in Jerusalem by a Jewish lawyer named Tertullus for being "a real pest and a fellow who stirs up dissension among all the Jews throughout the world, and a ringleader of the sect of the Nazarenes."[39] This of course raises the question of whether Paul can be taken as a representative of the "Jerusalem Church"—something I have disputed so far. Yet it is quite possible that the difference between Paul and the "Judaizing" followers of Jesus well may have not occurred to Tertullus, an outsider to the movement. It is also possible that Luke, who tells us about this incident, may have had good reasons to disregard that difference, which raises perplexing questions about the origin of the faith.

In any case, where did this term, "the Nazarenes," come from? Probably it came from nowhere other than the town of Nazareth. Jesus was widely called "Jesus of Nazareth," and those who followed him may well have adopted the definition for themselves. Or maybe other Jews began using the term for the followers of this strange Messiah from Galilee, as soon as they were a distinctive and significant enough group for others to need a word for them.[40]

The book of Acts tells us nothing about the fate of these Jerusalem-based Nazarenes, for it is a document interested only in the story of Paul. But from other sources we learn that James, the brother of Jesus and the leader of the movement, was executed sometime in the year AD 62. This must have been an important event for Judaea, for it is recorded by Josephus. In his *Antiquities of the Jews*, the Jewish historian reports that James and some of his fellow believers were brought to trial by high priest Ananus, a Sadducee, who was "a bold man in his temper . . . and very rigid in judging offenders." Then, Josephus notes:

> So [Ananus] assembled the Sanhedrin of judges and brought before them the brother of Jesus, who was called Christ, whose name was James, and some others; and when he had formed an accusation against them as breakers of the law, he delivered them to be stoned.[41]

The expression used here by Josephus, "the brother of Jesus, who was called Christ, whose name was James," is the second time he mentions Jesus in his chronicles, in addition to the *Testimonium Flavianum* we noted above. So, it is a very important source confirming that somebody named Jesus, "who was called Christ," really existed in first-century Judaea. It is also a very important source, meanwhile, confirming that the brother of Jesus, James, was a notable figure in the same time and milieu.

But for what exact "crime" was James, a pious Jew, punished by the Sanhedrin? The Christian chronicler Hegesippus, who also writes about the incident, relates that the story began when some Jews came to James for help in restraining people from believing that Jesus is the Messiah. James, a true believer, naturally refused this offer, rather testifying, "Christ himself sitteth in heaven, at the right hand of the Great Power, and shall come on the clouds of heaven."[42] This was a proclamation that Jesus was indeed the Messiah, but it was not, by Jewish standards, heresy or blasphemy. That is probably why James and his fellow believers were blamed by Ananus for "having transgressed the law"—a vague misdeed which was much less specific than blasphemy.

No wonder that other law-abiding, pious Jews refused to believe that James indeed deserved any punishment. "Those of the inhabitants of the city who were considered the most fair-minded and who were in strict observance of the law were offended at this," Josephus writes about the execution of James. He adds that these pious Jews, who were probably Pharisees, even appealed to the ruler of the time, King Agrippa, who ultimately deposed Ananus from the high priesthood.

The execution of James, in other words, turned into a scandal in first-century Judaea. For James was no apostate, no heretic, and even no transgresser of law. His "sect of Nazarenes" certainly disturbed some establishment figures such as Ananus and invited their wrath, but it was still a pious Jewish sect. No wonder there are clues that the real reason for the execution of James was his opposition to Ananus's shameless exploitation of the poorer priests, by taking tithes from them while they "starved to death."[43]

Losing James must have been a major blow to the sect of the Nazarenes, despite the fact that the leadership was assumed by Simon, another brother of Jesus, about whom we know very little. Even a bigger blow came soon, though, with the sacking of Jerusalem by the Roman military in AD 70, after a Jewish revolt led by Zealots that had begun four years earlier. The Romans, deciding this time to give the Jews a very bitter lesson, not only killed them in droves but also dealt the nation a mortal blow at its heart by destroying the Temple—a tragedy that Jews still mourn today on the annual fasting day, Tisha B'Av.

Among the Jews who had to flee Jerusalem there were the Nazarenes, who reportedly settled in Pella, an ancient city located in today's northwestern Jordan. Some of them went back to Jerusalem, only to be expelled again after the last Jewish revolt against Rome led by Simon bar Kokhba in AD 132–135, which led to an even bigger persecution of the Jews and the turning of Jerusalem into a pagan city.[44]

After that, like other Jews, Jewish Christians scattered around to form communities in northern Syria, Golan, and the Dead Sea region.[45] However they were becoming more and more a marginal Jewish sect, while Paul's teaching was proliferating among the Gentiles, establishing churches, communities, and documents that would become the basis of mainstream Christianity. This "Pauline Christianity," as some have called it, distanced itself more and more from its Jewish roots, to the extent of seeing Jesus' own story through an anti-Jewish, and implicitly pro-Roman, lens.[46] Moreover, it redefined Jewish concepts by giving them fundamentally new meanings—including the very meaning of who Jesus really was.

THE DE-JUDAIZED MESSIAH

As we saw in the previous chapter, for Jews, the Messiah was a human being chosen and blessed by God—but not God incarnate. This is still the meaning of the Messiah among Jews today. The

Orthodox communities in Israel and elsewhere await a *Mashiach* who will bring them the political and spiritual redemption promised by God—but not someone that they will worship *as* God.

This is the case, because for Jews—and also for Muslims, as we will see—the gap between God and man is unbridgeable. For the Hellenistic culture of the Roman world of the first century, however, this was not the case. Quite the contrary: in that "pagan" world— a term Christians coined later to define the polytheists—gods were visible and present beings, and not as just idols, but even disguised as men. We see this clearly in the book of Acts, which tells us that when crowds in Lystra, a city in Central Anatolia, saw the wondrous works of Paul, they got excited and declared: "The gods have come down to us in the likeness of men!" They had instantly decided that Paul was in fact Hermes and his companion Barnabas was Zeus.[47]

Quite a few of the scholars of the historical Jesus see this pagan background of the Greco-Roman world, in which Pauline Christianity not only thrived but also evolved, as the key to the core aspect of this new faith: the divinization of Jesus.

To see how this happened, just take a look at the key term, "Son of God." In Jewish texts, "Son of God" was merely "any one whose piety has placed him in a filial relation to God."[48] So the term could be used for angels, Israel itself as a nation, or the King of Israel.[49] In Psalms, for example, we read that God would make David his "firstborn and highest king of the earth," and, in return, David would cry, "You are my Father."[50] In this Jewish context, sonship to God implied "divine favour rather than the sharing of the divine nature."[51] In Greek culture, however, the term "Son of God" would imply nothing but God-the-Son—in the sense that Apollo was the son of Zeus.

Jesus in fact refers to himself in the gospels very rarely as "Son of God," but quite frequently as the "Son of Man," or *bar nasha*. The latter is a Jewish term that appears more than a hundred times in the Old Testament, most of them in the book of Ezekiel, where it is used by God to address the prophet Ezekiel, who is clearly a mortal human being. In this Jewish context, the title "Son of Man" implies not deity, but the quite contrary, "mortality, impotence, transientness as against the omnipotence and eternality of God."[52]

However, Gentile Christianity paid little attention to the title Son of Man. It is remarkable that Paul never used this title for Jesus in all his letters. He rather opted for "Son of God," or "the son," or "his son," and in a de-Judaized sense that implied deity for Jesus—such as defining Jesus as a preexistent being, receiver of prayers, and even creator.[53] In the meantime, the Son of Man gradually became "one of the most baffling problems confronting the New Testament scholar," for it did not fit the image of divine Jesus portrayed in mainstream Christianity.[54]

Other titles relating to the Jewish Messiah also got redefined or lost in its new Gentile setting. As the New Testament scholar Richard N. Longenecker explains in *The Christology of Early Jewish Christianity*:

> Christological titles appropriate in the Jewish Christian cycle of witness appear to have lacked meaning for Gentile believers. Thus Christ, while too firmly wedded to the person of Jesus to be set aside, became primarily a proper name; Seed of David and Son of God appear mainly in traditional portions; Suffering Servant comes to expression only by way of allusion; God's Salvation is translated into Saviour; and priestly and kingly motifs disappear almost entirely.[55]

In short, the more Christianity moved away from its Jewish roots and planted itself on Hellenistic soil, the more it perceived Jesus as divine. This was no preplanned scheme, but the natural result of transferring monotheistic Jewish concepts to a polytheistic Gentile setting.

That is probably why the more we move on from the earliest documents of the New Testament to the later ones, the more references we see to the divinity of Jesus.[56] Among the four gospels, the one that has the least allusions to Jesus' divinity, if any, is Mark, which widely is considered as the earliest, written probably sometime around AD 70.[57] Yet when we come to Matthew and Luke, written probably one to two decades after Mark, the emphasis on Jesus as a suprahuman being increases.

For an example, let's go back to the famous "Who do people say I am" passage that I quoted from Mark in the previous chapter. Here, to Jesus' question about his identity, Peter responded by only saying, "You are the Christ." In Matthew, however, Peter's testimony comes with a crucial addition: "You are the Christ, *the Son of the living God.*" Moreover, Jesus responds to Peter with another addition: "Blessed are you, Simon Bar-Jona! For flesh and blood has not revealed this to you, but my Father who is in heaven."[58]

My Father—a notable emphasis. To be sure, Jews did refer to God as "Father"—as in the ancient synagogue prayer, the *Kaddish,* which is probably the origin of the Lord's Prayer in Christianity. Thus Jesus the Jew might have easily prayed to "Father," or *Abba* in his own language, Aramaic, without implying any divinity for himself. We indeed see this in the Gospel of Mark, where Jesus prays, in human distress about his upcoming death, "Abba, Father, all things are possible unto thee; remove this cup from me." Yet the emphasized expression "my Father" never appears in Mark. It only appears in later gospels, Matthew and Luke, and quite repeatedly. Conspicuously enough, these two gospels also replace the words *Teacher* and *Rabbi* used for Jesus by fellow Jews in Mark, with the more elevated term *Lord.*

There is also a notable difference between the scenes of crucifixion in Mark, the earliest gospel, and Luke, a later one. In Mark, Jesus suffers in a very human way, in stress and anguish, and at the very end he cries: *Eloi, Eloi, lama sabachthani,* or, "My God, my God, why have you forsaken me?" In Luke, however, we see a more self-assured Jesus, and his call to "my God" is replaced by a very different line: "Father, into your hands I commit my spirit."[59]

Meanwhile, in Luke, we read about a Roman centurion who

oversaw the crucifixion of Jesus yet at the end realized, "Surely this was a righteous man." Matthew, however, elevates the christology in this testimony, making the centurion proclaim, "Surely he was the Son of God!"[60]

When we come to the Fourth Gospel—attributed to John the Apostle, but very unlikely to have been written by him—we meet an even more elevated Jesus. As the latest of all four gospels, written sometime around the turn of the first century, this document presents us with a Christ who existed before time with God, and that even *was* God, who came down to earth as Jesus to "dwell among men." In the Fourth Gospel, Jesus also constantly talks about who he is, what his identity is, and where he came from; whereas in the other three, he teaches not about himself but the Kingdom of God.[61] John's christology seems to be at a higher level in the evolution of the faith *of* Jesus into a faith *about* Jesus.

This evolution continued even after the formation of the New Testament gospels, as church councils kept elevating the nature of Christ and also condemning the "heretics" who subscribed to "lower" christologies. In his provocative book, *How Jesus Became God: The Exaltation of a Jewish Preacher from Galilee*, the Bible scholar Bart D. Ehrman sums up this process:

> In early Christianity the views of Christ got "higher and higher" with the passing of time, as he became increasingly identified as divine. Jesus went from being a potential (human) messiah to being the Son of God exalted to a divine status at his resurrection; to being a preexistent angelic being who came to earth incarnate as a man; to being the incarnation of the Word of God who existed before all time and through whom the world was created; to being God himself, equal with God the Father and always existent with him.[62]

Surely not all scholars would fully agree with this comment. Others rather argue, "a remarkable level of devotion to Jesus erupted in the earliest years of the Christian movement."[63] Some even argue, "the earliest christology was already the highest christology."[64] Moreover, even when the evolution of doctrine in early Christianity is granted, mainstream Christians can see it as the unfolding of God's mystery in time, through "inspired" men who established the truth about Christ. (In a somewhat similar fashion, Sunni Islam regards the evolution of its own doctrine in the formative centuries not as mundane history, but as a providential process expressed through the "infallible community."[65]) Mainstream Christians may also argue that Jews were too "rigid" in their monotheism and thus spiritually blind to see the divine Messiah among them as who he really was, whereas Gentiles came to Paul's preaching with a more open heart. "A partial hardening has happened to Israel," Paul himself argued, "until the fullness of the Gentiles has come in."[66]

Others, however, can see in this history rather a divergence from the traditional Abrahamic monotheism of a transcendent and unitarian God. Jews, the quintessential monotheists, are inevitably poised to think this way—exactly in the same way as Muslims do, as we shall later see.

THE TEXTS ABOUT THE HERETICS

While Pauline Christianity was going through its doctrinal evolution, Jewish Christianity was going through its existential decline. Uprooted from Jerusalem, it survived only as a growingly marginal strain, to be distrusted by mainstream Jews as a weird sect and to be condemned by Pauline Christians as a heresy. By the second and third centuries, this strain appears to be divided into factions, with such various names as Ebionites, Nazareans, Elkesaites, Cerinthians, and Symmachians. Perhaps these were different faces of Jewish Christianity—even Jewish Christianit*ies,* which lay on a thelogical spectrum—or perhaps they were just different names given to the same movement. It is hard to know, because we know these Jewish Christians less from their own sources than from the writings of Pauline church fathers who defined and condemned them as "heresies."

The first church father to note this problematic strain was Justin Martyr, also known as Saint Justin, who wrote around AD 150 about some Jews "who admit that [Jesus] is Christ, while holding Him to be man of men."[67] Some three decades later, the bishop of Lyon, Irenaeus, took up the same issue, more critically, in his famous book, *Adversus Haereses,* or *Against Heresies.* Among his targets were the Ebionites, whose name meant "the poor." These Ebionites had many erroneous beliefs, Irenaeus argued, which put them at odds with Pauline Christianity:

> They . . . repudiate the Apostle Paul, maintaining that he was an apostate from the law. As to the prophetical writings, they endeavour to expound them in a somewhat singular manner: they practice circumcision, persevere in the observance of those customs which are enjoined by the law, and are so Judaic in their style of life, that they even adore Jerusalem as if it were the house of God.[68]

More than a century later, sometime around AD 324, another church father, Eusebius, also wrote about the "Heresy of the Ebionites." The sect was called "poor," he claimed, "because they held poor and mean opinions concerning Christ"—whereas Ebionites most probably referred to themselves as "the poor" as an honorific title referring to their modesty, and in line with Jesus' beatitude, "Blessed are the poor in spirit, for theirs is the kingdom of heaven."[69] The sect's greatest deviation, Eusebius argued, was to "consider [Christ] a plain and common man, who was justified only because of his superior virtue." Some of the Ebionites accept the virgin birth, he explained, "but refuse to acknowledge that he pre-existed, being God, Word, and Wisdom."[70]

Eusebius added that the Ebionites "reject all the epistles of the apostle," who was none other than Paul, "whom they called an apostate from the law."[71] He also noted that the sect "used only the so-called Gospel according to the Hebrews."[72] Sadly we have no copy of that particular gospel, which exists only in the writings of church fathers as brief quotations. From the same sources, we also learn the existence of a "Gospel of the Ebionites" and a "Gospel of the Nazarenes," which may be just different definitions of a single Jewish Christian gospel, which reportedly was an adapted version of the Gospel of Matthew.

Two generations after Eusebius, another church writer who took up the issue was Epiphanius, the bishop of the city of Salamis, which was located on the Mediterranean island of Cyprus. Between the years 374 and 377, Epiphanius wrote a book titled *Panarion*, or "Medicine," in which he likened heresies to poisonous beasts whose bites needed to be cured. Among these serpents were "Ebionites" and "Nazarenes," names that Epiphanius seems to use interchangeably for the same people, who followed a "Gospel of the Hebrews," despised the Apostle Paul, denied the divinity of Jesus, and saw him rather as "the true prophet." They are "Jews and nothing else," Epiphanius demeaningly noted, yet even the Jews maligned them three times a day in their synagogues, praying "May God curse the Nazoraeans."[73]

A generation after Epiphanius, another prominent Christian figure, Jerome (347–420), a hermit, priest, and theologian, also wrote about the Jewish Christians he met in Antioch. He named them as Nazareans "who accept Christ in such a way that they do not cease to observe the old Law." These people used a Gospel of the Hebrews, Jerome noted, which was initially written in the Aramaic language with Hebrew letters but later translated into Greek. In this lost gospel, which we know only as much as Jerome reported, James the Just, who is downplayed in canonical gospels, was the most prominent disciple of Jesus. Jesus appeared after his crucifixion only to James, gave him bread, and said: "My brother, eat thy bread for the Son of Man is risen from among those who sleep."[74]

Unlike other church writers, however, Jerome's tone with regard to the Nazareans was curiously positive, because he found their view of Jesus acceptable. This has led to suggestions that perhaps there was a spectrum of Jewish Christians in which Ebionites represented the more Jewish wing, considering Jesus as the human Messiah, and the Nazareans represented the more Christian wing, accepting Jesus as the divine Son of God. Either this was really the case, or Jerome was not very well informed about the Jewish Christians. In any case, one of his observations helps elucidate the trouble of these unorthodox believers in Jesus:

> They believe in Christ, the Son of God born of Mary the virgin, and they say about him that he suffered and rose again under Pontius Pilate, in whom also we believe. But since they want to be both Jews and Christians, they are neither Jews nor Christians.[75]

In the same passage, Jerome also noted, "until now" the Jewish Christian heresy "is to be found in all parts of the East where Jews have their synagogues."[76] So Jewish Christianity was really no minor phenomenon in the beginning of the fifth century, when Jerome wrote these lines.

About half a century after Jerome, Theodoret of Cyrrhus (393–460), a city near Antioch, also wrote about the heretical Ebionites "who alone accept the Gospel according to the Hebrews, and regard the Apostle [Paul] as apostate." He seems to have just repeated Eusebius's views on these heretics, so it is not very clear whether he actually knew of an existing Ebionite community.[77]

THE TEXTS OF THE HERETICS

Besides the unfriendly descriptions by Pauline Church fathers, we also have a few texts used by Jewish Christians themselves which give us a sense of what they really believed in. The earliest of them is *The Teaching of the Twelve Apostles*, often simply called the *Didache*, from the Greek word for "teaching." It was probably written in the final decades of the first century somewhere in Syria. In fact, it was lost for centuries, known only in quotations in the works of Pauline church fathers. It was accidentally discovered in 1873, in a library in Istanbul, by Philoteus Bryennios, a Greek priest. Catholic scholars who later studied the text decided that it must be from "a very early period when Jewish influence was still important in the Church."[78]

No wonder that the *Didache* is quite reminiscent of the Epistle of James. It speaks of the Two Ways—of life versus death, of good versus evil, of piety versus sin. It has a heavy dose of emphasis on the observance of the Ten Commandments, righteousness, prayer, and ethics. Some parts are also very similar to Jesus' Sermon on the Mount. Notably, Jesus is mentioned in the document only four times—and always as the "servant" of God. "We thank Thee, Holy Father," one verse reads, "for the knowledge and faith and immortality which Thou hast made known to us through Jesus Thy Servant." Jesus' death and resurrection do not seem to be of concern, unlike in Pauline theology.[79] As Geza Vermes observes:

> The Jesus of the Didache is essentially the Servant of God, the great eschatological teacher who is expected to reappear soon to gather together and transfer the dispersed members of his church to the Kingdom of God. The ideas of atonement and redemption are nowhere visible in this earliest record for Jewish Christian life. Nor can one find any hint at the sacrificial character of Jesus' death and its Pauline symbolical re-enactment in the rituals of baptism and the Eucharist. Needless to say, the Johannine idea of the eternal and creative Logos is nowhere on the horizon either.[80]

Granted, the *Didache* includes an instruction to "baptize in the name of the Father, and of the Son, and of the Holy Spirit." This, obviously, is an allusion to the doctrine of the Trinity, which is very un-Jewish and unmistakably Christian. However, some scholars suspect that this trinitarian baptism formula, which seems to conflict with another line in the *Didache* that merely speaks of being "baptized in the name of the Lord," might be a later insertion by a "scribal editor."[81]

Another Jewish Christian source written some three centuries after the *Didache* is the "Pseudo-Clementine Writings," which give us a glimpse of the deepened gap between Pauline and Jewish Christianities. These are a set of some twenty books, which are often defined as "religious romance," or a "novel" in our modern literary definitions. Among their content, there is a specifically curious document called *Kerygmata Petrou*, or "Preaching of Peter," which is presented as a letter written by the Apostle Peter to none other than James the Just.

In this letter, Peter struggles with someone called Simon Magus, or "Simon the Magician," who is depicted as an imposter who joined the Jesus movement only to corrupt it. Of course, Simon Magus also appears in the book of Acts, as a Samaritan opportunist who was rejected by the disciples of Jesus. While reading the *Kerygmata Petrou*, however, it is hard not to conclude that this time Simon Magus is none other than Paul himself.[82] For Peter rejects the idea that "our Jesus" might have appeared to this man in a personal vision and asks him: "How are we to believe you when you tell us that he appeared to you? And how did he appear to you, when you entertain opinions contrary to his teaching?"[83]

In the same document, Peter also warns against "false prophets and false apostles, and false teachers," who speak in the name of Christ, but who "accomplish the will of the demon." Then he calls on all fellow believers: "Wherefore observe the greatest caution, that you believe no teacher, unless he bring from Jerusalem the testimonial of James the Lord's brother, or of whosoever may come after him."[84]

Most scholars do not believe that this fourth-century document is actually from Peter, the disciple of Jesus from the first century. Yet still, the document seems to be an echo of an acute tension within early Christianity between Paulines and the "Judaizers."

At this point, it could be asked whether we can really take the "heretical" Jewish Christians of the second, third, and fourth centuries as direct descendants of the "Jerusalem Church" led by James the Just right after the passing of Jesus. Christian authors have often given a negative answer to this question. They rather offer a later "re-Judaization" theory, suggesting that some latter-day Jewish Christians departed from Christian truth, without any precedent in the early church, to re-adopt Jewish ideas and practices.[85] Some even called early Jewish Christianity a "scholarly invention."[86]

James D. G. Dunn, a prominent theologian and a minister at the Church of Scotland, is among those who finds the re-Judaization theory unpersuasive. "The heretical Jewish Christianity of the later centuries," he rather argues, "could quite properly claim to be more truly the heir of earliest Christianity than any other expression of Christianity." The latter-day Jewish Christians, in particular the Ebionites, were only more strident in their anti-Paulinism, he adds, for in their time Pauline Christianity had developed into an unmistakably un-Jewish faith.[87]

At the end of the day, it seems astonishing how the vision of Paul, a man who had never seen or heard Jesus with his earthly eyes and ears, defined the Christ to the world and built the foundation of the greatest religion that has ever existed. The irony here, of course, is not a reason to suggest that Paul was insincere in his beliefs about Christ—an accusation brought upon him for centuries by theological rivals. The man devoted his whole life to spreading the Good News as he understood it, despite staggering odds, and we have no reason to think that he did this on cynical grounds.

Even more absurd is to see in Paul's mission a Jewish conspiracy, which some Muslim writers wrongfully have done in both the classical era and the modern day.[88] In fact, if there can be any informed Islamic critique of Paul, it can be that he parted ways with Judaism too much.[89] Meanwhile, his contribution to Western and ultimately global culture, with his emphasis on "faith" as a category in itself, must be acknowledged by all. For it was this Pauline emphasis, as one critic admitted, which "acquainted 'Western' minds with the emotional and intellectual universe that moderns call 'individual consciousness and belief.'"[90]

Whatever its exact explanation was, Paul's break with Judaism made Christianity the universalist religion that it is today. Both faiths suffered from persecution by Rome, but while Judaism remained as the national faith of a small people, Christianity, despite being a *religio illicita* (illegal religion), kept winning new converts from all over the Roman Empire.[91] By the early third century, Christians could be found "in all occupations and classes and ranks . . . from the intellectual elite and upper echelons of aristocratic nobility."[92] Finally, in the early fourth century, with the conversion of Emperor Constantine, Christianity conquered Rome. The impact of becoming the official religion of the unrivaled superpower on earth—the "Christendom shift"—would be earth-shattering and everlasting.

Meanwhile, Jewish Christians must have had a really hard time. As Jews, they were not fancied by Romans. As "Judaizers," they were not fancied by Gentile Christians. And as believers in an eccentric Messiah with avant-garde ideas, they were not fancied by other Jews either. Hence they became increasingly marginal and finally mute, as we hear nothing about them, even in the heresiology of the church fathers, after the middle of the fifth century. Theodoret of Cyrrhus, the last Church father to write about them in the 430s, even claimed that they were so completely forgotten that most people did not know their names.

So, the common view is that, by the end of the fifth century, Jewish Christians had already vanished from history.

Their creed, however, would not vanish.

CHAPTER THREE

A REBIRTH IN ARABIA

Say [Muhammad]: "I am nothing new among the Messengers."

—The Qur'an 49:6

In the year 610, on the western side of the Arabian Peninsula, in a small cave on a small mountain, something remarkable happened—remarkable and world-changing.

Inside the cave, a man was sitting by himself. It was his habit to come there alone, from his nearby hometown, Mecca, "the mother of cities," just to leave the city's busy market and find some free time to contemplate. He himself was a merchant at the market, with a good business, good reputation, and good marriage. He was forty—a late age, for his time—and probably did not expect any trouble for the rest of his life. But trouble was on its way.

His name was Muhammad, which meant "the praiseworthy" in his mother tongue, Arabic, a sister language to Aramaic and Hebrew. His people, the Arabs, were indeed distant cousins of the Jews. Legend had it that while Abraham's younger son Isaac became patriarch of the Israelites, the elder son, Ishmael, became the progenitor of the Arabs. Yet while Jews had remained loyal to the monotheism of Abraham, Arabs had developed a polytheistic religion, worshiping a plenitude of gods, which were often represented by idols. Uzza was the goddess of fertility, for example, Manat the goddess of fate, and Hubal the god of the moon.

Muhammad's city, Mecca, was the very hub of this Arab idolatry. At the heart of the town, there was a cube-shaped building called Ka'aba. (The word *cube*, arguably, comes from it.[1]) Arabs held that this was a temple built by Abraham and Ishmael, which could only be for monotheistic purposes, but the building had long ago turned into a pagan temple. During the time of Muhammad, there were more than three hundred idols inside the Ka'aba, to which pilgrims came every year from all over the peninsula to show their respect and to make their offerings. Idolatry was good for not only Mecca's prestige but also for its business.

Yet Muhammad was growingly uncomfortable with all of this. First, the idols did not make much sense to him—as they did not to the small group of Arab monotheists, called *Hanif*, who saw idolatry as a deviation from faith in one true God. Second, the extremely hierarchical social order of Mecca, where the arrogant rich trampled the underprivileged poor and the slaves, seemed unfair to Muhammad. In fact, his own tribe, the Quraish, had been a poor group themselves just two generations previously, barely surviving the harsh life in the desert. Yet their settlement in Mecca, and the city's bursting prominence, had made them quickly rich—nouveaux riches. Mecca had become a city of extremes, with prominent males selling their female slaves as prostitutes and exploitive usurers ripping people off.

Such matters bothered Muhammad when he withdrew from the city and came to the cave on that small mountain, only to sit silently for a bit and go back home. But on some day in the year 610, in the lunar month of Ramadan, something very strange happened. From the darkness of the cave, a voice suddenly called on him, telling him, "Recite!" The terrified Muhammad, thrown on the ground, replied, "I am no poet!" For poets were the orators in Mecca who would recite rhymes and collect tips. In return, the voice recited on his behalf:

Recite: In the Name of your Lord who created,
Created man from clots of blood.
Recite: And your Lord is the Most Generous,
He who taught by the pen,
Taught man what he did not know.[2]

Now Muhammad was even more terrified. He rushed out of the cave and headed directly home. He was convinced that he had been attacked by the *jinn*—the supernatural, and often demonic, creatures of the Arabian lore. When he finally threw himself in the arms of his wife Khadija, a businesswoman who was fifteen years older than he, he asked her, "Cover me." And he told her how the jinn had attacked him in the cave.

However, Khadija gave a bit more credit to the voice that had terrified her husband. She suggested consulting a man with a deeper knowledge about such mysteries, her cousin Waraqa ibn Nawfal. (In Arabic, the word *ibn* means "son of," just like the word *ben* in Hebrew.)

Islamic tradition tells us that Waraqa was initially a member of the *Hanif*. But the same tradition also tells us that Waraqa had converted to Christianity, apparently while traveling through Syria, where he studied the Bible, and had even become a priest. It is this Christian Waraqa who listened to what happened to Muhammad in the cave and who decided that the terrifying voice was not demonic but divine. "Surely, by Him in whose hand is Waraqa's soul," he exclaimed, "Thou art the Prophet of this people."

As we read in the biography of the Prophet penned by the Muslim historian Ibn Ishaq, Waraqa also told Muhammad: "There hath come unto thee the greatest law, who came unto Moses."[3] The original Arabic word here for "law" is *namus*, which is the equivalent of the Greek word *nomos*. The latter is frequently used in the New Testament, in the letters of Paul, and, with more approval, in the Epistle of James. Hence by using this powerful term, Waraqa seemed to imply that Muhammad was given not just one single revelation of a few words, but a whole divine law for a whole people.

No wonder the revelations continued. In the early stages, Muhammad still had a hard time convincing himself that he was a prophet chosen by God and not a madman haunted by demons. That is why a new revelation comforted him: "By the blessing of your Lord, you are not mad."[4] When revelations stopped for a while, he felt lost. A new revelation again assured him: "Your Lord has not abandoned you, nor does He hate you."[5] In other words, Muhammad's mission did not begin with a burning sense of self-importance and a premeditated triumph, as is often the case with religious charlatans. He rather found himself helplessly forced into an unforeseen struggle, as is often the case with true prophets and apostles.

The revelations went on for twenty-three years, gradually forming the scripture that was ultimately called the Qur'an, or "the Recitation." In the meantime, a community of believers emerged around Muhammad and went through a fascinating saga. In the beginning, for the first three years, there were just a few people quietly spreading the new faith. When they proclaimed it out loud, as a new revelation told Muhammad, they faced persecution from Mecca's pagan elites. By 622, twelve years after the first revelation, they all had to flee the city to save their lives. Only eight years and three big battles later, however, they came back with a huge army of conquest that took Mecca without bloodshed. They cleansed the Ka'aba of the idols and reestablished the building as a monotheist temple.

Soon the world would hear about their faith as a new religion called Islam. Islam itself was insisting, however, that there was nothing new about it.

MONOTHEISM FOR GENTILES

Theologically speaking, the birth of Islam was simply a victory of monotheism over polytheism. The idols the Arabs used to worship, as the Qur'an declared in one of its earlier verses, were nothing but "names which you and your forefathers invented."[6] They were no true gods that had true power over men. "If you call on them, they would not hear your call," the Qur'an noted, "and were they to hear, they would not respond to you."[7]

However, there was one specific god that both the pagan Arabs and the Qur'an honored: *Allah*. The term was a contraction of the article *al*, corresponding to the English word *the*, and the word *ilah*, corresponding to the English word *god*. Therefore, Allah was not just any god, but "*the* God." Pagan Arabs saw Him as the higher and unseen deity, far above all the other lesser gods that were represented by idols. In this view, Allah was the creator of the heavens and the earth, but he was distant from human beings, which was why humans had to worship the idols. "We only worship them so that they may bring us nearer to Allah," reasoned the idolaters of Mecca, as we read in the Qur'an.[8]

In return, the Qur'an declared that Allah is the only true God, to whom all worship should be devoted. Associating "partners" with Allah, or *shirk*, was defined as the gravest sin. From this, there emerged the basic credo of Islam, which is still recited every day across the globe, from the lips of believers to the minarets of mosques: "*La ilahe illallah*," or "There is no god, but The God." This bold, forceful, uncompromising monotheism was the very core of the new faith. That is why it would call itself "Islam," implying "submission" to that that one true God—and to no one else.

Yet who exactly was this one true God? The Qur'an's answer is straightforward: the God of Abraham, Ishmael, Isaac, and Jacob.[9] Also, the God of Noah, Lot, Moses, Joseph, Job, Jonah, Elijah, David, and Solomon. All such figures, known in the Judeo-Christian tradition as Jewish patriarchs, prophets, and kings—along with only three Arab prophets, Shuaib, Saleh, and Hud—are honored in the Qur'an as the harbingers of a monotheistic tradition. It is also acknowledged that Jews had a special role in this history. "O Children of Israel," God states in the Qur'an, "remember the blessing I conferred on you, and that I preferred you over all other beings."[10] Yet the Qur'an also teaches that monotheism is not a Jewish invention, but the archetypal religion proclaimed to many other nations by many other unidentified prophets.[11]

In this Qur'anic view of history, the Prophet Muhammad was no inventor of a new religion, but only a proclaimer of the ancient truths and a mere human being with no supernatural powers. "I am nothing new among the Messengers," a revelation told Muhammad to tell his people: "I have no idea what will be done with me or you. I only follow what has been revealed to me. I am only a clear warner."[12] Another revelation also noted that Muhammad was sent by God in order to "warn a people to whom no warner came before."[13] This was a reference to the Arabs, who, despite being distant relatives of Jews, never had their own versions of prophets and scriptures.

Moreover, other peoples who would accept Islam en masse over the centuries—such as Persians, Turks, Kurds, Berbers, Pashtuns, Indo-Aryans, Malays, Javanese, and many more—were all peoples with predominantly "pagan" backgrounds, to speak from within an Abrahamic perspective. As a result, you can meet millions of people in four corners of the world today whose name is Ishak (Isaac), Yusuf (Joseph), or Davud (David), and who revere Abraham for being obedient to God or Moses for standing up to the pharaoh, despite the fact that their own national histories have nothing to do with that of the Children of Israel.

In other words, the spread of Islam around the world amounted to a tectonic expansion of Abrahamic monotheism over the globe—as was also the case with Christianity. In fact, given the experience of these two branches, first Christianity and then Islam, one could say that Abrahamic monotheism, historically rooted in the tiny nation of Israel, conquered much of the world.[14]

A PASSION FOR SALVATION

What was the secret of Islam's astonishing success? How was it possible that what initially was a tiny cult in a tiny city in the Arabian desert so quickly spread and conquered a great part of the Old World, stretching from Spain to India?

Since the eighteenth century, when "Orientalist" studies fully began, many Western scholars have rightly asked these questions. Many of them found the answer in factors other than what Islam itself claims to be based on—faith. The French Orientalist Ernest Renan put this view most bluntly in 1881, claiming, "the Mussulman movement was produced almost without religious faith."[15] For him and other European writers, it was rather Arab nationalism, lust for power and empire, or even lust for sex (concubines and harems) that explained the motive at the origins of Islam.

That early Orientalist view is still very powerful today. Most modern social scientists already have the tendency to explain away all religious motivations as derivatives of something more "real," that is, material. Moreover, Islam's early marriage with power makes it easier to apply this secularist interpretation of the faith. Meanwhile, some Western Christians, who are understandably horrified by the violence of Muslim extremists, extrapolate from this current problem to claim that Islam is "a political ideology disguised as a religion."[16]

However, some recent academic views in the West challenge these popular narratives about Islam's origins. One powerful argument comes from Fred M. Donner, an American scholar of Islam, in his 2010 work, *Muhammad and the Believers*. Donner argues emphatically against the scholars who explained nascent Islam as a movement with earthly objectives. Quite the contrary, Donner says, Muhammad and his followers constituted a sincerely religious movement, focusing on one single powerful goal: personal salvation. "It is my conviction," he writes:

> that Islam began as a religious movement—not as a social, economic, or "national" one; in particular, it embodied an intense concern for attaining personal salvation through righteous behavior. The early Believers [in Islam] were concerned with social and

political issues but only insofar as they related to concepts of piety and proper behavior needed to ensure salvation.[17]

Donner is correct, for the fundamental concern of the Qur'an is the individual's relationship with God—the Creator and the Sustainer of the world and the heavens, and the Compassionate Lord of all humans. Belief in and servitude to God is the most fundamental duty of every person, along with the duty to obey and honor His commandments. Every human being is given a short time on earth and is then destined for the afterlife, where all will be judged by God. So the temporal life we know is nothing but a test—a test of choosing between truth and falsehood, good and evil. One of the very earliest revelations of the Qur'an emphasized this test, by reminding that God created the human being and showed him "the two ways":

> Have We not given him two eyes, and a tongue and two lips and
> shown him the two ways?
>   But he has not braved the steep ascent.
>   What will convey to you what the steep ascent is?
>   It is freeing a slave, or feeding on a day of hunger an orphaned
> relative, or a poor man in the dust.
>   Then to be one of those who have faith, and urge each other
> to steadfastness and urge each other to compassion.[18]

No one has yet noticed, to my knowledge, that this Two Ways teaching in the Qur'an is strikingly similar to another Two Ways teaching that we find in another sacred text: the *Didache*, or *The Teaching of the Twelve Apostles*, the Jewish Christian document from the late first century. This is how the very beginning of the *Didache* reads:

> There are two Ways, one of Life and one of Death, and there is
> a great difference between the two Ways. The Way of Life is
> this: First, thou shalt love the God who made thee, secondly, thy

neighbour as thyself; and whatsoever thou wouldst not have done
to thyself, do not thou to another.[19]

The two passages above, from the Qur'an and the *Didache*,
are curiously similar—not verbatim, obviously, but theologically.
Both teach that God shows Two Ways to humans, and that the good
way is defined by devotion to God and benevolence to other humans.
Both, in other words, offer salvation to humankind through the
right faith *and* good works—unlike the Pauline doctrine of being
saved by "faith alone," or *sola fide*, a theological term coined later
by Martin Luther.

This emphasis on faith and works is so powerful in the Qur'an
that it defines its believers as "those who have faith and do right
actions." This expression is used in some forty-five different verses
and often as the definition of the very formula of salvation. "Those
who have faith and do right actions," one of those verses promises,
"the All-Merciful will bestow His love on them."[20]

We will come back to the question of how the *Didache*'s theology of monotheism and piety, reflecting first-century Jewish Christianity, reappeared in the Qur'an six centuries later. It will be helpful
before that, however, to look a bit deeper into the birth of Islam and
its connection to its Abrahamic sisters.

INTERRELIGIOUS CONNECTIONS

Idolatry, as we noted before, was the norm in the Arabian Peninsula
of the early seventh century. Yet there were other faith communities. Besides the monotheist *Hanifs*, about which we know very
little, there were also Jews and Christians. Judaism had come to
Arabia in fact quite early, probably right after the Roman destruction of the Temple in Jerusalem in AD 70. Hence, at the time of
Muhammad, there were Arabic-speaking Jewish communities in
the oasis-based towns of the northwestern side of the peninsula—
such as Tabuk, Tayma, Khaybar, and Yathrib.[21] Yathrib was the city

to which Muhammad migrated in 622, to flee the persecution in Mecca that had come very close to killing him. Hence Yathrib became the second home of Muslims, and later became known as the City of the Prophet, or *Madinatu an-Nabi*. The term *madina* here, meaning "city," soon replaced Yathrib as the town's name.

In this Medina there were three Jewish tribes, and the Prophet of Islam signed a significant charter with them soon after his arrival. One of the clauses of this charter declared, "To the Jews their religion, and to the Muslims their religion." Interpreted today by Muslim intellectuals as a basis for pluralism, the charter unfortunately did not live long, as the secret connections of the Jewish tribes with the pagans of Mecca led to their tragic expulsion from Medina.[22] Yet still the interaction of Muslims with the Jews in the city, which can be traced in many verses of the Qur'an, allowed both interfaith dialogue and dispute.

Meanwhile, Christianity was present in the southern part of Arabia, or Yemen, in the east, and in the north, bordering present-day Iraq and Syria. Therefore, Muslims had less direct acquaintance with Christians than with Jews during the formative years of Islam, but they had contacts nonetheless. Muhammad himself had met Christians during commercial trips to Syria, before the beginning of his prophetic mission. As the Islamic tradition tells us, it was on one of these trips that a Christian monk named Bahira saw and identified the adolescent Muhammad, taken there by his uncle, as the awaited Prophet. This story, along with that of the priest Waraqa, highlights not only the Muslim idea that "true Christians" saw the light of the Prophet Muhammad. It also highlights, regardless of the historical accuracy of the story, that Islam saw a light in Christianity that it could take as its precursor.

In fact, as a monotheistic revolution in a polytheistic society, Islam clearly perceived former monotheisms, especially Judaism and Christianity, as sister faiths and even allies. The Qur'an defined Jews and Christians as the "People of the Book," respecting their scriptures—the *Tawrat,* which is the Torah, the *Zabur,* which is the Psalms, and the *Injil,* which is the gospel, derived from the Greek word *evangelion.* The Qur'an held that it was not a major novelty, but a confirmation of those older books, or "what was there before it."[23]

Hence the older monotheists were not called to convert to Islam necessarily, but to follow their own scriptures wholeheartedly. "The people of the Gospel," the Qur'an openly decreed, "should judge by what God sent down in it."[24] Jews and Christians, in other words, were called to be better Jews and Christians. A Qur'anic verse promised salvation to them, as long as they had faith and good deeds:

> Surely those who believe, and those who are Jews, and the Christians, and the Sabians, whoever believes in God and the Last day and does good, they shall have their reward from their Lord, and there is no fear for them, nor shall they grieve.[25]

The term "Sabian" here, which apparently refers to a religious community known to the earliest Muslims, has been much discussed. The common view is that the Qur'an's Sabians were Mandaeists, the members of a gnostic Mesopotamian religion that bore influences of Zoroastrianism but also of Christianity, with John the Baptist being a central figure. The fact that the Qur'an promised salvation for them, along with Jews and Christians, reflects a theological liberality in early Islam that most contemporary Muslims would have a hard time even to consider.

In *Muhammad and the Believers,* Donner argues that this theological liberality was so wide in early Islam that it was in fact a movement of believers—*mu'minun,* a term used almost a thousand times in the Qur'an—which was a broad umbrella that could incorporate all monotheists. The specific believers who followed Muhammad were called Muslims—*muslimun,* a term used in the Qur'an seventy-five times. But these Muslims spearheaded a "confessionally open religious movement," which "enjoined all monotheists to live in strict observance of the law that God had repeatedly revealed to humankind—whether in the form of the Torah, the Gospels, or the Qur'an."[26]

One should consider that Islam did not have to follow this pluralistic path. "It would have been much simpler for the early Muslim community to make a clean, harsh break from the Jews and Christians," notes Zachary Karabell, an American historian. Muhammad simply "could have dismissed them as apostates and adversaries, and presented them with the choice to convert or be eliminated."[27] This was clearly not the case and, while one can find pragmatic reasons to explain why, there is also a theological reason—a shared commitment to monotheism.

This affinity for older monotheisms in early Islam led to some interesting political alliances as well. In 615, the fifth year after the first revelation, the nascent Muslim community in Mecca faced severe persecution from the city's idolatrous establishment. Those without strong clan ties were especially vulnerable, and thus the Prophet told some eighty-four among them to migrate to save their lives. Their destination was the Christian Kingdom of Aksum in Abyssinia, today's Ethiopia, which was just on the other side of the Red Sea. The Christian king there, Muhammad said, "would not tolerate injustice and it is a friendly country."[28] And the king, called the Negus, indeed welcomed the Arab refugees who sought refuge in Abyssinia, and proved happy to discover that they believed in one God—and, also, even in the virgin birth of Christ, a point which we shall examine later. These Muslim refugees lived in Abyssinia for fifteen years before returning to Arabia when it became safer for them.

A more significant political event of the time was the series of wars between the Byzantine and the Sassanid Empires—or, in religious terms, Christians and Zoroastrians. During the first decade of Islam, from 610 to 620, the Sassanid armies had the upper hand in this drama, inflicting on the Byzantines a series of crushing defeats. The Sassanid armies captured Jerusalem in 614, massacring thousands of its Christian inhabitants, burning churches, and confiscating the True Cross—on which Jesus was believed to have been crucified. Soon the Sassanids conquered Syria and Egypt as well and reached the gates of the Byzantine capital, Constantinople. Arabia itself was not touched by these Byzantine-Sassanid wars, but the Arabs followed the clash of the two superpowers of the world with fascination. Back in Mecca, there was even more interest, for Muslims identified with the Christian Byzantines, also called "Romans," whereas the idolaters sympathized with the Zoroastrian Sassanids. The victories of the latter, therefore, only disillusioned the Muslims. But then, probably sometime in the year 615, soon after the sacking of Jerusalem, Muhammad declared a new revelation from God, which promised a joyful turn of events:

> The Romans have been defeated in the land nearby, but after their defeat they will themselves be victorious in a few years' time. The affair is God's from beginning to end. On that day, the believers will rejoice in God's help. He grants victory to whomever He wills. He is the Almighty, the Most Merciful.[29]

Curiously enough, the Romans did indeed soon defeat the Sassanids, in the battle of Nineveh in 627. The victory led to their retaking Syria and Mesopotamia, including Jerusalem, and recovering the True Cross, which had been taken to Persia as a trophy. Meanwhile, the revelation just quoted was included in the Qur'an as the opening verses of the chapter titled "*Rum*," or "The Romans." Today it is evidence that at the very beginning of Islam, Muslims saw Christians as allies.

Moreover, the Roman emperor who defeated the Sassanids, Heraclius, achieved an interesting sympathetic portrayal in Muslim literature. His Christian piety and virtuous rule received praise from early exegetes of the Qur'an. Muslim historians also wrote about a letter sent by the Prophet Muhammad to Heraclius, "the great leader of the *Rum*," inviting him to accept Islam, or, at least, follow the

Qur'anic call to Jews and Christians: "O People of the Book, let us arrive at a word that is common to us all: we worship God alone, we ascribe no partner to Him, and none of us takes others beside God as lords."[30] Heraclius responded to the letter warmly, as we read in Muslim sources, and, while this might be a pious fiction, it is also a notable witness to the attitude toward the Christian *Rum* in the early Muslim imagination.[31]

Rome (that is, Byzantium) was to the north of Arabia. In the south, another notable contact took place in 631, just a year before the passing of Muhammad, when a group of Christians from Najran, a city between Mecca and Yemen, came to Medina. Led by a man named Abdul Masih, or "the Slave of the Messiah," the delegation stayed in the Muslim capital and were allowed by the Prophet to pray in the mosque. (The Saudi kingdom, which does not allow a single Christian to set foot in Mecca and Medina today, somehow doesn't glean the right lesson from this episode.) As Muslim historians later reported, these Christians both felt moved by the Muslims' respect for Jesus but also objected to the Qur'an's assessment of their doctrines about the nature of Christ. Yet still Muhammad signed a pact with them, which included the following clauses:

> Najran has the protection of God and the pledges of Muhammad, the Prophet, to protect their lives, faith, land, property, those who are absent and those who are present, and their clan and allies. They need not change anything of their past customs. No right of theirs or their religion shall be altered. No bishop, monk or church guard shall be removed from his position.[32]

Yet the tolerance of Islam toward other religions that we find in the Qur'an and the Prophet's life gradually declined, as Muslims defined themselves as a new religion that is totally distinct from, and even at odds with, other monotheistic traditions.[33] This "cult of Islam as the one true religion," as Karen Armstrong puts it, lost

sight of its founder's claim not to found "a new, exclusive religion."[34]
Meanwhile mundane geopolitics led to bitter conflicts between the
expanding Muslim empire and the Christian states—and to the
latter's counterattack, the Crusades.

Yet the early affinity between Muslims and their older monotheist relatives still had a lasting legacy with some practical results.
While the Qur'an banned Muslims from eating the food of pagans,
which could have been unclean and even slaughtered for idols, it
declared the food of the Jews and Christians permissible.[35] That is
why most conservative Muslims living in the West today, who feel
unsure about ritual uncleanness of common food, safely opt for ko-
sher products. Similarly, the Qur'an banned Muslims from marrying
polytheists, but allowed Muslim men to marry Jewish or Christian
women, without their converting to Islam.[36]

Moreover, a certain level of respect for the People of the Book
remained in Islam, allowing Judaism and Christianity to survive
under Muslim rule. This rule did spread "by the sword," as often
noted, but it did not impose Islam by the sword.[37] Both written
and archeological evidence today show that after the Islamic conquest of Syria, the stronghold of eastern Christianity in the seventh
century, churches remained untouched and new churches were built.
There are even records of places of worship shared between Muslims
and Christians in the first century of Islam—in cities like Jerusalem,
Damascus, and Homs.[38]

That is why the head of the East Syrian Church, Catholicos
Isho'yahb III, wrote positively about the Muslim conquerors around
the year 650, noting: "Not only are they no enemy to Christianity,
but they are even praisers of our faith, honorers of our Lord's priests
and holy ones, and supporters of churches and monasteries."[39]
There were contrary Christian views as well, yet writing some four
decades later, John bar Penkaye, a Syriac Nestorian monk, also
sounded happy with the replacement "kingdom of the Persians"
with "kingdom of the children of Hagar," as he called the Muslims.

"[God] had previously prepared them to hold Christians in honor," he even suggested. "Thus there also carefully came from God a certain commandment that they should hold our monastic order in honor."[40]

Islam's spread in the Middle East helped the Jews as well—including ending their longing for Jerusalem. The mere Jewish presence in the holy city was banned by the pagan Romans in AD 135 after the disastrous Bar Kokhba revolt. When Rome adopted Christianity in the fourth century, the ban continued with a specifically Christian bias. The church father Jerome in fact blessed the Roman persecution of the Jews as "the wrath of the Lord" on "the children of this wretched nation . . . [who] are not worthy of compassion." Yet when Caliph Umar conquered Jerusalem in 637, to bring the holy city under Islamic rule, Jews were not only allowed but even encouraged to go there. The Jewish scholar Daniel al-Qumusi wrote about this resettlement appreciatively in the late ninth century, noting that after the coming of "the king of Ishmael," or the Arab caliph, "Israel come from the four corners of the earth to Jerusalem to preach and pray."[41]

Beyond Jerusalem, too, Muslims proved hospitable to Jews—at a time when Christians typically denigrated them as "god killers." Hence, during the Muslim conquests in the Middle East and North Africa, including Spain, "the Jews usually rejoiced when Christian territory fell into Islamic hands."[42] In return, Christians often "considered the Jews allies of the Muslims and Islamic fifth columnists in Christian territory."[43]

Today, the disturbing strains of hostility toward Christians in the Muslim world derive less from Islam's core texts but more from the political grievances against the West, which leads to a selectively negative reading of those texts. Similarly, the ugly echoes of anti-Semitism in the contemporary Muslim world are produced less by the traditional sources of Islam than by the Arab-Israeli conflict and the fifty-year-old Israeli occupation of Palestine.

THE JEWISH CONNECTION

Everything we have noted so far in this chapter tells us, in a nutshell, that Islam was born as a new episode of Abrahamic monotheism, with remarkable connections to its predecessors. But the more curious question is how this Abrahamic rebirth in pagan Arabia exactly came to be. What was its true origin?

For Muslims, including myself, this question has a metaphysical answer: Islam's origin is divine revelation. The voice that spoke to Muhammad in that cave was really not a demon or a hallucination, but the Angel Gabriel. God had revealed His word to Abraham, Moses, and Jesus before, and He revealed it to Muhammad as well. Thus the parallels between Islam and older monotheisms are easy to explain: they reflect the continuation of the same revealed wisdom that comes from the same God.

For non-Muslims, however, who would understandably not accept this faith-based answer, the question is how Muhammad accumulated and incorporated the knowledge of older religious traditions into the Qur'an along with his own sayings—which later were collected as the hadiths, making up the secondary textual source of Islam. The question, in other words, is what the "historical Muhammad" inherited and from whom.

This question has been tackled over the past two centuries by various Orientalists who studied Islam's origins, and much emphasis has been put on a possible Jewish connection—that the Prophet of Islam borrowed heavily from the teachings of Judaism. And it is a persuasive thesis, to a great extent, for Islam indeed is a religion that strongly resembles Judaism and includes many of its elements.

To see how, let's begin with the Qur'an. It is *not* a book like the New Testament, which reports the sayings and deeds of Jesus. It is rather a book like the Torah, which is believed to be revealed by God. And like the Torah, the Qur'an tells its reader about God, His creation of the world in seven days, His rules, and His prophets.

Just as the Qur'an resembles the Torah, so the Prophet Muhammad resembles Moses, who is notably the most frequently named and most extensively narrated character of the whole Qur'an.[44] Yet both Moses and Muhammad are mortal human beings who happen to be lawgivers; not the "son of God" in a divine sense, let alone God incarnate. Hence neither Judaism nor Islam has a doctrine of the Trinity, or anything like it, as their monotheism is similarly strict and uncompromising. In both religions, the nature of God is also unknown, and man can know God only by knowing his "attributes"—such as His justice, His mercy, and His majesty.

Also, neither Judaism nor Islam recognizes any "saints," who are, in Catholicism, intermediaries between God and men. Similarly, neither Judaism nor Islam accepts the doctrine of original sin and the related notion of redemption. In both religions, humans just have to ask forgiveness from God for their individual sins— not seek atonement for some inherent guilt that they carry as Adam's children.

Both religions have a strong tradition of religious law—Halakha in Judaism, Shariah in Islam. This law covers the rules of personal observance, such as dietary laws or the dress code. It also covers public matters, such as the penal code. (The punishment for adultery in the Torah, for example, is stoning. In the Qur'an, it is lashes, although stoning was later incorporated into the Shariah via certain hadiths.) How literally this law should be understood and whether it should be really implemented or not are questions that tend to divide both religions according to orthodox, conservative, reformist, or secular points of view.

Some of the parallels in the Judaic Halakha and the Islamic Shariah are also striking. *Sadakah* in Islam, the term for "alms," is *tzedakah* in Judaism. In both traditions, pork is strictly banned, even reviled. There are certain dress codes for both men and women. Ritual slaughter of the animals—called *shechita* in Judaism and *dabihah* in Islam—is a must for any meat to be "clean." Circumcision for males is another must—and "the uncircumcised" can be a derogatory term for the heathen. Lately such common practices in Judaism and Islam led to controversies in Europe, as some governments banned circumcision and ritual animal slaughter out of concern for human rights and animal rights. As a response, European imams and rabbis gathered in 2015 to form a Muslim-Jewish Leadership Council to defend these practices as part of their "religious freedom."[45]

Worship in Judaism and Islam has also similarities. The Prophet Muhammad and his followers in Medina used to pray three times a day, by turning their faces—guess where—to Jerusalem, in the same manner with the Jews in the city. This direction of prayer, or *qibla*, changed only in the fifteenth year of Muhammad's prophecy, when a new revelation told Muslims to turn their faces to the Masjid al-Haram—the Ka'aba and its surroundings—marking a difference, and perhaps a departure, from Judaism. Yet today the mosque and the synagogue are analogous temples: there is no graven image, no object of devotion such as the cross. That is why while Orthodox Jews are forbidden to pray in Christian churches, let alone even enter them, they are allowed by their rabbis to pray in Muslim mosques.[46]

Due to all such similarities between Judaism and Islam, medieval Nestorian Christians had perceived Muslims as "the new Jews."[47] In the modern era, some Western scholars argued that Islam is nothing but an adaptation of Judaism to an Arab context. With his 1833 landmark work, *Was hat Mohammed aus dem Judenthume aufgenommen?*, or "What did Mohammed take from Judaism?," the German rabbi and scholar Abraham Geiger argued that Hebrew scripture and rabbinical sources shaped the worldview of the Qur'an. In a 1927 article, "The Influence of Judaism in Islam," Alfred Guillaume wrote about the Qur'an's "Jewish fibre." Writing in 1925, John C. Blair suggested that the Qur'an is in fact "a compendium of Talmudic Judaism."[48] In his 1954 book, *Judaism in Islam*, Abraham I. Katsh advanced the argument, asserting that Prophet Muhammad "borrowed extensively from Jewish sources."[49]

Yet there is another powerful theme in the Qur'an that not only has no place within Judaism, but has been often avidly rejected by Jews throughout the past two thousand years: that their much-awaited Messiah has already come—and that he is none other than Jesus of Nazareth.

THE QUR'ANIC MESSIAH

In the Qur'an, there is a long chapter called "*Al-Ma'ida*," which means "The Table"—a table that relates to Jesus and his disciples, as we will see later. A part of its content is about the religious history of Jews and Christians. In one passage, God explains this history, referring to Himself with the pronoun *We*, which is often used in the Qur'an as an expression of magnanimity:

> We sent down the Torah containing guidance and light, and the Prophets who had submitted themselves gave judgment by it for the Jews—as did their scholars and their rabbis—by what they had been allowed to preserve of God's Book to which they were witnesses.[50]

In other words, all the Jewish prophets were sent by God—the God of the Qur'an, who was also the God of the Torah. He was the One, as the next verse explains, who prescribed to Jews: "A life for a life, an eye for an eye, a nose for a nose, an ear for an ear, a tooth for a tooth, and retaliation for wounds; but if anyone forgoes that as a charity, it will act as expiation for him." But finally, the same God sent another prophet to the same Jews, with a new scripture that confirmed the Torah but brought some new guidance as well:

> And We sent Jesus son of Mary following in their footsteps, confirming the Torah that came before him. We gave him the Gospel containing guidance and light, confirming the Torah that came before it, and as guidance and admonition for those who fear God.[51]

Jesus, son of Mary—or, in its Arabic original, *Isa ibn Maryam*—is how the Qur'an most typically refers to Jesus. The etymological origin of the word *Isa* has led to different theories, but it most likely seems to be derived from the original Hebrew name of Jesus, which is *Yeshua*, by first turning into *Yeshu* in Syriac, then *Yasu* among Arab Christians, and finally taking the form *Isa*.[52] *Maryam*, meanwhile, is the clearly original Aramaic name of Mary.

Jesus appears in some ninety-three verses of the Qur'an in fifteen different chapters. Some of these verses narrate the miraculous birth of Jesus—from a virgin mother, Mary, and no father. Others explain the message he gave to his people, the Jews. "I come confirming the Torah," Jesus reportedly says, for example, "and to make lawful for you some of what was previously forbidden to you."[53] In other words, the Islamic Jesus is a reformer within Judaism, who offers Jews a less strict and restrictive Halakha. Jesus' miracles are also narrated in the Qur'an; some of these accounts seem parallel to the New Testament gospels and others parallel to what Christians call the Apocrypha. Finally, the Qur'an has its own perspective on the nature of Jesus and the crucifixion and, with a bit of a stretch of the imagination, even on the Second Coming.

We will look into such details of the Qur'anic Jesus in the chapters ahead. At this point, it is just worth underlining the crux of the matter: the Qur'an emphatically declares that Jesus is the Messiah. The term *al-Masih* is used eleven times in the Qur'an and always to refer to Jesus. He is *Isa al-Masih*, which could best be translated as Jesus the Christ. In a few verses, Jesus is mentioned not by his name but only with this title. "The Messiah said," one such verse reads, "Children of Israel; worship God, my Lord and your Lord."[54]

The Qur'an never explains what "the Messiah" means, which gives the impression that the term was already known at the time and milieu. Notably, all the verses that mention "the Messiah" were revealed in Medina, which, as we noted before, was also the home of a large Jewish community.[55] One thus gets the impression that the verses about "the Messiah" could be, at least in part, a polemic against these Jews: Are still you expecting a Messiah? It was the Jesus whom you denied!

However, the Qur'an's polemic about the Messiah targets another faith community as well: Christians. They are not blamed for denying the Messiah, as the Jews did, but, quite the contrary, for venerating the Messiah excessively, to the extent of seeing him as divine. A long passage in the Qur'an calls on those among the People of the Book who define the Messiah as the Son of God and speak of a trinitarian godhead:

> People of the Book! Do not go to excess in your religion. Say nothing but the truth about God. The Messiah, Jesus son of Mary, was only the Messenger of God and His Word, which He cast into Mary, and a Spirit from Him. So have faith in God and His Messengers. Do not say, "Three." It is better that you stop. God is only One God. He is too Glorious to have a son. Everything in the heavens and in the earth belongs to Him. God suffices as a Guardian. The Messiah would never disdain to be a servant to God, nor would the angels near to Him.[56]

These verses present some interesting parallels to Christian texts—such as Jesus being the Word of God, reminiscent of the Logos in the Fourth Gospel. But they also present a bold rejection of Jesus as the Son of God and the very notion of a triune God. Jesus is the son of Mary, not of God, and like other messengers before him, he is ultimately a servant of God.

With such arguments against both Judaism and Christianity, the Qur'an takes a middle ground between them: To Jews, it says that Jesus was the legitimate Messiah that they should have honored and obeyed. To Christians, it says that Jesus was still a human who worshiped God—and not an object of worship himself. Jacques Jomier, a Dominician priest, once observed the peculiarity of this middle ground, noting:

> Faced with the problem of its Christian background, the Koran takes a position when it pronounces against the divinity of Jesus

Christ. In that, it is close to Rabbinic Judaism, which in its turn
has denied Christ's divinity. Still this Judaism should not be confused with that professed by Orthodox rabbis. The Koranic tendencies are so Christianizing that the Koran contains something
about the person of Jesus that goes beyond simple respect. In effect,
who in the circles of Orthodox Jews would have been able to call
Jesus Word of God and Messiah, when one knows the force of
understanding lying beneath such titles?[57]

Curiously, this middle position that seemed to be confusing to
Jomier, and to many other observers, is not just *any* position between
Judaism and Christianity. It is rather the very doctrine upheld by
Jewish Christians, centuries before Islam. For Jewish Christians,
as we saw in the previous chapters, Jesus was the awaited Messiah,
but only as the last great Jewish prophet, not as God.

Those who noticed the theological connection here include
Hans Küng, the Swiss Catholic scholar who has been dubbed the
"greatest living theologian." In his majestic 2007 book, *Islam*,
he notes: "The analogies between the Qur'anic picture of Jesus and
a christology with a Jewish–Christian stamp are perplexing. These
parallels are irrefutable and call for more intensive historical and
systematic reflection."[58]

And now is the time for such a reflection.

CHAPTER FOUR

THE MISSING LINK

Here is a paradox of world-historical proportions: Jewish Christianity indeed disappeared within the Christian church, but was preserved in Islam.

—Hans-Joachim Schoeps, religious historian and philosopher

IN SEVENTEENTH-CENTURY IRELAND, THERE LIVED A MAN named John Toland. He was a "freethinker," as secular intellectuals were called at the time, and a controversial writer. His very first book, *Christianity Not Mysterious*, published in 1696, argued that biblical miracles could actually all be natural phenomena—an argument that got him into trouble. He was prosecuted by a grand jury in London for "heresy" and authorities in Ireland demanded that he be burned at the stake. Luckily, it was just the copies of his book that were publicly burned in Dublin. The British Isles at the time, like all of Europe, were not terribly liberal places.

Yet Toland did not give up writing and penned other books that questioned church dogma. In 1718 he published a new volume: *Nazarenus: Or Jewish, Gentile, and Mahometan Christianity*. It was a book that proposed religious tolerance to Europeans by showing them the invisible links between the three Abrahamic faiths.

For this noble goal, Toland highlighted two themes that were quite unknown to his contemporaries: the "Nazarenes" and "Mahometan

Christianity." The "Nazarenes," or Jewish Christians, Toland explained, were the Jews who believed in Jesus but did not cease to observe the Jewish Law. They were not heretics, he stressed, but "Primitive Christians most properly so called, and the only Christians for some time"—even the representatives of the "the Original Plan of Christianity." The lesson for contemporary Christians, Toland argued, was that "hatred to the Jews," and of the Jews' practice of their law, was terribly wrong.[1]

The second theme of the book, the more provocative one, concerned "Mahometan Christianity." The term *Mahometan*, derived from "Muhammadan," was the usual English designation for Muslims—apparently due to the misperception that the Prophet Muhammad was as central to Islam as Jesus Christ was to Christianity. Yet the notion of a "Mahometan Christianity" was simply unheard of.

Toland had discovered this phenomenon, to his amazement, in 1709, in Amsterdam, when he read "a Mahometan Gospel, never before publicly made known among Christians." This was a reference to the *Gospel of Barnabas*, which is considered by most scholars as a pseudepigraphal work, indeed a pious forgery, apparently written in the fifteenth century by some unknown Muslim author to help support the Qur'anic view of Jesus. But the document was still helpful to see that view, about which Toland was fascinated to learn. "What Mahometans believe concerning Christ and his doctrine were [not] the inventions of Mahomet," he concluded, disagreeing with the then-common view of Islam's origin. Muslim beliefs were rather quite Nazarene, he wrote, making these beliefs "as old as the time of the Apostles."[2]

Toland, as far as we know, was the first person in the West ever to highlight the curious link between Islam and Jewish Christianity—although another British writer, Henry Stubbe, also had offered similar thesis, only in passing, half a century previously.[3] Yet the idea did not have a great impact at the time and remained buried in the bookshelves. About a century and a half after Toland, the German scholar Ferdinand Christian Baur (1792–1860), founder of the famous Tübingen School of New Testament studies, took up Toland's thesis, but only on the issue of Jewish Christianity, which he called "*Judenchristentum.*" Baur's work, which highlighted the tension between Pauline Christianity and the "Jerusalem Church" led by James, proved to be a groundbreaking basis for "historical Jesus" studies. Yet the connection of this story to Islam remained unexplored.

Nearly a century after Baur, however, one of the scholars of the Tübingen School, Adolf von Harnack (1851–1930), reopened the discussion about the origins of Islam. He focused on the doctrines of the Jewish Christian sect called Elkesaites, which he defined as "Gnostic Judeo-Christianity," and found it "in many and decisive regards as congenial and on a par with Islam."[4] Harnack summed his conclusion in what later become a famous quote: "Islam is a transformation of the Jewish religion already transformed by the gnostic Jewish-Christians on Arabic soil."[5]

Harnack's thesis was later picked up and developed by other German scholars, first by Adolf Schlatter and then, more notably, by Hans-Joachim Schoeps. The latter focused on the most well-known Jewish Christian sect, the Ebionites, and traced their views in the Qur'an in a 1949 article. What he discovered, in his own words, was "a paradox of world-historical proportions." It was the paradox that "Jewish Christianity indeed disappeared within the Christian church, but was preserved in Islam and thereby extended some of its basic ideas even to our own day."[6]

In the 1960s the discussion was reopened by the Israeli scholar Shlomo Pines, based on his study of the medieval Muslim writer Abd al-Jabbar's critique of Pauline Christianity. Al-Jabbar's arguments, Pines argued, prove the existence of a continuous Jewish Christian tradition as late as the twelfth century.[7] But his own colleague, S. M. Stern, wrote a powerful rebuttal against Pines and, to a great extent, discredited the argument.[8]

In 1971 Martiniano Pellegrino Roncaglia, a scholar at the Arab Institute for East and West Studies in Beirut, extended the discussion in "Ebionite and Elkesaite Elements in the Koran."[9] In the 2000s, other scholars such as François de Blois, Edouard M. Gallez, Joachim Gnilka, and Joseph Azzi also explored the connection between Jewish Christianity and Islam, in academic books and scholarly journals.[10] Finally famed Danish-American scholar of Islamic studies Patricia Crone took up the issue. Yet her comprehensive two-part article on "Jewish Christianity and the Qur'an" was published only after her death in July 2015.[11]

Despite all this academic work, the continuum between Jewish Christianity and Islam, this "paradox of world-historical proportions," as Schoeps put it, is largely unnoticed, even by most of the experts in the academia. "It is really astonishing," as François de Blois observed in 2002, "that this discussion has had virtually no resonance among specialists in Arabic and Islamic studies."[12] The eminent theologian Hans Küng also found it astonishing that the "unmistakable parallels between the Qur'an and the understanding of Christ in Jewish-Christian communities" have found only "few echoes." One major reason, Küng argued, is the common unwillingness to ask disturbing questions: "Not only Muslim theologians but also Christian dogmatic theologians of all confessions often simply ignore inconvenient results of exegetical and historical research."[13]

The inconvenient results of research are often the most eye-opening ones, though. And now is our time to look at them.

THE DOCTRINAL CONNECTION

For anyone who ponders the link between Jewish Christianity and Islam, there are two major areas of investigation. The first is the doctrinal connection, or the parallels between the teachings of two faiths. The second is the historical connection, or the channels through which these parallels might have been established. And, as we will now see, the first of these two connections is much easier to establish than the second one.

In fact, I have been probing the doctrinal connection since the very beginning of this book. As I explained in the Introduction, it was my accidental discovery of the Epistle of James, as an ordinary Muslim who had known just the Qur'an and other Islamic texts before, that struck me with a powerful sense of familiarity. As discussed earlier, the view of Jesus as a great prophet and the awaited Messiah, but not a divine "Son of God," is quite parallel in Jewish Christianity and in Islam. Similarly parallel is the teaching in both traditions that men are saved by both faith and acts—and not by faith alone.

But there is even more that connects the two faiths doctrinally, and we begin to see them when we read the Qur'an in comparison to Jewish Christian texts—such as the Epistle of James, the *Didache*, or the "Pseudo-Clementine Writings."

We have already noted one interesting parallel between these texts in the previous chapter: both the Qur'an and the *Didache* speak of Two Ways, of good and evil, teaching that men are called upon to chose between them, to be either rewarded or punished by God. But an even more impressive parallel to the Qur'an comes from the "Pseudo-Clementine Writings," in the collection called *Homilies*. Here, in one passage, Simon Peter, the apostle, proclaims: "God is one, and there is no God but Him."[14] Notably, this is nothing but the basic credo of Islam, and repeated almost verbatim in "*al-Baqara*," the second chapter of the Qur'an: "Your God is One God. There is no god but Him."[15]

Besides God—whose absolute unity leaves no room for any trinity—the ways that the prophets are seen in both traditions are also very similar. We know this, in part, from the Book of Elchasai, which was apparently a second-century Aramaic text followed by the Jewish Christian sect called Elchasaites. The book is only available in the writings of the Church fathers who condemn it, but the fragments they report are enough to indicate that these Jewish Christians had a doctrine about prophecy. Accordingly, God had ordained a "True Prophet" to appear and reappear among men to call them to truth, and Jesus Christ was the last reincarnation of this divinely ordained seer.[16] The Qur'anic notion of the chain of prophets, the last of which is Muhammad, is unmistakably similar.

The images of Jesus in Jewish Christianity and Islam are very similar, if not identical, as well. We mentioned that the Qur'an insists that Jesus was the Messiah—which is interesting, for it was probably an alien concept for seventh-century pagan Arabs. Also interesting is the Qur'an's emphasis that Jesus was sent to Jews—that he was, as a Qur'anic verse noted, "a Messenger to the Children of Israel."[17] The seemingly insignificant but actually impressive point here was captured by Patricia Crone, who suggested, "That Jesus was sent to the Israelites is an astonishing claim for a seventh-century preacher to make."[18]

Why astonishing? Because unless one had a sense of historical Jesus, one would rather think that Jesus was sent to the Christians. That is, in fact, what most Muslims readily think today—imagining that Moses is the prophet of Jews, Jesus is the prophet of Christians, and Muhammad is the prophet of Muslims. Therefore, Crone suggests, from her perspective:

> One would have expected the Messenger [Muhammad] to say that Jesus was sent to the *Christians*. Of course there were no Christians before Jesus, but this would hardly have prevented the Messenger from seeing God as sending Jesus to them; and even if we assume his historical sense to have been too well developed for him to do so, one would have expected him to say that the Israelites responded to his preaching by dividing into Jews and Christians, which is historically correct. But what he actually says is that they divided into believing and unbelieving *Israelites* (61:14): in religious terms they split, but ethnically they remained the same.[19]

Alas, according to Jewish Christian texts as well, the impact of Jesus on Jews was exactly the same: dividing them into "believing" and "unbelieving" factions. One document in the "Pseudo-Clementine Writings," the *Ascents of James*, speaks of "us who believe in Jesus, and the unbelieving Jews."[20] That is a very Qur'anic perspective. Or, to frame it in the reverse direction as Crone does, the Qur'an's perspective "is unquestionably Jewish Christian."[21]

Another aspect of the Qur'an that resonates with Jewish Christianity is the great emphasis on Moses as "the paradigmatic prophet."[22] He is by far the most prominent character in the whole Qur'an.[23] His name is mentioned 136 times, whereas Muhammad's name is mentioned only four times. The Qur'anic narrative concerning Moses includes most of the details one finds in the Old Testament—from his being abandoned on the Nile as a baby, to his adoption by the pharaoh's wife, to his escape to Midian, to the burning bush, to his defiance of the pharaoh and his miracles, to the Exodus, to the parting of the sea, and to the golden calf.

Besides views about God and the prophets, there are also some striking similarities between the practices of Jewish Christianity and Islam. The former, being an extension of Judaism, of course had dietary laws that banned pork and carrion, and prescribed circumcision for all males. These practices, as we noted before, all continued in Islam. Beyond these well-known examples, however, Jewish Christians seem to have a practice that is found in neither Judaism nor Christianity, but only in Islam: the prohibition of wine.

We infer the Jewish Christian position on wine from the writings of church father Irenaeus. In his famous book *Adversus Haereses*, or *Against Heresies* (c. AD 180), he wrote that the Ebionites "reject the commixture of the heavenly wine and wish it to be water of the world only."[24] We also know from Hegesippus, the Christian chronicler of the second century, that James the Just, the brother of Jesus and the pioneer of all Jewish Christians, "drank no wine or other intoxicating liquor."[25] These two pieces of information led some scholars to suggest the Jewish Christians, at least some of them, strictly refrained from alcohol. And, of course, the Qur'an also tells Muslims to refrain from "wine," a word often interpreted as a reference to all intoxicants.[26]

Another interesting practice of the Ebionites was daily ablutions, as Epiphanius noted about them. The "Pseudo-Clementine Writings," too, noted a Jewish Christian practice of "ritual ablutions . . . before prayer." Moreover, Jewish Christian males washed themselves after sexual intercourse, and avoided sex during their wives' monthly periods.[27] All of that fits perfectly into the Islamic practices of ablutions before daily prayers (*wudu*), the washing of the whole body after sex (*ghusl*), and abstaining from intercourse during menstruation.

Finally, while the Ebionites did uphold the Jewish Law, they also accepted a certain reform to it introduced by Jesus. "Nor do they accept Moses' Pentateuch in its entirety; certain sayings they reject," Epiphanius wrote about them, disparagingly. He also added that the Ebionites would defend this selective approach to law by claiming, "Christ has revealed this to me."[28] This, too, perfectly fits the Qur'anic image of Jesus, who came to "confirm the Torah" but also to "make lawful for you some of what was previously forbidden to you."[29]

Such parallels between Jewish Christianity and Islam have been noticed by Muslims as well. *İslam Ansiklopedisi* (The Encyclopedia of Islam), published by Turkey's Islamic Directorate of Religious Affairs, has a long entry on "Jewish Christians," which gives a detailed evaluation of their creed. "Jewish Christians," the article concludes, "represented the real message of Jesus, and their image of Jesus is the same with that of Islam."[30]

Therefore, the question facing us is not whether a doctrinal connection between Jewish Christianity and Islam exists. It certainly does exist. The question is how in the world this connection was possible.

THE HISTORICAL CONNECTION

The question about the historical connection is simple: is there a chance that Jewish Christianity, which seems to have vanished in history by the end of the fifth century, might have survived to have an impact in early seventh-century Arabia, to have influenced the "historical Muhammad"?[31]

At first sight, the answer to this question is negative: we have no record of a Jewish Christian community that continued to exist to the time and in the milieu of the Prophet Muhammad. We of course know that certain Christian sects, with their own distinct doctrines, did exist within or near Arabia. Among them were the Melkites, who followed the Byzantine tradition and who accepted the teaching of the Council of Chalcedon, that Christ had two natures—both human and divine, which came together in one person to form one *hypostasis*. There also the Jacobites, who espoused Monophysitism, or the doctrine that Christ had one single nature—a synthesis of divine and human. Then there were Nestorians, who espoused Dyophysitism, or the doctrine that Christ has two separate natures—human and divine, which remained separate. Despite these schisms over the nature of Jesus, which led to bitter disputes at the time, all these Christians were "Pauline." They all believed, in other words, that Jesus was the divine Christ—unlike most Jewish Christians who continued to see him as the human Messiah.

That is why various scholars have been tempted to hypothesize the existence of Jewish Christianity in the time and milieu of the Prophet Muhammad, by simply looking at the doctrinal connection between Jewish Christianity and Islam and then assuming that there must be a historical connection behind it. In the words of Sidney H. Griffith, professor of early Christian studies at the Catholic University of America and an expert on Arab Christianity:

> Unwarrantedly assuming that the Qur'an must have inherited its own teachings from some Christian group in its milieu, these scholars have often looked for, and found, references to Christian groups mentioned in the ancient heresiographies. On that basis they then postulated the presence of remnants of such groups as the Nazarenes or other Judeo-Christian communities in the

Arabic-speaking milieu in the first third of the seventh century, even when there is no confirming historical evidence of their presence there at the requisite time or place.[32]

Among these assumptions, there is the theory that Waraqa, the Christian cousin-in-law of Muhammad who confirmed his prophethood, was in fact an "Ebionite priest."[33] Yet Waraqa is traditionally assumed to be a Nestorian, and there is really no trace of evidence that he was in fact a member of, or even influenced by, a Jewish Christian community. Another assumption is that there must have been "a community of Nazoraean Christians in central Arabia, in the seventh century, unnoticed by the outside world."[34] A more modest version of this theory is that at least "Judaeo-Christian oral traditions could have survived until the time of the Qur'an's origins."[35] Another possibility is that maybe the *Hanif,* the pre-Islamic Arab monotheists, were in fact "semitically oriented Christians."[36] Yet all these theories are postulations without conclusive evidence.

On the other hand, there is some evidence for the existence of sects with Jewish Christian tendencies arising in the Middle East *much later than* the birth of Islam. One is Isawiyya, a Jewish sect that spread in eighth- and ninth-century Iraq and Syria, and which honored Jesus as "a prophet or wise man."[37] There is also a record by the eleventh-century Muslim writer Abd al-Jabbar, whom we have already met, of an unusual sect among Qaraite Jews—those who diverged from rabbinical Judaism by accepting only the authority of the Torah, but not that of the the Talmud, reminiscent of the *sola scriptura* doctrine in Protestanism. This particular Qaraite sect, Jabbar approvingly noted, respect Jesus as "a just and pious [man] and to have had a leading position among the Jews."[38] He also wrote about "Judaizing" Christians who "believe that their Lord is a Jew, the son of a Jew, born from a Jew, and that his mother is a Jewish woman."[39]

Based on such anecdotal evidence, Crone at some point had turned the theory upside down, suggesting that even if we don't have evidence of Islam's flourishing thanks to the legacy of Jewish Christianity, we can argue for a latter-day flourishing of Jewish Christianity thanks to the impact of Islam. "Islam made Judaeo-Christianity a polemically viable position," in her words, "and accordingly the Judaeo-Christians came out of hiding and began to recruit."[40] Yet where these people were really "hiding" before, and what this means for the origin of Islam, still remains unclear.

With their eye on Islam's scripture rather than its history, however, some scholars think that they already have found the key to the hiding place: the very text of the Qur'an. Or, more precisely, the very term the Qur'an uses for "Christians."

THE MYSTERY OF AL-NASARA

If you speak to any native Arab speaker today, and ask him about "Christians," you will probably learn that he refers to them as *al-Masihiyya*. The word comes from *Masih*, or "Messiah," and literally means "those who follow the Messiah." It is thus the perfect equivalent of the term "Christian," which comes from the word *Christ*, or the Greek original, *Christós*, which of course means "Messiah."

Yet for some curious reason, you can never find the term *al-Masihiyya* in the Qur'an. The Qur'an rather consistently uses a different term to designate Christians: *al-Nasara*.

Since the earliest centuries of Islam, Muslims engaged in exegeses pondered the exact meaning of this term. One common explanation was found in the fact that Jesus was from the town of Nazareth. So, some Qur'anic commentators reasoned, Christians were called *al-Nasara* as a reference to the fact that they were the followers of the prophet from Nazareth. Another explanation was found in the consonantal root of the term, *N-S-R*, which means "to help." A verse in the Qur'an quotes Jesus asking his disciples, "Who will be my helpers to God?" The disciples reply, "We will be the helpers of God."[41] So, according this view, the Qur'an called Christians "*al-Nasara*," because they were the "helpers" (*ansar*) of Jesus and God.

Yet we also know that there is a non-Arabic term that fits very well with al-Nasara: the Nazarenes. This was the term used to designate the earliest followers of Jesus, as known from the Book of Acts. Moreover, in the heresiology of Pauline church fathers, Nazareans—also spelled Nazaraeans, Nazoreans, or Nazoraeans—were listed as one of the deviant Jewish Christian sects.

Therefore, some scholars wondered, could the Qur'an's al-Nasara be a reference not to all Christians, but only to Jewish Christians, who could still be present at the time of the Prophet Muhammad, right in the vicinity of Mecca? Could that be our missing link?

This question gets even more interesting when we look at the ways the word *al-Nasara* is used in the Qur'an, where it appears in fourteen different verses. In two of these verses, the people in question are referred to not just as al-Nasara, but as "those who say, 'We are al-Nasara.'" In other words, the term is used as a self-designation of the group. And while we do not know any Christian sect that called itself al-Nasara, we do know a Jewish Christian sect that called itself the Nazarenes.

More interestingly, when the Qur'an condemns belief in the divinity of Jesus, along with the doctrine of the Trinity, which are of course hallmarks of Pauline Christianity, it defines its adherents not as al-Nasara, but rather merely as "those who say" these things:

> *Those who say that the Messiah, son of Mary, is God* are unbelievers. The Messiah said, "Children of Israel! worship God, my Lord and your Lord. If anyone associates anything with God, God has forbidden him the Garden and his refuge will be the Fire." The wrongdoers will have no helpers.
>
> *Those who say that God is the third of three* are unbelievers. There is no god but One God. If they do not stop saying what they say, a painful punishment will afflict those among them who are unbelievers. [Emphases added.][42]

These two verses of the Qur'an have been much discussed. Some interpreters suggest that what the Qur'an condemns here is not exactly the doctrine of the Trinity, but tritheism, or belief in three separate Gods, which would be a heretical belief for Pauline Christians as well. It has been also noted that the precise phrase, "God is the third of three," is not exactly how Pauline Christians express their creed. These suggestions are worth considering, especially for seeking a more lenient interpretation of the Qur'an regarding mainstream Christianity. Yet what is most curious for us, at this point, is that the Qur'an does not condemn al-Nasara as "those who say that the Messiah is God" and "those who say God is the third of the three."

Quite the contrary, the Qur'an actually has very nice things to say about al-Nasara. In one remarkable passage, Jews and polytheists are disparaged for being "the most hostile to the believers," but al-Nasara are generously praised: "You are sure to find that the closest in affection toward the believers are those who say, 'We are al-Nasara,' for there are among them people devoted to learning and ascetics."[43] Then the verses go on to explain how these people fall into tears when they hear the message of the Qur'an:

> When they listen to what has been sent down to the Messenger, you will see their eyes overflowing with tears because they recognize the Truth [in it]. They say, 'Our Lord, we believe, so count us amongst the witnesses. Why should we not believe in God and in the Truth that has come down to us, when we long for our Lord to include us in the company of the righteous?' For saying this, God has rewarded them with Gardens graced with flowing streams, and there they will stay: that is the reward of those who do good.[44]

According to most traditional Muslim exegetes, these Qur'anic verses praising al-Nasara described the situation of the priests of the Negus, the king of Abyssinia who had welcomed the Muslim refugees from Mecca, when they heard the Qur'an. One wonders, therefore, exactly what kind of Christians these Christians of Abyssinia, or Ethiopia, were.

The Ethiopian Church, which still exists today, is considered a part of Oriental Orthodoxy. Hence, it accepts the Council of Nicaea, which defined Christ as divine. Thus, at least at the first sight, it cannot be considered as having a Jewish Christian character. Yet still, the same Ethiopian Church also has unmistakably Jewish practices, such as the observance of the Sabbath and circumcision of males— precisely on the eighth day, as in Judaism. No wonder such un-Pauline features have led European Christians throughout history to blame their Ethiopian coreligionists for "Judaizing tendencies." A Portuguese Jesuit of the eighteenth century even went as far as claiming that "Ethiopian religion" is "nothing but a hotch-potch of Jewish and Moslem superstitions."[45] A more modern and objective comment is that the Ethiopian Church has many traditions that "stem from Judaism," but "have undergone a process of re-shaping and re-forming them consistent with the basic Christian ideas."[46] But when did this "re-shaping and re-forming" take place? Could the Ethiopian Church of the seventh century have been closer to Judaism, and Jewish Christianity, than it is today? These are interesting questions, but because of the lack of literary or archeological data, they can only be answered by historical speculation.

The historian Samuel Zinner attempts such a speculation by arguing that "the Ethiopian Church's fundamentally Jewish character" might be traced back to "Ebionites who together with their Jewish compatriots may have fled the destruction of Jerusalem in 70 CE."[47] Accordingly, Ebionitism, as quintessential Jewish Christianity, might have survived within the Ethiopian Church for centuries in a stealth form. According to another historian, Schlomo Pines, that can be also true for the Nestorian Church, which was allegedly joined by many suppressed Jewish Christians after the fourth century in order to preserve their faith clandestinely. For

Pines, the Nestorian Church must have been the channel through which Jewish Christian teaching reached out to seventh-century Arabia.

Another scholar who studies Islam's origins, François de Blois, a scholar at the School of Oriental and African Studies in London, also thinks that al-Nasara are in fact Jewish Christians, who might have survived and reached Arabia as "an isolated outpost."[48] But the real evidence, de Blois suggests, is in another Qur'anic verdict about al-Nasara: that Muslims can eat their food. "The food of those given the Book is permitted to you," the Qur'an declares, "and your food is permitted to them."[49] This is a nice liberality that makes Muslim life less complicated, but it raises a complication regarding the precise nature of "those given the Book." As de Blois explains:

> If nasara means "catholic Christians," then it is very difficult to see how their food should be "permitted to you," seeing that the catholic canon contains statements to the effect that Jesus "declared all food clean" (Mark 7:19) and that catholic Christians are notorious for their porcophagy. But if the nasara of the Quran are indeed Nazoraeans, who observed the Jewish laws of purity, then the statement that "the food of those to whom the book was given is permitted to you" would make very good sense.[50]

So far, the theory that the Qur'an's al-Nasara are in fact Jewish Christians sounds good. But in fact there are also serious problems with this theory. First, there is a Qur'anic verse that runs contrary to the more sympathetic verses about al-Nasara, condemning them for saying "The Messiah is the Son of God."[51] This must be a reference to not Jewish but mainstream Christianity. Also problematic is the fact that in one of the sympathetic verses about al-Nasara, the Qur'an speaks highly of "people devoted to learning and ascetics" among them, a phrase which has also been translated as "priests and monks." The latter term seems to refer to a monastic class, which is a hallmark of Pauline Christianity, not its Jewish counterpart.[52]

That is why the theory that the Qur'an's al-Nasara could be Jewish Christians is not accepted by all experts on nascent Islam. Critics also note that in Syriac, a language very close to Arabic, the notable word *Nasraye* is used to designate Christians of all kinds. So, they reason, this Syriac term might have easily made its way to the Arabic language, turning Nasraye into Nasara, and that the Qur'an might have simply adopted this Arabic term, without any intention of designating Jewish Christianity.[53]

Sidney H. Griffith, an expert on Arab Christianity, is of this latter persuasion. "The Qur'an's seeming espousal of positions earlier held by some Jewish Christians," he notes, "hardly constitutes evidence for the actual presence of one or another of these long-gone communities in its seventh-century Arabian milieu."[54] Similarly, Gabriel Said Reynolds, professor of Islamic studies at the University of Notre Dame, also argues that the Qur'an's al-Nasara are most probably all Christians and those who argue otherwise are reading too much into the text of the Qur'an. Reynolds also criticizes the "motif of Orientalist scholarship on the Qur'an," which was "to seek out Christian heretics whom Muhammad might have met as a way of explaining Qur'anic material on Christianity." Such scholars, he argues, miss the fact that the Qur'an has its own language, with its own creative use of rhetorical tools such as irony and hyperbole.[55]

In short, the academic discussion on who the Qur'an's al-Nasara really were is far from being resolved. The thesis that they could be identical with Nazarenes, or Jewish Christians, remains an interesting postulation—but not much more.

Does this mean, then, that the historical connection for which we are looking—the missing link between Jewish Christianity and Islam—is doomed to be missing?

Before giving an answer, there is one more piece to add to the puzzle.

A MESSAGE ON A ROCK

In the 1980s the late Israeli archeologist Yehuda D. Nevo carried out interesting work in the Negev Desert in southern Israel. His focus was the rock inscriptions scattered in the area, which were all in the Arabic language and dated back to the seventh or eighth centuries. In particular, near Sde Boke, a kibbutz founded in 1952 to cultivate the arid Negev and still the home of a few hundred Israelis, Nevo discovered something remarkable. Something which could shed some new light on early Islam.

Nevo died in 1992, but his work was published the following year, in a posthumous article titled "Towards a Prehistory of Islam." He began by frankly noting that he was inspired by the "late origins" hypothesis about Islam, which suggested that the Qur'an was actually a much later document than what Muslims believed, that it was created around the eighth century in Mesopotamia by the "Arab empire," which needed a pious fiction for its political claims. In the next few decades after Nevo, however, this late origins hypothesis would be largely discredited, as linguistic research showed the Qur'an to be "the product of the earliest stages in the life of the [Muslim] community in western Arabia."[56] Moreover, German studies in the 1980s of an ancient manuscript of the Qur'an found in Yemen a decade earlier also discredited the "late Qur'an hypothesis," as the parchment proved to be from the early seventh century, making it quite "early."[57]

Yet more important than Nevo's theoretical framework were his actual findings. All the inscriptions he found and examined, some of which included their dates, dated from the mid-first century of Islam (AD 660 to 680) to the second century of Islam (the 780s). But there were categoric differences in their context. The earliest inscriptions were merely monotheist, with devotion to *Allah*, the Arabic word for *God*, but with no exclusive Islamic content, such as reference to the Prophet Muhammad. Hence Nevo called these inscriptions "pre-Muhammadan texts." Later inscriptions, however, were unmistakably Islamic: "There is no God but Allah alone," one of them read, "and Muhammad is His servant and messenger."[58]

Among the pre-Muhammadan texts, one was exceptionally remarkable. Discovered on a rock near Sde Boker, this was a short prayer for forgiveness. And it ended with this line:

> *Amin rabb-l-alamin rabb Musa wa 'Isa.*[59]
> Or, "Amen, the Lord of Worlds, the Lord of Moses and Jesus."

Muslims who just read the Arabic line above might experience a moment of awe, as I personally did the first time I read it. Because the term here, *rabb-l-alamin*, "the Lord of the Worlds," is very familiar to almost every Muslim on the face of the earth. It is in the very first line of the very first chapter of the Qur'an, the "*Fatiha*," or the "Opening," which reads: "Praise be to God, the Lord of the Worlds." It is a line repeated over and over every single day around the globe, in every single Muslim prayer.

Yet, lo and behold, in this very Islamic-sounding line, there is no mention of the Prophet Muhammad. God is honored as "the Lord of Moses and Jesus," not the Lord of Muhammad, which is not an omission that one would normally expect from a Muslim author. That is why Nevo classified this prayer as a "pre-Muhammadan text." It was written by someone, in other words, who was not a Muslim. But by whom?

A Jew would not praise "the Lord of Moses and Jesus," because he would not treat Jesus as a great prophet on a par with Moses. But a Christian would not write it, either, for the exact same reason: Jesus was *not* a great prophet on a par with Moses—he was something much greater, the divine Son of God and Lord himself. Therefore, as Nevo observed, here was the glimpse of a creed that differed from both Judaism and Christianity:

> Coupling Jesus with Moses, the lawgiver who spoke to God face-to-face, gives to Jesus the highest rank attainable by the most pious

of human beings, and has him sharing with Moses the honor of serving as an identifier of God. Nonetheless, it makes Allah's supreme position, and Jesus' subordination, quite clear.[60]

We know that, outside Islam, there is only one tradition that would see Moses and Jesus in this light: Jewish Christianity. Nevo, too, had the same feeling about the source of the pre-Muhammadan texts. "They were certainly left by a Judaeo-Christian group," he argued, which seem to have existed "in the Negev at least, in the late first and early second centuries A.H."[61] (AH stands for "After Hijra," *hijra* being the Prophet Muhammad's migration to Medina in AD 620, which is also the beginning of the Muslim calendar.) Another scholar also stressed that the inscriptions indicate the presence of "a form of Judaeo-Christianity not identifiable with Judaism, Christianity or Islam."[62]

This, indeed, may be the greatest clue we have available regarding the possible existence of a Jewish Christian community at the dawn of Islam.

To add to this archeological evidence, we also have a literary clue that Jewish Christians could really have been in the Negev region at that time. This comes from the writings of "Cyril," who wrote under the name of Cyril of Jerusalem (d. 386), but who is believed to be an author from the sixth or seventh century, and hence is commonly called Pseudo-Cyril. This Christian writer noted a "heretical" Samaritan living in Palestine, who believed "the son of Mary was a prophet of God"—an unmistakably Jewish Christian view of Jesus. He also referred to a monk named Annarichos who lived in the Gaza area and who followed the "Gospel of the Hebrews"—a lost Jewish Christian text.[63]

Yet while these clues are impressive, it is impossible to judge whether they point to just some eccentric individuals or to an active Jewish Christian community that could have transmitted its teachings. Even if such a community existed, it is also impossible to know whether it could have had any influence in the Hijaz region in western Arabia, where Islam was born. Very little archeological research has ever been made in the Hijaz, and our sources for the history of the region are very limited. Hence we have very little material at hand to reconstruct its distant past.

THE ABRAHAMIC ARCHETYPE

After all the search for a historical connection between Jewish Christianity and Islam, we still are left with the observation that Guillaume Dye, one of the experts on the topic, shared in late 2015: "We have no evidence of Jewish Christian groups in Arabia in the early 7th century, and no evidence either that other putative Jewish Christian groups elsewhere in the Near East played a role in the emergence of early Islam."[64]

The "evidence," as Dye pointed out, is offered by circular reasoning: certain teachings in the Qur'an resemble those of Jewish Christians; therefore Jewish Christians must have directly influenced the making of the Qur'an. In fact, with such reasoning, Western researches have found many other "heresies" that must have been present in or nearby seventh-century Arabia. A short list includes Nestorianism, Monophysitism, Tritheism, Antideco-Marcianites, Manichaeism, and Gnosticism.[65] And this is a bit too much, unless one is ready to imagine Arabia "as a kind of Jurassic Park for ancient 'heresies.' "[66]

That is why we should perhaps entertain the possibility that such a Jurassic Park never existed, and the doctrinal connection between Jewish Christianity and Islam is *not* based on a historical connection. Samuel Zinner, one of the Western scholars who have pondered this issue deeply, precisely makes that point, criticizing the "historicist view," which:

> Would not sufficiently take into account the possibility of similar ideas and rites arising independently in two separate religious variants, issuing forth from a single transcendent archetype underlying the Abrahamic faiths.[67]

The transcendent Abrahamic archetype—that is how Zinner, consciously introducing a Platonic philosophical category into the history of religion, explains the doctrinal connection between Jewish Christianity and Islam. Accordingly, the connection doesn't have to be rooted in the Prophet Muhammad's exposure to preexisting religious traditions. It can rather be explained as the rebirth of the Abrahamic archetype unto him—through intuition, if one prefers a secular concept, or through revelation, if one is open to a religious one.

Whichever leap of faith one takes here—the mishaps of history, the archetypes of Platonism, or the metaphysics of religion—it is notable that Islam stands on a "straight path," as it claims, descending all the way from Abraham: a path of pure, simple, austere monotheism. Christian scholar Martiniano Pellegrino Roncaglia put this elegantly in his 1971 article, in which he found in the Qur'an "the crystallization of an Arabized form of Jewish Christianity." Therefore, he explained:

> When the old Christian apologists and heresiologues saw in Islam a Christian heresy, they were not far from the truth; their way of expressing themselves was somewhat simplistic, but they had grasped the kernel of truth of a religious phenomenon that they poorly understood. From the Ebionite standpoint, the dialectical movement that goes from Adam, Abraham, and Moses up to Jesus then found in Muhammad its culmination, historically and theologically.[68]

The mapping of this Abrahamic genealogy could help modern Christians, Roncaglia added, realize that Islam is not too alien to their own tradition, and, in fact, reflects an echo from its earliest phase:

> Some in the West think that Islam, in its cultural expression, represents a religious phase inferior to Christianity, but this is

justified only in that our Western Christianity has been "re-elaborated" and re-thought within Greco-Roman culture. But if we reinsert Christianity within the historical and cultural framework that was originally its own, that is to say, within the Jewish Christian framework, if we set aside the Platonization of Christology in order to return to the forms of the Mother Church of Jerusalem under the leadership of Saint James, "the Lord's brother," and if we reinsert the whole within the Semitic context, then Islam would appear to us in a more favorable light, even in the West.[69]

Such a rethinking of Islam is certainly needed in the contemporary West, where the perception of this great religion has unfortunately been tainted by the misdeeds of its latter-day Zealots. Meanwhile, however, a rethinking of Islam's place in the Abrahamic genealogy is needed for Muslims themselves as well. For quite a few present-day Muslims see the world in a simple dichotomy of us versus them, the followers of truth versus the followers of falsehood, where the latter category includes everything outside of Islam, or even outside their specific sect of Islam.

Yet this parochialism is a far cry from the pluralism one finds in the Qur'an. For example, after stating "the people of the Gospel should judge by what God sent down in it," the Qur'an explicitly notes that the existence of different religious traditions on earth is not an aberration but, quite the contrary, the very will of God:

And We have sent down the Book to you [Muhammad] with truth, confirming and conserving the previous Books. So judge between them by what God has sent down and do not follow their whims and desires deviating from the Truth that has come to you.

We have appointed a law and a practice for every one of you. Had God willed, He would have made you a single community, but He wanted to test you regarding what has come to you. So compete with each other in doing good. Every one of you will return to God and He will inform you regarding the things about which you differed.[70]

In other words, different religious traditions should "compete with each other in doing good," while agreeing to disagree about their differences, deferring the ultimate judgment to God, to be given in the afterlife. Notably, this idea of deference was further developed by a medieval school of thought in Islam, which made the "postponement," or *irja*, of religious disputes to the afterlife its main doctrine. Hence its advocates were called "the Postponers," or the *Murjia*. Unsurprisingly, they have been despised for centuries by intolerant Muslims—including most lately the notorious ISIS—who wish to punish their opponents by claiming authority from God.[71]

Today we need more *irja*, or religious tolerance, both among Muslims themselves and between Muslims and adherents of other faiths. And realizing that Islam does not simply begin with the Prophet Muhammad in seventh-century Arabia, but is rather rooted in former manifestations of the Abrahamic archetype, from Abraham to Moses, from James the Just to the Ebionites, would help. It would help build, at the very least, a deeper, wider, and wiser Muslim historical imagination.

Most important of all, of course, is Jesus. Islam has the utmost respect for him, along with his mother, and places him in a very exalted place. But how does this idea of Jesus exactly differ from his place in Christianity? Or is it as different as it is often assumed? Moreover, what does Islam's connection to Jewish Christianity tells us about the Islamic image of Jesus?

In the rest of this book, I will focus on these questions. And I will begin with the very beginning of the Jesus story: his miraculous birth from his immaculate mother.

CHAPTER FIVE

MARY AND HER BABY

Remember the one who guarded her chastity. We breathed into her from Our Spirit and made her and her son a sign for all people.

—The Qur'an 21:31

In the whole Qur'an, which has more than six thousand verses, there is only one woman mentioned by name. There is even a long chapter named after her. Even more, there is a longer chapter named after her family. And yet that woman is not Aminah, the mother of the Prophet Muhammad; or Khadijah, his first wife; or Fatima, his daughter, as one could have expected to see.[1] She is rather Mary, the mother of Jesus.

Mary is not just named repeatedly in the Muslim scripture—some thirty-four times, compared to nineteen times in the New Testament. She is also exceptionally praised. "God has chosen you and purified you," angels tell Mary in the Qur'an. "He has chosen you over all other women."[2] Consequently, Mary became highly respected in all Muslim cultures, as her Arabic name, *Maryam*, has been given to countless baby girls. There are shrines in her name in the Middle East, which are visited by not just Christians but also Muslims. Among the Sufis, the mystics of Islam, Mary has enjoyed an even deeper adoration, as a perfect example of devotion to God.

In the twentieth century, a group of Sufis even established an order
named *Maryamiyya*, or "the followers of Mary," whose members
include some prominent American academics, such as the Iranian-
born philosopher Seyyed Hossein Nasr.[3]

Even Mary as she appears in Christian texts and contexts has received Muslim respect. Legend has it that when the Prophet Muhammad smashed the hundreds of idols in the Ka'aba in the year 630,
toward the end of his life, he spared only the frescoes of Jesus and
Mary. In 1187, when the Muslim ruler Salahaddin reconquered Jerusalem, he destroyed the churches built in the city by the Crusaders—not
those built by Eastern Christians, with which he had no problem—but
he still spared a Crusader relic: the Church of Saint Anne, which was
believed to be the childhood home of Mary. "The preservation of this
Church demonstrates the Islamic devotion to Mary," a Catholic source
appreciatively notes, "as the Muslims' great reverence for Our Lady
precluded [them] from destroying her birthplace."[4]

The Qur'anic story of Mary, which is impressively detailed for a
scripture whose main focus is elsewhere, is placed in two separate
chapters: the chapter "Mary," which is accepted to be "Meccan" (revealed in Mecca) and thus relatively earlier; and the chapter "Family
of Imran," which is accepted to be "Medinan" (revealed in Medina)
and thus relatively later. There are parallels between the Mary accounts in these two chapters, but also some differences. Moreover,
there are both parallels and differences between them and the New
Testament and Christian Apocrypha.

Let's begin with the chapter "Mary," which presents us a storyline
that largely resembles the beginning of the Gospel of Luke. The plot
begins with "an account of your Lord's grace towards His servant,
Zachariah."[5] We meet him, whose name is Zakariyya in Arabic, without any introduction, without any explanation. But we are still drawn
into his story, when we learn about the secret prayer he gave to God:

> When he called to his Lord secretly, saying, "Lord, my bones have
> weakened and my hair is ashen grey, but never, Lord, have I ever

prayed to You in vain: I fear [what] my kinsmen [will do] when I am gone, for my wife is barren, so grant me a successor—a gift from You—to be my heir and the heir of the family of Jacob. Lord, make him well pleasing [to You]."[6]

In return, to Zachariah's surprise, God answers his prayers and heralds him a blessed son:

O Zachariah! surely We give you good news of a boy whose name shall be Yahya: We have not made before anyone his equal.

He said: "O my Lord! when shall I have a son, and my wife is barren, and I myself have reached indeed the extreme degree of old age?"

He said: "So shall it be, your Lord says: It is easy to Me, and indeed I created you before, when you were nothing."[7]

The son promised to Zechariah is John the Baptist, who is named in the Qur'an as *Yahya*.[8] The word seems to be a derivative of the Syriac name *Yohannan*. Since Zechariah is still surprised by the news of this baby boy, he asks God: "My Lord, give me a Sign." God says, 'Your Sign is not to speak to people for three nights despite the fact that you are perfectly able to."[9] Notably, the Gospel of Luke also notes this detail, reporting that Zechariah was told, "thou shalt be silent and not able to speak."[10] But it is the Qur'an which specifies the period as "for three days."

Angels also call on Zechariah, telling him that his baby boy will be no ordinary son, but will precede someone even more extra-ordinary: "God gives you news of John, confirming a Word from God. He will be noble and chaste, a prophet, one of the righteous."[11] The noteworthy term here, "Word from God," is used for none other than Jesus. For John, the Qur'an also notes the following:

[We said], "John, hold on to the Scripture firmly." While he was still a boy, We granted him wisdom, tenderness from Us, and purity. He was devout, kind to his parents, not domineering or rebellious. Peace was on him the day he was born, the day he died, and it will be on him the day he is raised to life again.[12]

The emphasis here that John the Baptist "held on to the Scripture firmly" fits the doctrinal line of both Jewish Christianity and Islam: that there is a chain of prophets whose primary mission is to uphold the revealed Word of God. Meanwhile, the Qur'anic emphasis on John being "chaste" seems to resonate with the note in the Gospel of Luke that John drank "no wine nor strong drink."[13]

That is all that we learn from the Qur'an about John the Baptist. Actually he is not called "the Baptist," as the concept of baptism never occurs in the Qur'an. Neither do we learn from the Qur'an about John's encounter with Jesus or his execution by Herod. As is the case with most Old Testament figures, such as Elijah and Job, the Qur'an briefly touches on the story of John the Baptist and highlights only its own key theological message: there has been a chain of prophets, from time immemorial, who all proclaimed the same monotheistic message.

MARY'S PREGOSPEL

To proceed with the Qur'anic story of Mary in its correct chronology, we need to go to the other relevant section, "The Family of Imran."[14] This is one of the longest chapters of the Qur'an, and a considerable part of it is about the story of Mary. In fact the very name of the chapter is closely related to Mary, because Imran is none other than the father of Mary. This may sound strange, for while the New Testament never mentions the names of Mary's parents, Christian Apocrypha has established that her mother's name was Anna and her father's name was Joachim, from the Hebrew *Yehoyaqim*. Therefore, how Yehoyaqim became Imran in the Qur'an has led to a scholarly discussion, to which we shall return.[15]

For now, let's see what the Qur'an says about the family of Imran.

Interestingly, the person we really meet here is not Imran, who is totally obscure aside from the mere mention of his name, but his wife, who is quoted at length:

> Imran's wife said, "Lord, I have dedicated what is growing in my womb entirely to You; so accept this from me. You are the One who hears and knows all."
>
> But when she gave birth, she said, "My Lord! I have given birth to a girl." God knew best what she had given birth to: the male is not like the female. "I name her Mary and I commend her and her offspring to Your protection from the rejected Satan."
>
> Her Lord graciously accepted her and made her grow in goodness, and entrusted her to the charge of Zachariah. Whenever Zachariah went in to see her in her sanctuary, he found her supplied with food. He said, "Mary, how is it you have this food?" and she said, "They are from God: God provides limitlessly for whoever He will."[16]

Bible readers might be a little surprised with this passage. For unlike the other Qur'anic passages concerning Mary and her kin that we have quoted so far, this one has no parallels in Luke or any other canonical gospel. There are many details here that are simply unknown to the whole New Testament, such as Mary's devotion to God in her mother's womb, Zachariah's guardianship of the young Mary who stayed at a "sanctuary," or the miraculous food with which she was supplied.[17]

Yet, lo and behold, all these details are found somewhere else: the apocryphal gospel called the *Protoevangelium of James.*

Also called the Book of James, this document should not be confused with the Epistle of James, which is in the New Testament and to which I have referred many times so far. The *Protoevangelium* is a totally separate document, although it is attributed to the same person: James the Just, the brother of Jesus and the leader of the

"Jerusalem Church." However, scholars have established that the document must have been written in the middle of the second century, and in Greek, only to be falsely attributed to James. It is called *Protoevangelium*, or "pregospel," because it addresses the birth and upbringing of Mary along with the delivery of Jesus in a much more detailed way than the New Testament gospels, whose real focus is the mission of Jesus the adult.

As noted by scholars since the seventeenth century, many details in the *Protoevangelium* unmistakably match with the Qur'anic account of Mary.[18] For example, in the former text, Mary's mother, who is named as Anna, praises God for conceiving an unexpected baby and vows, "If I beget either male or female, I will bring it as a gift to the Lord my God."[19] This sounds very similar to the vow one hears from the same person, Mary's mother, in the Qur'an: "Lord, I have dedicated what is growing in my womb entirely to You."[20] Moreover, in both texts, it is Mary's mother, not the father as was typical, who names the newborn baby.

The *Protoevangelium* also tells us that after the birth of Mary, her mother "made a sanctuary in her bed-chamber, and allowed nothing common or unclean to pass through her."[21] This, again, sounds similar to the Qur'anic account, which speaks of Mary's "sanctuary." Then, at the age of three, Mary is dedicated by her parents to "the Temple of the Lord," to live and worship there as a kind of nun, and Zachariah becomes her caretaker. But Mary has heavenly caretakers, too, who provide her with miraculous nourishment. The *Protoevangelium* notes this from the vantage point of the third person: "Mary was in the temple of the Lord as if she were a dove that dwelt there, and she received food from the hand of an angel."[22] The Qur'an notes this detail by means of a dialogue between Mary and Zachariah. "Mary, how is it you have this food?" asks the latter. She answers, "They are from God: God provides limitlessly for whoever He will."[23]

And there is even more. The *Protoevangelium* tells us that when

Mary came of age, Zachariah went out to "assemble the widowers of the people, and let them bring each his rod."[24] The point was to organize a drawing of lots to designate the the future husband of Mary, assuming a divine hand behind things. "To whomsoever the Lord shall show a sign," the *Protoevangelium* explains, "his wife shall she be."[25] And this occurrence, too, of which there is no hint in the New Testament, is mentioned in the Qur'an, albeit in passing. After telling some other news about Mary, the Qur'an, in a monologue to the Prophet Muhammad, tells him:

> This is an account of things beyond your knowledge that We reveal to you [Muhammad]: you were not present among them when they cast lots to see which of them should take charge of Mary, you were not present with them when they argued [about her].[26]

It is interesting that in this verse the Qur'an does not explain who "they" were. Mary's future husband, Joseph, is not in the scene, as he never appears in the Qur'an, and we don't know anyone else around her other than Zachariah, who is her godfatherly protector. Hence major Muslim exegetes such as Tabari wrote that the casting of lots for Mary was not about her marriage but about her custody at a much younger age. According to his account, some nineteen and twenty-nine scribes of the Torah threw their long pens on the water. Only that of Zachariah floated, and hence he took Mary into his custody.[27]

What can be said by looking at all these parallels between the Qur'an and the *Protoevangelium*? It can be said safely that the Qur'an is "closely in conversation with the *Protoevangelium*."[28] Yet the nature of this conversation can be interpreted in different ways. One can assume a historical connection, arguing that the Qur'an must have "borrowed" elements from this earlier Christian document, as Christian writers have often done. Or one can assume, as the Catholic scholar Sidney Griffith suggests:

the Qur'an presumes in its audience a familiarity with the Christian narrative of the annunciation to Mary as it circulated in the largely oral, intertextual, Christian kerygma as it was preached in Arabia in the late sixth and early seventh centuries.[29]

No matter how we interpret the parallelism, we should also take a moment to look at which Christian communities might have being using the *Protoevangelium* at the time and in the milieu in which the Qur'an originated. The book was largely unknown to Western Christians until the sixteenth century, but it had been widely used among Eastern Christians since the fifth century, when it was translated from Greek into Syriac. Despite some of its conflicts with the New Testament gospels—like its suggestion that Mary gave birth to Jesus in a cave in the wilderness, not in Bethlehem—it was widely accepted in Eastern churches. A powerful testimony to this is the Chora Church in Istanbul, now a museum, which has breathtakingly beautiful mosaics that date from the thirteenth century and depict the birth and life of Mary exactly as described in the *Protoevangelium*.

But what about Jewish Christians, the usual suspects in our story? Could they have been among those who used and preserved and perhaps transmitted the *Protoevangelium*? The common scholarly answer to this question would be negative, because it has been assumed that far from being Jewish, the author of the *Protoevangelium* actually has a limited and flawed sense of Judaism, its rites and customs. More recent work, however, has challenged this view, arguing that the author of the document is actually well-versed in Judaism.[30] Some have suggested that the work was penned to "advance the Christian message of Jesus as the Messiah in a way that resonated with a Jewish audience."[31] Some even have suggested that, besides Greek, Coptic, and Armenian churches, the book must have been used "above all among the Ebionites."[32]

We can suggest, therefore, that the parallelism between the *Protoevangelium* and the Qur'an fits into the parallelism between Jewish Christianity and Islam.

QUR'ANIC ANNUNCIATION

In Christian terminology, "the Annunciation" refers to the announce-ment by the Angel Gabriel to Mary that she will have a blessed son: "Thou shalt conceive in thy womb, and bring forth a son, and shalt call his name Jesus. He shall be great, and shall be called the Son of the Most High: and the Lord God shall give unto him the throne of his father David."[33]

This incident, which we learn only from Luke among the four canonical gospels, exists in the Qur'an as well, in both the chapter "The Family of Imran" and the chapter "Mary." The latter, which is more detailed, reads as follows:

> Mention Mary in the Book [Qur'an], how she withdrew from her people to an eastern place, and veiled herself from them.
>   Then We sent Our Spirit to her and it took on for her the form of a perfect man.
>   She said, "I seek refuge from you with the All-Merciful if you have fear of Him."
>   He said, "I am only your Lord's messenger so that He can give you a pure boy."
>   She said, "How can I have a boy when no man has touched me and I am not an unchaste woman?"
>   He said, "It will be so! Your Lord says, 'That is easy for Me. It is so that We can make him a Sign for mankind and a mercy from Us. It is a matter already decreed.'"

There are several striking aspects of this passage, but the most important is that the Qur'an confirms the virginity of Mary—"no man has touched me and I am not an unchaste woman." But how did Mary, the virgin, exactly conceive Jesus? In two other verses of the Qur'an, which use the exact same expression, we hear God stating: "We breathed into her from Our Spirit."[34] The verses do

not explain how this took place, and hence classical Muslim exegetes have offered their various explanations. Some wrote that Gabriel, as God's agent, breathed into Mary's bosom until the Spirit
reached her womb. Others wrote that Gabriel blew into the sleeve
of Mary or the side of her chemise. Yet any consideration of a sexual relation between Mary and Gabriel has been almost unani-
mously ruled out by Muslim exegetes.[35]

One key question here, which would be theologically significant, is whether the Spirit of God impregnated Mary or gave life
to an embryo which was already formed, again miraculously, in
her womb. A close reading of the related verses show that the latter
is the case, making an important difference between the Islamic
and Christian christologies—a topic to which we shall return
later.[36]

Another detail in the Qur'anic story of the Annunciation is that
immediately before the coming of the angel, Mary "withdrew from
her people to an eastern place, and veiled herself from them."[37] This
unspecified "eastern place," or "a place to the east"—*mashraqa* in
its original Arabic—has naturally sparked discussion.[38] Suggestions
by Muslim exegetes include an area east of Jerusalem, an area in
Jerusalem east of the Temple Mount, or merely the easternmost
chamber of the Temple itself.[39] The latter explanation, remarkably,
resonates with an Old Testament emphasis on the eastern side of
the Temple: in Ezekiel, we read, "The glory of the Lord entered the
temple through the gate facing east."[40] Moreover, a fifth-century
Christian writer, Hesychius of Jerusalem, in his homilies, writes of
Mary's "Closed door" as "located in the East."[41]

If the "eastern place," was somewhere in the Jerusalem Temple,
then it would also be easy to explain how Mary "veiled herself," in
line with Christian tradition. For the *Protoevangelium of James* says
that immediately before the Annunciation, the priests at the Temple
said, "Let us make a veil for the temple of the Lord," and Mary got
to work spinning it.

QUR'ANIC NATIVITY

After the Annunciation of Jesus, the Qur'an immediately moves on to the Nativity—as the birth of Jesus is called in the Christian tradition. And Mary's drama continues with the following episode in the Qur'an, which, again, may sound quite unfamiliar to Bible readers:

> So she conceived him and withdrew with him to a distant place. The pains of labour drove her to the trunk of a date-palm. She said, "Oh if only I had died before this time and was something discarded and forgotten!"
>
> A voice called out to her from under her, "Do not grieve! Your Lord has placed a small stream at your feet. Shake the trunk of the palm towards you and fresh, ripe dates will drop down onto you. Eat and drink and delight your eyes. If you should see anyone at all, just say, 'I have made a vow of abstinence to the All-Merciful and today I will not speak to any human being.'"[42]

This remarkable passage from the Qur'anic chapter "Mary" includes themes that are totally absent from the New Testament: a "distant place," Mary's agony and stress, a palm tree that relieves her hunger, and a miraculous spring of water that relieves her thirst. Probably, these are all news to Western Christians.

Yet, lo and behold, all these themes are in fact present in a much-forgotten Christian text: The *Gospel of Pseudo-Matthew*, which is also called the *Infancy Gospel of Matthew*. This, again, has nothing to do with the Gospel of Matthew found in the New Testament. It is rather an apocryphal work written under the name of the gospel author Matthew; it is believed to have been authored sometime in the early seventh century, or perhaps the eighth or even ninth centuries.[43] Much of its content seems to be an edited reproduction of *Protoevangelium of James*, but it has an additional part presenting a unique version of the flight into Egypt—the escape of Joseph, Mary, and the infant Jesus from King Herod's massacre of the innocents. And in this version of the flight into Egypt story, on the third day, something interesting happens:

> Mary was fatigued by the excessive heat of the sun in the desert; and seeing a palm tree, she said to Joseph: Let me rest a little under the shade of this tree ... And as the blessed Mary was sitting there, she looked up to the foliage of the palm, and saw it full of fruit, and said to Joseph: I wish it were possible to get some of the fruit of this palm ...
>
> Then the child Jesus, with a joyful countenance, reposing in the bosom of His mother, said to the palm: O tree, bend thy branches, and refresh my mother with thy fruit. And immediately at these words the palm bent its top down to the very feet of the blessed Mary; and they gathered from it fruit, with which they were all refreshed ...
>
> Then Jesus said to it: Raise thyself, O palm tree ... and open from thy roots a vein of water which has been hid in the earth, and let the waters flow, so that we may be satisfied from thee. And it rose up immediately, and at its root there began to come forth a spring of water exceedingly clear and cool and sparkling.[44]

So, here, in the *Gospel of Pseudo-Matthew*, we have all the themes of the Qur'anic story of the Nativity: Mary feels extremely uncomfortable, she sits down under a palm tree that feeds her with dates, and she is even hydrated by a miraculous spring of water. Yet, alas, there is also a major discrepancy here. The Qur'an uses these themes while telling us how Mary, alone by herself, gave birth to Jesus. But the *Gospel of Pseudo-Matthew* uses them while telling us a much later episode, a time when Jesus was a child fleeing to Egypt with his parents, Mary and Joseph.

This, naturally, led many Christian writers to conclude that the Qur'an "wrongly borrowed" from the *Gospel of Pseudo-Matthew*, but only by misquoting or distorting it. On the other hand, others recalled that this apocryphal gospel was "composed at a date too late to have had an impact on the Qur'anic text," and also was written in the Latin language somewhere in the Christian West, a medium far removed from the Arabic Qur'an.[45] Yet one could still assume that it relied on earlier Christian narratives, which may have circulated in the pre-Islamic Near East.[46]

So, it seemed plausible to think that the Qur'an "wrongly borrowed" from preexisting Christian lore. But then came an archeological discovery that added a totally new element to the puzzle. It suggested, in the words of the Belgian scholar of early Islam Guillaume Dye, "what might look like a strange mistake can be explained in a different and much more fascinating way."[47]

A CHURCH WITH A PALM TREE

In 1992 Israeli authorities were constructing a wider road between Jerusalem and Bethlehem, which are only five miles apart. At a midpoint between the two cities, they unexpectedly came across the remains of an ancient church buried underground. Five years later, the ruins were carefully excavated by the Israel Antiquities Authority, whose archeologists realized that they had found a famed yet lost Byzantine church: Kathisma of the Theotokos, or Seat of the God-bearer.

Since *God-bearer* was the title given to Mary in Eastern Christianity, this church was clearly related to Mary. But exactly how? According to the legend, during the flight into Egypt, Mary, accompanied by her child, Jesus, and her husband, Joseph, rested on a rock located between Jerusalem and Bethlehem. That rock gradually became a place of Christian pilgrimage, and an octagonal church was built on top of it in the fifth century—the church that the Israelis accidentally found.

Moreover, in its initial centuries, there was also a spring of water coming from that rock. We know this from a pilgrimage guide written sometime between AD 560 and 570, by an anonymous writer known as the Piacenza Pilgrim, who wrote:

> On the way to Bethlehem, at the third milestone from Jerusalem . . . I saw standing water which came from a rock, of which you can take as much as you like up to seven pints . . . It is indescribably sweet to drink, and people say that Saint Mary became thirsty on the flight into Egypt, and that when she stopped here this water immediately flowed. Nowadays there is also a church building there.[48]

This, of course, surprisingly reminds us of the Mary stories in both the *Gospel of Pseudo-Matthew* and the Qur'an. But there is even more reason for surprise, for the floor of the Kathisma Church has beautiful mosaics, one of which represents something quite interesting: a large date palm, flanked by two smaller palms, all of which are laden with dates. "Since this is the church's only pictorial mosaic," notes Stephen J. Shoemaker, the American academic who studied the matter in detail, "this is almost certainly a representation of the date palm from which the Virgin Mary was miraculously fed."[49]

So, in summary, at this ancient church called Kathisma, we seem to have a tradition that depicts Mary with a miraculous water spring and a palm tree with dates—the very two elements found in both *Pseudo-Matthew* and the Qur'an. That is truly remarkable.

However, we still do have the problem mentioned before: the Qur'an presents the palm tree and the water spring scene as the setting of the Nativity—the very birth of Jesus. However, *Pseudo-Matthew* depicts the same scene as a moment in the flight into Egypt, which took place *only after Jesus was born*. This major gap still needs an explanation.

To find one, we have to add one more piece of information to the puzzle: the *Protoevangelium of James*, whose parallels with the Qur'an we have seen, also says something about the Nativity of

Jesus. But remarkably, it does not place his holy birth in Bethlehem, as it is located in the gospels of Matthew and Luke and in the popular Christian imagination. It rather places it in the wilderness, somewhere between Jerusalem and Bethlehem. Actually, in a cave exactly in "the middle of the road."[50] In other words, exactly the area where the Kathisma church is.

So, one wonders, could the Kathisma church actually be the place at which Mary gave birth to Jesus?

We can never exactly know, for we only have different accounts of something that happened more than two thousand years ago. But it is interesting that, in the Christian tradition, there are elements that place the birth of Jesus not in Bethlehem but somewhere out of the city, and that also place a palm tree and a water spring in the same vicinity.

No wonder that a deeper look into the Christian folklore surrounding the Kathisma Church reveals that in the very beginning, "the location of the Kathisma church was primitively connected with the Nativity."[51] In other words, it was venerated as the very birthplace of Jesus. Only later, when Bethlehem became established among Christians as the birthplace of Jesus, the significance of the location of Kathisma got reinterpreted, and it evolved into a resting place in the midst of the flight into Egypt.[52] That is how the birth of Jesus in the wilderness as told in the *Protoevangelium* and Mary's rest under the palm tree as told in *Pseudo-Matthew* got combined and located in the very same place.

This makes Kathisma, in the words of Shoemaker, "the only place in the Christian tradition where the two legends that were the Qur'an's sources meet."[53] From this, he concludes that the Kathisma traditions must have "influenced the formation of the Qur'anic traditions of the Nativity."[54] However, one can think the other way around too. One can take "the correspondence of the Qur'an with the traditions of the Kathisma shrine," in Shoemaker's words, as "a happy coincidence."[55] Or, perhaps, even a confirmation. It depends on toward which direction one is willing to take a leap of faith.

On the other hand, Shoemaker's thesis is not without problems—and critics.[56] First of all, Israeli archeologists have actually found on the Bethlehem road not one but two churches within a couple of hundred meters of each other, which might have narratives of their own. Moreover, Christian sources about Mary's birthgiving are quite diverse, and some even see echoes of the Qur'anic story in the New Testament's Book of Revelations.[57] Finally there is another verse of the Qur'an, which reads, "We made the son of Mary and his mother a sign; We gave them shelter on a peaceful hillside with flowing water."[58] Whether this refers to the Nativity or a later episode—such as flight to Egypt—is unclear.

Therefore, the question of how the Qur'anic account of the Nativity fits into Christian accounts and archeological findings is not entirely answered. But it seems certain that the Kathisma Church is an important piece in this puzzle.

"SISTER OF AARON"?

When we go back to the Qur'anic story of Mary, we see that the birth of Jesus was only the beginning of her ordeal. For now she had to go back to her people, a morally judgmental society, to put it lightly, with a fatherless baby in her arms. No wonder her situation immediately caused reactions, as we read in the Qur'anic chapter "Mary":

> She brought him to her people, carrying him. They said, "Mary! You have done an unthinkable thing! Sister of Aaron, your father was not an evil man nor was your mother an unchaste woman!"[59]

Note a curious expression here that has raised much controversy: "sister of Aaron." There is only one Aaron in the Qur'an, as in the Old Testament, and he is the brother of Moses. So, Mary, who lived more than a thousand years later, could certainly not be a sibling to Aaron. Meanwhile, Aaron did have a sister, whose name was Miryam. This led to accusations that the Qur'an "confused" the two women, Miryam and Mary, whose names sound all too similar.

In return, Muslim scholars have argued either that Mary had an otherwise unknown brother named Aaron or, more persuasively, that being a "sister of Aaron" can merely mean being a descendant of Aaron—which Mary arguably was.[60] After all, Jesus was proclaimed to be the "son of David" as well, which implied not direct sonship but lineage. Suleiman A. Mourad, who supports this argument, also adds:

> The expression sister of Aaron, moreover, occurs in the Qur'anic reference to the questioning of Mary in the Temple. It is especially appropriate in this context for the questioners, the Temple's priests, to magnify Mary's moral transgression (her pregnancy) by appealing to her ancestor Aaron, whose descendents are the only Israelites qualified to serve in the Temple, where Mary herself was raised. In other words, Mary as a descendent of Aaron is expected to keep the purity of the sanctuary, rather than defile it by supposedly committing the shameful act that would lead to a pregnancy. Here too, there are no grounds on which to argue that the Qur'an is identifying Mary as literally the sister of Aaron.[61]

Yet the puzzle here is not limited to Mary's being the "sister of Aaron." There is also the question of Imran and Imran's wife, who appear in the Qur'an as Mary's parents. The problem is that Imran seems to be a reference to the biblical Amran, who was the father not of Mary but of Moses, Aaron, and Miryam. As a result, there is an additional claim of the Qur'an being "confused" about biblical characters and their relations.

However, there is an alternative explanation to this riddle that seems to put everything in place: that the Qur'an merely employs "typology," which is "an approach of Scripture whose basic principle is to see former characters or events as prefiguring, announcing, later figures or events."[62] This approach is used in the Christian tradition as well and, remarkably, we even have a case of it being used to connect Mary and Aaron. It is in the *Lection of Jeremiah*, a very short and largely unknown document that dates from the first decades of the seventh century and was used in liturgical celebrations in Jerusalem. The text quotes oracles from the Hebrew prophet Jeremiah, who uses the Ark of the Covenant as a metaphor for the crib of the infant Jesus. In one place, it reads:

> And the prophet [Jeremiah] said: "His coming will be a sign for you, and for other children at the end of the world. And nobody will bring forth the hidden Ark from the rock, except the priest *Aaron, the brother of Mary*."[63]

"Aaron, the brother of Mary" clearly resonates with the Qur'anic "Mary, sister of Aaron." Guillaume Dye, the scholar who brought this "fascinating yet much neglected text" to attention, argues:

> The *Lection of Jeremiah* always speaks of Mary, and not Miryam, and since the author is patently a (clever) monk, he would not mistake Miryam for Mary. The formula priest brother of Mary is an addition of the *Lection*. Its typological and symbolic signification is obvious.[64]

To this, Dye also adds that the *Lection of Jeremiah* was read at the Kathisma Church near Jerusalem as a liturgical text. Then, by recalling the parallels between the Kathisma Church traditions and the Qur'an's story of the Nativity, he suggests that the *Lection of Jeremiah*, in terms of identifying Mary, might well be "the source of the Qur'an." However, from the Muslim point of view, it could be taken as a confirmation of the Qur'an as well—that the Qur'an's typological identification of Mary as "the sister of Aaron" was not without any historical basis.

Moreover, there is one more possibility as to why the Qur'an identifies Mary as "the sister of Aaron"—and it is fascinating as well.

First, note that the Qur'an calls Mary "the sister of Aaron," but not of Moses, which may reflect an emphasis on an Aaronid lineage of Mary. This, by extension, would mean that Jesus was of Aaronid descent as well. That, naturally, would conflict with Jesus' Davidic descent, which traditionally has been accepted as a basis of his claim to Messiahship. For most Jews believed that the Messiah would be a "son of David."

Yet some Jews had an alternative view: They believed that the Messiah would be from the line of Aaron. The earliest source in which this idea can be found is the Dead Sea Scrolls of Qumran, believed to be used by the Essenes, the ascetic Jewish sect of the time of Jesus. But, lo and behold, a branch of the Elchasaites, a later Jewish Christian sect, also believed that Mary was "from the tribe of Levi, from which the priests came."[65] They believed, in other words, that Mary was from the bloodline of Aaron.

So, the Qur'an's designation of Mary as "the sister of Aaron" may perhaps be a reflection of "the idea of an Aaronid Messiah." And this would be yet another parallel between Jewish Christianity and Islam.[66]

AN ARTICULATE NEWBORN

When you read the Qur'an and the New Testament side by side and focus on the Nativity, you will see one significant difference in the cast of characters: Joseph. According to the gospels, he becomes engaged to Mary before the Annunciation and marries her soon after, whereas he never appears in the Qur'an. That is why Muslims are often surprised to learn that Christians believe that Mary had a husband. For the plain impression one gets from the Qur'an is that Mary was always single, always unmarried. A Christian scholar even sees a "subtle ascetic hint" here, in the sense that "no male figure is needed to be closely associated with Mary because God sufficiently meets her needs."[67]

Yet the absence of Joseph from the Qur'an leads to a question: How could Mary prove that her fatherless son was not an illegitimate child? How could she prove that she had not "done an unthinkable thing," as she was accused of by her people when they saw a baby in her arms?

The canonical gospels that narrate the birth of Jesus—Matthew and Luke—do not deal with this question, for the presence of Joseph solves the problem. Although Joseph is not the biological father of Jesus, he appears as such and hence Mary is saved from any suspicion. In the Qur'an, however, the single-mother Mary immediately receives the stigma of unchastity. Moreover, as we also learn from the Qur'an, at the very moment of Jesus' birth, Mary takes a vow of silence ordered by God: "today I will not speak to any human being."[68] So, the poor woman is accused of fornication and cannot even speak to defend herself. That is a dangerous situation, especially in a society where the penalty for fornication can be no less than stoning.

That is why Mary is saved from this stigma only through a miracle—a miracle by the very newborn Jesus. As the Qur'anic chapter "Mary" tells us:

> She pointed towards him. They said, "How can a baby in the cradle speak?"
>
> He said, "I am the servant of God, He has given me the Book and made me a Prophet. He has made me blessed wherever I am and directed me to do prayers and give alms as long as I live, and to show devotion to my mother. He has not made me insolent or arrogant. Peace be upon me the day I was born, and the day I die and the day I am raised up again alive."
>
> That is Jesus, son of Mary, the word of truth about which they are in doubt.[69]

A baby Jesus who speaks in his cradle . . . For Bible readers, again, this may be a very unfamiliar theme. In fact, this was brought up as an argument against the Qur'an by medieval Catholic Christians. Since no Christian had heard about this story, they argued, it must be a myth.[70] In return, the Muslim exegete Fakhraddin al-Razi discussed why "Christians have denied that Jesus spoke in the cradle," despite this being "one of the most astonishing and most unusual events." He argued that perhaps the miracle had taken place in the presence of only a few people, who could have decided to conceal it, only to be disclosed by another miracle, which is the revelation of the Qur'an.[71]

However, this astonishing and unusual theme of the baby Jesus speaking from his cradle *does* exist within the Christian tradition—in an apocryphal and much-forgotten text: the *Syriac Infancy Gospel,* which is also known as the *Arabic Infancy Gospel.* This document is believed to be a seventh-century invention popular among Syrian Nestorians. It is in the same genre as the *Protoevangelium of James* and the *Gospel of Pseudo-Matthew*, and in fact borrows from them heavily. Like them, it is an infancy gospel, focusing on the life of the baby and the child Jesus. And like them, it tells many miracle stories about Jesus, one of which is reported right at the beginning of the text:

> Jesus spoke . . . when He was in His cradle, said to His mother:
> I am the Son of God, the Logos, whom you have brought forth, as
> the Angel Gabriel announced to you; and my Father has sent me
> for the salvation of the world.[72]

Clearly, this passage is quite different from the Jesus-in-the-cradle story in the Qur'an. Here the newborn Jesus speaks to his mother. But in the Qur'an, he speaks to the Jews who question the chastity of his mother. Here the newborn Jesus says, "I am the Son of God, the Logos." But in the Qur'an, he says, "I am the servant of God . . . He made me a Prophet." Both texts, in other words, make Jesus speak from the outlook of their respective christologies.

The rest of the *Syriac Infancy Gospel* is also quite dissimilar to the Qur'an. But still it is the only source in the Christian tradition that depicts an infant Jesus who speaks in his cradle. In the Qur'an, however, we see this as an important and emphasized theme. Besides the passage just quoted from the chapter "Mary," we also hear about an incident in the chapter "Family of Imran," from the mouth of the angels:

> Mary, your Lord gives you good news of a Word from Him. His name is the Messiah, Jesus, son of Mary, of high esteem in the world and the hereafter, and one of those brought near. He will speak to people in the cradle, and also when fully grown, and will be one of the righteous.[73]

Also, in the Qur'anic chapter "Table," we hear God himself calling to Jesus: "Jesus, son of Mary, remember My blessing to you and to your mother when I reinforced you with the Holy Spirit so that you could speak to people in the cradle and when you were fully grown."[74]

All this emphasis in the Qur'an about Jesus' speech in the cradle, a theme that never appears in the New Testament and only once in the *Syriac Infancy Gospel*, is curious. "Why would Islam have Jesus speaking from the cradle," hence asks a modern-day Evangelical source, detecting "an agenda here."[75] The agenda, it adds, must be to make Jesus himself renounce trinitarian christology, which is probably not off the mark. However, the adult Jesus could also do that, as we already see in other verses of the Qur'an.

The real "agenda," I believe, in line with some traditional Muslim exegetes, is to defend Mary against accusations of unchastity.[76] This seems to be quite an important matter for the Qur'an, for in a separate chapter we also see that certain Jews are condemned for "their utterance of a monstrous slander against Mary."[77] That may be a reference to an ancient Jewish rumor that Jesus was the illegitimate son of a Roman soldier named Pantera.[78]

Moreover, the newborn Jesus who speaks from the cradle not only defends his mother, but also affirms his God-given mission to "show devotion to my mother"—or "cherish my mother," in other translations. This is a powerful statement, which seems to diverge from a puzzling attitude one finds in the New Testament: there, especially in the Gospel of Luke, there is a subtle tendency to portray Jesus as distant from his family. When a woman is impressed by Jesus and proclaims, "Blessed is the mother who gave you birth and nursed you," he responds: "Blessed rather are those who hear the word of God and obey it."[79] And when Jesus is told in a crowd, "Your mother and brothers are standing outside, wanting to see you," he answers: "My mother and brothers are those who hear God's word and put it into practice."[80] In the fourth gospel, there is an even colder episode, in which Mary asks for Jesus' help at the wedding in Cana but gets the response: "Woman, why do you involve me? My hour has not yet come."[81]

For sure, Christian scholars have offered nuanced interpretations of these passages, and have also pointed out Jesus' care for his mother at the Cruxifiction, committing her to the care of his disciple John.[82] Others, however, see in the same passages a tendency to "marginalize the family of Jesus"—as a backdrop of the tension between Paul and James.[83]

In contrast to the latter view, the Qur'an does not mention the siblings of Jesus, but still puts an unmistakable emphasis on Jesus' love for and devotion to his mother. This, at the very least, seems to be an example of the ideal parent-child relationship of the Qur'an, which is defined by mutual love and the child's gratitude to the parents, especially the mother. "We have instructed man to be good to his parents," a verse reads. "His mother bore him with difficulty and with difficulty gave birth to him; and his bearing and weaning take thirty months."[84]

VIRGIN MARY, UNDIVINE JESUS

Most Muslims in the world today may not be aware of all the details of the Qur'anic story of Mary, but they probably know its gist:

that the birth of Jesus was a virgin birth and that Jesus was conceived miraculously, without a father. This has been a universally accepted credo since the beginning of Islam, and has been taken seriously and respectfully. Reportedly, Caliph Umar, a companion of the Prophet and his second "successor," or caliph, as the leader of the Muslim community, once rebuked a man who named his son Isa, or Jesus, and then kept calling himself Abu Isa, or "the father of Jesus." Apparently Umar was angry because he felt that a human being calling himself "the father of Jesus" could be denigrating Jesus.[85]

Throughout Muslim history, almost all interpreters of the Qur'an took the virgin birth story as a literal fact. A twentieth-century exegete even dubbed it as "the strangest event that humanity throughout its history has ever witnessed."[86] A handful of modern-day Muslim exegetes tried to offer naturalistic interpretations of the virgin birth, while affirming Mary's chastity, yet this view has not gained much popularity.[87] Hence today, the standard Muslim view is that Jesus, of course, was born without a biological father.

Two American Baptist ministers appreciate this point in their coauthored book of apologetical theology. "Ironically," they note, "Muslims extend more respect to Jesus as a high prophet than do most liberal 'Christians.'" Those liberal Christians reject the virgin birth, they add, unlike the Muslims who really do believe in it.[88]

However, the same Qur'an that strongly affirms the virgin birth also emphatically denies what many Christians see as its logical outcome: the divinity of Jesus. In a very commanding passage, the Qur'an calls on Christians to actually stop seeing Jesus as divine:

Those who say, "God is the Messiah, son of Mary," are unbelievers. Say: "Who possesses any power at all over God if He desires to destroy the Messiah, son of Mary, and his mother, and everyone else on earth?" The kingdom of the heavens and the earth and everything between them belongs to God. He creates whatever He wills. God has power over all things.[89]

Christians may find the Qur'anic fine-tuning here—affirmation of virgin birth coupled with the renunciation of Jesus' divinity—a bit odd. It has even been suggested as an inconsistency in the Qur'an.[90] That is because, in the Christian imagination, belief in the virgin birth and belief in the divinity of Jesus often go hand in hand. Once you accept the former, you also accept the latter.

However, the Qur'anic position on this matter has a precedent within Christianity as well—within, not too surprisingly, Jewish Christianity. We know this from the church father Eusebius of Caesarea, who wrote in the early fourth century that the Ebionites were divided into two groups. The first one held that Jesus was "a plain and common man" and "the fruit of the intercourse of a man with Mary." But the second group, Eusebius explained, "did not deny that the Lord was born of a virgin and of the Holy Spirit." Nevertheless, he added, they "refused to acknowledge that he pre-existed, being God, Word, and Wisdom."[91]

Similarly, Origen, writing a century before, noted that some Jewish Christians "admit [Christ's] birth from Mary and the divine Sprit, [but] they deny His divinity."[92] That is why Gentile Christians rebuked Jewish Christians "for their low view of the person of Christ."[93] Other church writers, Epiphanius and Jerome, also noted that some Jewish Christians accepted the virgin birth whereas others denied it. They also suggested that the first group was called "Nazarenes," the latter "Ebionites," raising the possibility of a diversity of views among Jewish Christians as well.[94]

Therefore, the Qur'an's stance on the virgin birth seems to be yet another example of the doctrinal connection between Jewish Christianity and Islam—the two main traditions on earth that affirm that Jesus was indeed "incarnate by the Holy Ghost of the Virgin Mary," as said in the Nicene Creed, but that he was *not* "very God of very God, begotten, not made."

MARY AS GOD?

Besides the divinity of Jesus, the Qur'an seems to refute another theological claim as well: the divinity of Mary. We see this in a very interesting rhetorical conversation in the Qur'an, where God questions Jesus, apparently in the afterlife, about what happened back on earth:

> When God says, "Jesus, son of Mary, did you say to people, 'Take me and my mother as two gods alongside God?'" he will say:
>
> "May You be exalted! I would never say what I had no right to say. If I had said such a thing You would have known it. You know all that is within me, though I do not know what is within You. You alone have full knowledge of things unseen.
>
> "I told them only what You commanded me to: 'Worship God, my Lord and your Lord.' I was a witness over them during my time among them. Ever since You took my soul, You alone have been the watcher over them.
>
> "You are witness to all things. And if You punish them, they are Your servants. If You forgive them, You are the Almighty, the Wise."[95]

There are two remarkable points in this passage. First, it makes Jesus speak against the doctrine of the very people who claim to follow him—the Christians. This is the only example of such polemic in the Qur'an, in which somebody whom the Qur'an identifies as a prophet disavows the theology of his followers.[96] The same cannot be seen with Abraham, Jacob, or Moses, probably because their image among the Jews as mortal prophets is not in conflict with the austere monotheism of the Qur'an.

The second and more curious point in the Qur'anic passage is the line about Mary, in which Jesus is asked whether he told people, "Take me and my mother as two gods alongside God." With this line, the Qur'an seems to target the divinization of both Jesus and

Mary. However, Christians, at least the ones we know of, do not see Mary as divine. Hence, for centuries they have objected to this accusation by the Qur'an. Many Christian or Orientalist critics of the Muslim scripture argued that its author "misunderstood" the Christian doctrine. Since the Qur'an, in a separate verse, also seems to condemn the doctrine of the Trinity—or the idea that "God is the third of three"—the argument went further: that the Qur'an's author got the doctrine of the Trinity scandalously wrong, assuming that it refers to a triune family of God the Father, Jesus the Son, and Mary the Wife.[97]

Yet there are two counterarguments to this argument. The first of them comes from the Qur'an itself, from a verse that reprimands both Jews and Christians for their theological errors:

> They have taken their rabbis and monks as lords besides God, and also the Messiah, son of Mary. Yet they were commanded to worship only one God. There is no god but Him. Glory be to Him above anything they associate with Him.[98]

What is notable here is that the veneration of "rabbis and monks" is rebuked along with the veneration of Jesus, and in the very same line. The accusation is that these clerics are taken by Jews and Christens as "lords." The term here, *rabb*, does not equal "god," *ilah*, but the two concepts are closely related. No wonder taking someone other than God as "lord" is portrayed as the opposite of "worshiping only one God."

Yet how could Jews and Christians take their "rabbis and monks" as "lords," although they certainly don't claim that? According to a hadith (saying attributed to Muhammad), this very question was posed to the Prophet, and he gave an explanatory answer: "They [rabbis and monks] prohibited the allowed for them [Jews and Christians], and allowed the prohibited, and they obeyed them. This is how they worshiped them."[99] So, in the Qur'an's conceptual universe, accepting someone as a god apart from God can happen without formally declaring them as gods but still venerating and obeying them at a level that is only appropriate for God. The Qur'anic accusation against Christians that they took Mary as a god "alongside God" can be understood in this sense, especially in light of the tradition of veneration of Mary found in Catholic, Anglican, and Eastern Christianity—although not in Protestantism. No wonder Martin Luther accused Catholics of having lapsed into "idolatry" for praying to Mary.[100]

We should also recall that the veneration of Mary raised controversy among Middle Eastern Christians as well. In the fifth century, the Nestorian Church, popular in Syria, Iraq, and eastern Anatolia, refused to call Mary *Theotokos*, or "God-bearer," and gave her the more modest title, *Christotokos*, or "Christ-bearer." This dispute, along with a controversy on the nature of Christ, led to the condemnation of Nestorianism as a heresy at the First Council of Ephesus in 431 and at the Council of Chalcedon in 451. Hence it has been argued that this controversy between Nestorians and other churches is behind the Qur'an's denunciation of Mary's divinity.[101]

The second argument to support the Qur'an's denunciation of Mary's divinization as not so off the mark is that there were nonorthodox Christians at the time who really did worship Mary. We know this thanks to Epiphanius of Salamis, who in his late-fourth-century work *Panarion* condemned a plenitude of heretics including the Collyridians, who "came to Arabia from Thrace and northern Scythia." This was a sect composed mainly of women, he explained, who presented "small cakes" to the Virgin Mary as sacred offerings. To argue against their heresy, Epiphanius had to remind his readers that "Mary is not God and does not have her body from heaven but by human conception."[102] Arguably this fourth-century trace of the Collyridians was just "the tip of the Marian iceberg," and, in fact, "there was an organized and widespread Marian religion during the first centuries of the Christian era."[103]

So, in summary, the Qur'an's position on Mary is to condemn such a "Marian religion" at one extreme and condemn the denigration of Mary as an unchaste woman at the other. The Islamic take on Mary elevates her to the highest possible human level—a woman "over all other women"—but also opposes any possible deviation from Islam's passionate monotheism.

But what about Mary's son? How does this passionate monotheism deal with him? What does it say about his identity and mission? Now is the time to look deeper into these questions.

CHAPTER SIX

THE QUR'ANIC JESUS

The Qur'anic portrait of Jesus is not so remote from the New Testament as might seem to be the case at first glance.

—Hekki Räisänen, Finnish biblical scholar[1]

THE QUR'ANIC STORY OF JESUS IS REMARKABLY CONCISE WHEN compared to the New Testament story. In the Qur'an, one never learns about the temptation in the wilderness, the preaching in Galilee, the cleansing of the Temple, the agony at Gethsemane, the trial at Pilate's court, the drama of the crucifixion, or the joy of the Resurrection. Such themes about Jesus' life and ministry simply do not exist in the Qur'an, and for a simple reason: Jesus is not the main character of the Qur'an.

As a matter of fact, the Qur'an has no main character—other than God himself. Everything else is given attention only with regard to its relationship with God. Among humans, the most noteworthy ones are the prophets, who, by divine revelation, are "sent" to their peoples to call them to believe in God and follow his commandments. In fact, the usual Qur'anic word for prophet, *rasul*, literally means "the one who is sent." The other Qur'anic word for prophet, *nabi*, means "news giver."

According to a hadith, the number of all the prophets sent to humankind is as high as twenty-four thousand—suggesting that not just the Children of Israel or Muslims themselves are the receivers of divine guidance. All these known and unknown prophets must be respected by Muslims, the Qur'an reminds believers, and they should "not differentiate between any of them."[2] Yet still, another verse of the Qur'an notes that God Himself elevated certain messengers:

> We favoured some of these messengers above others. God spoke to some; others He raised in rank. We gave Jesus, son of Mary, Our clear signs and strengthened him with the holy spirit.[3]

The term "holy spirit" here may catch the attention of Christians, and rightly so. For while describing Jesus, the Qur'an uses some of the powerful concepts of Christian theology—but often not exactly with the same meaning, as we shall see. It also uses its own theological concepts to praise Jesus—an exceptionally sublime praise given to no one else, including the Prophet Muhammad. In one of the best short summaries of the Qur'anic picture of Jesus, Geoffrey Parrinder, the late British scholar of religion and a Methodist minister, observed:

> The Qur'an gives a greater number of honourable titles to Jesus than to any other figure of the past. He is a "sign," a "mercy," a "witness" and an "example." He is called by his proper name Jesus, by the titles Messiah (Christ) and Son of Mary, and by the names Messenger, Prophet, Servant, Word and Spirit of God. The Qur'an gives two accounts of the annunciation and birth of Jesus, and refers to his teachings and healings, and his death and exaltation . . . Jesus is always spoken of in the Qur'an with reverence; there is no breath of criticism, for he is the Christ of God.[4]

"Christ of God," or God's Messiah. The latter term, *Masih*, although repeatedly used for Jesus in the Qur'an, is never explained, as we noted before. Hence Muslim exegetes put some thought to its meaning. Since it seems related to the verb *masaha*, which means "wipe," prominent exegete al-Tabari took it to mean that God Himself had wiped the sins off Jesus, so "the Messiah" may be equated with "the Truthful One" (*al-Siddiq*). Others have suggested that the name Messiah referred to someone who was touched by blessings (*musiha bi'l-baraka*).[5]

So, what did the Messiah aim to do and what did he accomplish?

The first answer we get to these questions from the Qur'an is that Jesus was not a founder of a new religion, but "a Messenger to the Children of Israel."[6] The Qur'an also tells us that this new messenger did not abolish the religion of the Children of Israel, but rather brought some liberality to it. To his fellow Jews, he said:

> I come confirming the Torah I find already there, and to make lawful for you some of what was previously forbidden to you. I have brought you a Sign from your Lord. So have fear of God and obey me. God is my Lord and your Lord; so worship Him. That is a straight path.[7]

The notable expression here, "my Lord and your Lord," is quoted four more times in the Qur'an from the mouth of Jesus.[8] It seems to emphasize the Islamic view that Jesus was not God, but rather a servant of God. This may sound contrary to mainstream Christian theology, but it also sounds remarkably parallel to a passage in the New Testament, in the Gospel of John: "I am ascending to my Father and your Father," Jesus says, "to *my God and your God*."[9]

The second answer we get from the Qur'an about Jesus' mission is that he came to the Children of Israel at a time of religious disputes. "I have come to you with Wisdom," we hear him saying to his people, "and to clarify for you some of the things about which you have differed; therefore have fear of God and obey me."[10] (If one substituted "have fear of God and obey me" with "have faith" and "follow me," it would sound very much like the gospels.) Notably, the Jews of the first century "differed" a lot. As we learn from the writings of Josephus, they were indeed a nation haunted by religious disputes and divided into conflicting parties.

The third key point we learn about Jesus' mission from the Qur'an is that he came to Jews with *bayyinat*, or "clear signs."[11] This is a term used in the Qur'an more than fifty times, and it refers to the proofs prophets present to their people to show their divine mandate. "We gave Moses nine clear signs" God says in one of these verses, in an apparent reference to the miracles of Moses— the flood, locusts, vermin, frogs, blood, Moses's staff, Moses's hand, death of the firstborn, and the parting of the sea.[12]

So, what were the "clear signs" of Jesus? And what do they tell us about his portrait in the Qur'an and the relation of this portrait to the different Christianities that preceded Islam?

BIRDS CREATED OUT OF CLAY

We have already seen two major Qur'anic miracles of Jesus: he was born of a virgin, without a biological father, and he spoke to people soon after his birth, from his cradle. Yet there is more in the Qur'an on this matter, narrated in two similar yet distinct passages. The first one is in the chapter "Family of Imran," where we hear angels speaking to Mary, at the Annunciation, telling her about the wondrous works of her future son. This son will be "a messenger to the Children of Israel," and will tell them:

> I have brought you a Sign from your Lord. I will create the shape of a bird out of clay for you and then breathe into it and it will be a bird by God's permission. I will heal the blind and the leper, and bring the dead to life, by God's permission. I will tell you what you eat and what you store up in your homes. There is a Sign for you in that if you are believers.[13]

The second passage about Jesus' miracles is from the fifth chapter of the Qur'an, entitled "The Table"—a title also related to Jesus, as we shall see. This time, we hear God Himself speaking to Jesus, in the past tense, in a dramatic scene of reckoning that takes place in the afterlife:

> On the day God gathers the Messengers together and says, "What response did you receive?" they will say, "We do not know. You are the Knower of unseen things."
>
> [And God will say]: "Jesus, son of Mary, remember My blessing to you and to your mother . . . And when you created a bird-shape out of clay by My permission, and then breathed into it and it became a bird by My permission; and healed the blind and the leper by My permission; and when you brought forth the dead by My permission; and when I held back the Children of Israel from you, when you brought them the Clear Signs and those of them who were unbelievers said, 'This is nothing but downright magic.'"[14]

In both of these Qur'anic passages, Jesus performs several miracles—always with God's permission, emphatically, in case we forget.[15] Some of these are what Christians call "healing miracles"—healing the blind and the leper and bringing the dead to life—and they must be quite familiar to all readers of the New Testament. However, the notion of Jesus telling "what you eat and what you store up in your homes" may sound unfamiliar to the same readers. Some have suggested an echo of it in a passage in the Gospel of Matthew: "Lay not up for yourselves treasures upon the earth, where moth and rust consume, and where thieves break through and steal."[16] But, honestly, this similarity seems a bit too far-fetched. Meanwhile, we should note that the post-Qur'anic Islamic literature includes some detailed stories about Jesus' clairvoyance about what people eat and store up.[17]

What is most striking in these Qur'anic passages, though, is a third genre of miracle attributed to Jesus, which is quite remarkable, but which is totally absent from the New Testament: that he gave life to birds made of clay. Or that he declared, to quote his words again, "I will create the shape of a bird out of clay for you and then breathe into it and it will be a bird by God's permission."

Both Muslim and Christian commentators have been intrigued by this miracle, for in both religions giving life to inanimate matter is seen as a power that belongs only to God. To add more awe to the matter, the Qur'an's terminology here has interesting parallels. First, the verb used to denote that Jesus "created" the shape of a bird from clay is *khalaqa*, the very verb that the Qur'an uses almost exclusively to refer to God's creative act. Second, the substance that Jesus used, which is clay, or *tin*, is the exact same substance from which God created the first man. Third, the verb used to refer to Jesus "breathing" into clay, *nafakha*, is again the exact same word indicating God's "breathing" into clay to create the first man, or His "breathing" into Mary to create Jesus himself.[18]

Looking at these clues, the prominent twelfth-century exegete of the Qur'an Fakhraddin al-Razi argued that perhaps Jesus' breath had some unusual power—that God might have "endowed Jesus' breath with particular efficacy so that when he blew into things it caused them to come to life."[19] Others suggested that Jesus was "allowed to exercise the divine prerogative of creating life"—which was the case with neither Abraham, nor Moses, nor Muhammad himself.[20] Hence the life-giving breath of Jesus, *dam-i Isa*, became a mystical concept in Islam, especially among the Sufis. The great Sufi Ibn al-Arabi wrote the following to describe the Christ:

> A Spirit from none other than God,
> So that he might raise the dead and bring forth birds
>   from clay.
> And become worthy to be associated with his Lord
> By which he exerted great influence, both high and low.

God purified him in body and made him transcendent
In the spirit, making him like Himself in creating.[21]

Another question relating to the clay birds miracle is whether it is known only to Muslim sources. It certainly has no trace in the whole New Testament. But, as in some other Qur'anic themes about Jesus, this story too has a parallel in the Christian Apocrypha: it is narrated in the noncanonical *Infancy Gospel of Thomas*.[22]

This document, which scholars believe to have been written in the second century, should not be confused with the *Gospel of Thomas*, another apocryphal text, which was lost for centuries until being accidentally found in 1945, near Nag Hammadi, a city in upper Egypt. The *Gospel of Thomas*, which has attracted lot of attention because of its Gnostic tendencies, is a "sayings gospel," which includes only the teaching of Jesus. In contrast, the *Infancy Gospel of Thomas*, or *IGT*, is a text that narrates, in its own words, "the works of the childhood of our Lord Jesus." And right at its beginning, it tells this interesting story of the child Jesus making birds out of clay:

> This little child Jesus when he was five years old was playing at the ford of a brook: and he gathered together the waters that flowed there into pools, and made them straightway clean, and commanded them by his word alone. And having made soft clay, he fashioned thereof twelve sparrows. And it was the Sabbath when he did these things . . . And there were also many other little children playing with him.
>
> And a certain Jew when he saw what Jesus did, playing upon the Sabbath day, departed straightway and told his father Joseph: Lo, thy child is at the brook, and he hath taken clay and fashioned twelve little birds, and hath polluted the Sabbath day. And Joseph came to the place and saw: and cried out to him, saying: Wherefore doest thou these things on the Sabbath, which it is not lawful to do? But Jesus clapped his hands together and cried out to the sparrows and said to them: Go! and the sparrows took their flight

and went away chirping. And when the Jews saw it they were amazed, and departed and told their chief men that which they had seen Jesus do.[23]

This long story has some differences from the Qur'anic story of the clay birds: First, when you read the Qur'an, you can get the impression that creating clay birds was the work of an adult Jesus, but the *IGT* narrates it as the work of the child Jesus. Second, the Qur'an speaks of Jesus creating a "bird"—although some exegetes argued that this could be read as plural—whereas the *IGT* speaks of Jesus creating "twelve sparrows." Third, in the Qur'an, Jesus breathes into the clay birds to give them life, but in the *IGT* he just claps his hands and cries to them. And fourth, as if to underline Islam's nuanced theological difference from Christianity, the Qur'an stresses that Jesus performed this miracle "by God's permission," whereas the *IGT* does not see the need to make that point.[24]

Yet, such differences aside, the parallel between the Qur'an and the *IGT* with regard to this particular story is unmistakable and striking.[25] This parallel, therefore, has raised the question of how this clay birds story might have made its way into the Qur'an.

As in other parallels between the Qur'an and preexisting Christian (or Jewish) texts, one can have three different approaches to this question: The first is to wonder and investigate how the Qur'an might have "borrowed" from earlier sources, as non-Muslim critics would typically do. The second is to assume that the Qur'an is divinely revealed, as Muslims would do, and then to see the textual parallels as the Qur'an's confirmation, or correction, of certain themes in preexisting traditions. A third approach, which is theologically neutral, is to accept that since the Qur'an was "in dialogue" with the traditions present at its time and milieu, it naturally referred to them, no matter how one explains the Qur'an's origin.

Whichever of these approaches one may take, it still is interesting to explore the transmitters of the Christian texts with which the Qur'an seems to be "in dialogue." It is interesting, for example, to explore which particular strain of Christianity was the transmitter of the *IGT*.

In academia, the common answer to this question has been found in Gnosticism—the "heretical" movement within second-century Christianity that focused on a more esoteric reading of the Jesus message. Yet according to Andries van Aarde, professor of theology at the University of Pretoria, the Gnostic tendency can be found in only one of the manuscripts of the *IGT*, of which there are many. Meanwhile the more authentic manuscript, found in the collection of *Codex Sinaiticus*, he argues, reflects a different theology: the theology of the early Ebionites—our usual suspects.[26]

According to Van Arde, this Jewish Christian trace is detectable at the very beginning of the *IGT*. The author identifies himself as "I, Thomas the Israelite," who appeals to "all the brothers living amidst the heathen." Then throughout the text, three themes stand out: "Jesus' obedience to the law, the restriction of salvation to Israel, and Jesus' close and positive relation with his biological family."[27]

It also interesting that James, the brother of Jesus, shows up in the *IGT*. The little James, as the story goes, is sent out by his father Joseph to collect wood for the fire. The young child Jesus follows his younger brother and, when the latter is bitten by a viper, saves him from death by breathing on the bite and healing the wound.[28] In a deeply religious context where every event was seen as theologically meaningful, this strong bond the *IGT* presents between Jesus and James could be meaningful, too.

In summary, we can safely assume a parallel between the Qur'an and the *IGT*, as seen in the clay birds story. Moreover, we can reason that the *IGT* was a text that reflected Jewish Christian themes, and therefore fits into our quest for the theological precursors of Islam.

A PROPHECY BY JESUS

One of the remarkable passages about Jesus in the Qur'an is where
he is quoted as making a prophecy about the future—a prophecy
that has fascinated Muslims for centuries. In the chapter "Solid
Lines," which is one of the latest in the Qur'an, we read Jesus say:

> Children of Israel, I am sent to you by God, confirming the Torah
> that came before me and bringing good news of a messenger to
> follow me whose name will be Ahmad.[29]

A messenger after Jesus whose name will be "Ahmad" . . . Traditionally, Muslims have taken this as a reference to the Prophet
Muhammad. The two words, Ahmad and Muhammad, both come
from the Arabic triconsonantal root *H-M-D*, or "praise." The only
difference is that while Ahmad means "the praised one," Muhammad means "the most praised one."

However, there seems to be a problem with this Qur'anic prophecy by Jesus: It does not exist in the New Testament. So, some
Muslim scholars found the solution in arguing that the prophecy
did originally exist in the gospels, but the Christians cunningly
took it out. This really was not a great solution, however, as it can be
neither proved nor disproved, only asserted.

Other Muslim scholars opted for another solution: They actually
found the prophecy in the New Testament—albeit in a different
wording. In the fourth gospel, Jesus foretells, four times, that God
will send an "Advocate" or "Comforter" after him, "to help you and
be with you forever."[30] The original Greek word here is *paraclete,* on
which Muslim literature paid much attention. One suggestion was
that the word is a misspelling of another Greek word, *periklutos,*
which means "celebrated," and thus sounds similar to "praised," or
Ahmad. Another suggestion was that the Aramaic original word
for *paraclete* could be *menahhemana*, which sounded a bit like
Muhammad.[31]

Yet these theories seem a bit overstretched, too. Moreover, when Jesus proclaims a "Comforter," he already identifies it as "the Holy Spirit, whom the Father will send in my name."[32] Hence that is how the Christian tradition understood the term—a reference to the Holy Spirit.

Therefore, maybe we should look for another explanation—and do this by turning our attention from the New Testament to the Qur'an itself. It is actually curious that the Qur'an makes Jesus foretell "a messenger . . . whose name will be Ahmad." Why Ahmad, one wonders, and not Muhammad? For although the words are similar, they are not identical. And while the word *Ahmad* is just another name for the Prophet Muhammad in the Islamic tradition, this seems to be a later development, not a legacy from the time of the Qur'an.[33] So, the question remains: Why Ahmad, not Muhammad?[34]

A solution lies in a much-overlooked grammatical alternative: The word *Ahmad*, or "praised," can simply be an adjective rather than a proper name. In other words, Jesus can be foretelling not a messenger "whose name will be Ahmad," but a messenger "whose name will be praised."[35]

If this is the case, then we would have room for multiple interpretations. The messenger "whose name will be praised" can still be the Prophet Muhammad, for Muslims who believe in him as a praised prophet. For Christians, it can still be the Holy Spirit—who is also mentioned in the Qur'an as an agent with which God "strengthened" Jesus, albeit not as the third person of a trinity.[36]

THE GOSPEL OF JESUS

When Muslims get their hands on a copy of the New Testament for the first time, they are often surprised. They expect a book like the Qur'an, but find something quite different. For in the Qur'an, the author is none other than God Himself. In the New Testament, however, there are several authors, and they are neither God nor even Jesus. They are rather mortal men who either reported Jesus'

works and teachings in four different "gospels" or merely commented about these in almost two dozen "epistles."

This fundamental difference between the Qur'an and the New
Testament has in fact an understandable rationale. In Islam, the
Qur'an is taken as the "Word of God." In Christianity, however, the
"Word of God" is not a book, but Jesus himself. The New Testament
merely narrates that Word, which became flesh in the form of
Jesus.

Yet still, there remains a discrepancy between the New Testament and the way Islam defines it: the Qur'an speaks of "the gospel"
as a single book like itself. "He has sent down the Book to you with
truth confirming what was there before it," a Qur'anic verse tells
Muhammad. "And He sent down the Torah and the Gospel."[37] The
word translated here as "Gospel" is *Injil* in its Arabic original. It is
a word that occurs twelve times in the Qur'an, nine of them in con-
juncture with *Tawrat*. Scholars have little doubt that both words
came into Arabic from foreign sources—*Tawrat* from the Hebrew
Torah, and *Injil* from Greek *Evangelion*, or its Ethiopian derivative,
Wangel.

The Qur'an shows great respect for both the Torah and the
Gospel—and also for *Zabur*, which is the Arabic word for "Psalms."[38]
In a remarkable passage, God speaks, as often in the Qur'an, as
"We":

> We revealed the Torah with guidance and light, and the proph-
> ets, who had submitted to God, judged according to it for the
> Jews. So did the rabbis and the scholars in accordance with that
> part of God's Scripture which they were entrusted to preserve,
> and to which they were witnesses . . .
>
> In the Torah We prescribed for them a life for a life, an eye for
> an eye, a nose for a nose, an ear for an ear, a tooth for a tooth, an
> equal wound for a wound: if anyone forgoes this out of charity, it
> will serve as atonement for his bad deeds. Those who do not judge
> according to what God has revealed are doing grave wrong.

We sent Jesus, son of Mary, in their footsteps, to confirm the Torah that had been sent before him: We gave him the Gospel with guidance, light, and confirmation of the Torah already revealed—a guide and lesson for those who take heed of God.[39]

The rest of this passage is even more interesting: "So let the followers of the Gospel judge according to what God has sent down in it."[40] This seems to suggest that, instead of calling Christians to convert to Islam, the Qur'an rather asks Christians to follow their own scripture firmly—offering a vision of religious pluralism that many contemporary Muslims will have a hard time accepting.

Yet the problem still remains: The Qur'an speaks of a single "Gospel" "given" to Jesus by God. But we rather have several gospels written by different evangelists. Muhammad Husayn Tabataba'i, a prominent Shiite exegete of the twentieth century, also pointed to this contradiction:

> As for the *Injil* (Gospel), which means "good tidings," the Qur'an indicates that it was one single scripture revealed to Jesus, and is his specific revelation. But as for the Gospels which are attributed to Matthew, Mark, Luke and John, they are books written after Jesus, peace be upon him.[41]

So, how do we make a sense of this difference? Some of the early Muslim exegetes of the Qur'an found the solution in suggesting that the Qur'an's "Gospel" merely refers to the whole New Testament, as the Qur'an's "Torah" might be a reference to the whole Old Testament.[42] Some Western scholars rather suggested that the Qur'an was perhaps referring to the *Diatessaron*, the "gospel harmony" compiled by Tatian, a second-century Christian theologian. This was a combination of the four gospels into a single text and was widely used among Syrian Christians until the fifth century, perhaps by Jewish Christians as well.[43] Yet we don't have any evidence of being it used in the time and milieu of the Qur'an.[44]

A third explanation is that the Qur'an was perhaps referring to an "original gospel," a text written before Mark, Matthew, Luke, or John.[45] One candidate could be the "Gospel of the Hebrews" that the Jewish Christians reportedly used. But that is a lost document buried deep in history. The other candidate, however, is buried in a more accessible place: the New Testament itself.

What I am referring to is the famous "Q Gospel." It was "discovered" in the nineteenth century, when some German scholars of the Bible noticed a formerly unknown interconnection between the three Synoptic Gospels—Mark, Matthew, and Luke. First, they realized that the earliest among these was Mark—not Matthew, as the traditional view held. Second, they realized that Matthew and Luke borrowed heavily from Mark. Third and most important, they also realized that Matthew and Luke have many identical parts that do not appear in Mark. Since Matthew and Luke were most probably written around the same time but in different places, these scholars reasoned, their "common material" must have come from a separate source. One of the scholars, theologian Johannes Weiss (d. 1914), called this source the Q Gospel, Q standing for the German word *Quelle*, which means "source."

Since then, this theory has been widely accepted. The hypothetical Q Gospel, which scholars constructed by mapping out the common material in Matthew and Luke, has been published as a text in itself and has taken on a life of its own. Many books have been written about it, with titles calling it "the earliest gospel" or "the lost gospel."

Now, there is a very important feature of Q that makes it very relevant to our discussion: It is strictly a sayings gospel. In other words, its content is nothing but the sayings of Jesus. They include some of the most fundamental moral teachings of Christianity, such as the Sermon on the Mount, the Lord's Prayer, loving one's enemies, turning the other cheek, the Beatitudes, the parables of the mustard seed, the yeast, the invited dinner guests, and more.[46]

Moreover, there is nothing in Q that is explicitly Pauline. In other words, there is nothing that reflects the theology offered by Paul about the crucifixion and resurrection of Christ, which would form the basis of Christianity as a new religion detached from Judaism. A mere reading of Q rather gives an impression of Jesus as a reformer within Judaism—a reformer who reemphasized the spirit of the law to those who were blinded by the letter of the law.

That is why James M. Robinson, cochair of the International Q Project, argues that Q was the product of the "Jewish Jesus movement."[47] This movement was devoted to the teaching of its Messiah, which they collected as "sayings"—probably first in Aramaic, but then also in Greek, the lingua franca of the time, producing the "source" that Matthew and Luke would use as the basis of their texts.

In a striking contrast, for Paul the focus was not Jesus' sayings, but his crucifixion and resurrection. Throughout his thirteen letters, which make up almost one third of the New Testament, Paul never quoted a saying from Jesus—not even a single one.[48] For him, the Good News was not the teaching *of* Jesus, but the teaching *about* Jesus.

The academic and popular literature on Q is huge, and there are naturally various views about it, but few among those who admit the existence of Q doubt that it reflects a more Jewish stage of Christianity. Less noticed is the fact that Q seems to match perfectly with the *Injil*, the gospel to which the Qur'an refers, both in form and in theology. This view would not render the New Testament irrelevant for Islam, for, quite the contrary, that is the source in which Q is present. It would rather call for a selective reading of the New Testament.

THE DISCIPLES AND THEIR "TABLE"

The details the Qur'an gives about the life of Jesus are scarce, yet there is a remarkably generous focus on the disciples—or, in Arabic, the *hawariyun*. Some Muslim scholars have argued that the word comes from the Arabic word *hawira*, which means "pure

white," which they took as a reference to the moral cleanliness of
Jesus' followers. It seems more accurate, however, to think that the
term has a non-Arabic origin: A very similar term, *hawarya*, meaning "messenger," had been used for the disciples in Ethiopian Christian sources.[49]

What is more interesting is that the disciples, whose image in
the New Testament is not always very bright, have a very positive
image in the Qur'an. In three separate passages of the Qur'an, they
are pictured as ideal believers that Muslims should emulate. The
first passage is in the chapter "Family of Imran," and tells us how
the disciples believed in Jesus in spite of some other fellow Jews:

> When Jesus realized they [still] did not believe, he said, "Who will
> help me in God's cause?" The disciples said, "We will be God's
> helpers; we believe in God, witness our devotion to Him. Lord,
> we believe in what You have revealed and we follow the messenger:
> record us among those who bear witness."[50]

Notably, the term used above, "helpers," or *ansar*, has become a
powerful term in Islamic tradition. The Medinan Muslims who
hosted the refugees from Mecca, who just like the Prophet himself
had migrated to save their lives, were called helpers. In the modern
era, various Muslim parties, some of them violent, also labeled
themselves as helpers—such as Ansar al-Islam in Iraq or Ansar al-
Sharia in Libya, which are terrorist groups that unfortunately have
a very militant notion of "helping" God and His cause.

The second Qur'anic passage about the disciples of Jesus is
located in one of the late and short chapters of the Qur'an titled
"Solid Lines," or *Saff*, which tells believers to be steadfast in the heat
of the battle with pagans. It again refers to the disciples as helpers:

> You who believe, be God's helpers. As Jesus, son of Mary, said to
> the disciples, "Who will come with me to help God?" The disci-
> ples said, "We shall be God's helpers." Some of the Children of

Israel believed and some disbelieved: We supported the believers against their enemy and they were the ones who came
out on top.[51]

The last part of this verse is admittedly a bit perplexing. For it is
hard to explain how, in the context of Jesus and disciples, God "supported the believers against their enemy and they were the ones
who came out on top." The history of early Christianity rather is the
history of the suppression of Christians—whether they were Jewish
or Gentile. That is why some Muslim commentators have offered a
very long-term solution to this problem, arguing that the believers'
victory was realized only with the advent of Islam.[52]

The third Qur'anic passage about the disciples introduces another
curious theme, indeed a miracle. Here, disciples ask Jesus whether
God can send down a heavenly "table" for them—a table with food,
which will be the basis of a feast:

> When the Disciples said, "Jesus son of Mary! Can your Lord send
> down a table to us out of heaven?" He said, "Have fear of God if
> you are believers."
>
> They said, "We want to eat from it and for our hearts to be at
> peace and to know that you have told us the truth and to be
> among those who witness it."
>
> Jesus son of Mary said, "God, our Lord, send down a table to
> us out of heaven to be a feast for us, for the first and last of us, and
> as a Sign from You. Provide for us. You are the Best of Providers."
>
> God said, "I will send it down to you but if anyone among you
> is an unbeliver after that, I will punish him with a punishment
> the like of which I will not inflict on anyone else in all the
> worlds."[53]

This episode is located in the fifth chapter of the Qur'an, titled
"Ma'ida." Not all Muslims might be aware of it, but this very title
comes from the episode above: *ma'ida* is the word used for *table* in

the sentence "Can your Lord send down a table to us from heaven?" Some interpreters of the Qur'an translated the word also as "table with food" or "feast."

For the Christian, however, this table miracle is likely to sound odd. For it has no fitting parallel in the New Testament. For an allusion, some have pointed out Jesus' miracle of feeding the five thousand with only five loaves of bread and two fish. Others, including the early twentieth-century Muslim scholar Rashid Rida, saw a resonance with the Bread of Life discourse in the Fourth Gospel, where Jesus speaks of "the true bread from heaven."[54] Yet the most significant allusion seems to be to the Last Supper, at which Jesus gathered the disciples, gave them bread and wine, and established the *Eucharist*, the ceremony of bread and wine. This view is further strengthened by the fact that a very similar term, *ma'edd*, was used by Ethiopian Christians, before and during the birth of Islam, to refer to the table of the Eucharist, which was also called the Lord's Table.[55]

So, we can assume that the *ma'ida* in the Qur'an is a different version of the Last Supper. However, it is a very different version. There is neither a bread-and-wine ceremony in the Qur'an nor their consecration as the body and blood of Christ. As a Western scholar has observed:

> In this reinterpretation, the person of Jesus loses its paramount importance and his being the son of God is expressly denied. Instead, the Eucharist is interpreted as confirmation and remembrance of God's covenant with the apostles. With that, the Eucharist is added to the line of covenants God has made both with the Children of Israel previously and with the new community of believers afterwards.[56]

In other words, the Qur'an presents us an unusual Eucharist that lacks the exclusively Christian themes, but that asserts the ancient Jewish theme of covenant with God.

Moreover, the Qur'anic passage that defines this unusual Eucharist has a line which sounds quite similar to a line in the Old Testament that describes the Jewish Passover. In the Qur'an, we read Jesus asking, "God, our Lord, send down a table to us out of heaven to be a feast for us, for the first and last of us, and as a Sign from You." In Exodus, we read the Lord Himself declare: "This is a day you are to commemorate; for the generations to come you shall celebrate it as a festival to the Lord."[57] Furthermore, there is an additional parallel with the Psalms. In the Qur'an, we read the disciples asking Jesus, "Can your Lord send down a table to us out of heaven?" In Psalms, we read Jews asking Moses, "Can God prepare a table in the wilderness?"[58]

The point is that the unusual Eucharist we see in the Qur'an seems to present Jesus and his disciples in a distinctly Jewish framework. Here we have, one could even say, not a Christian Eucharist but a Jewish-Christian Eucharist.

Should we be surprised, then, to note that the Jewish Christians, the "heretics" of mainstream Christianity, had really their own, self-styled Eucharist? We learn this, again, from the heresiology of Church fathers. "These men reject the commixture of the heavenly wine and wish it to be water," Irenaeus wrote, as we noted before while stressing that Ebionites abstained from wine. Yet this was not a mere replacing of liquids, as we understand from Irenaeus, for he added: "[They are] not receiving God as to have union with Him."[59] In other words, Ebionites were not celebrating the Eucharist in order to "eat the body" and "drink the blood" of the Messiah—an idea totally alien and even repugnant to the Jewish mind.[60] For them, the Last Supper was rather "a mere remembrance of the table fellowship with Jesus."[61] It was probably also fashioned on the Jewish Passover, with themes from the Old Testament.

So, we can argue that the *ma'ida* story in the Qur'an, as a reinterpreted Last Supper, is theologically compatible with the Ebionite version of the Last Supper. It suggests, once again, that Jewish Christianity and Islam are somehow congruous.

THE MAN ON THE CROSS

The Qur'an is not a work of literary narrative, as is the Bible. As a scripture that provides guidance (*huda*) and a reminder (*tadhkira*) to humankind, it gives more emphasis to spiritual edifications than to providing a full account of facts. So, the Qur'an's main concern with the Jesus story, too, is not to give a full account of the Jesus story, but rather to put it in the right theological perspective. That is probably why, although it contains detailed narratives about the birth and mission of Jesus, it tells us almost nothing about his passing. For it does not consider the passing of Jesus—just like that of Abraham, Moses, or Muhammad himself—as an event with major theological significance.

In contrast, the passing of Jesus—or, more precisely, his Crucifixion, Resurrection, and Ascension—is crucial for Christianity. "If Christ has not been raised," Paul famously wrote to the Corinthians, "then our preaching is vain, your faith also is vain."[62] No wonder what ultimately became the very symbol of Christianity was the sign of the cross, which stands for the crucifixion—and not the sign of the fish, as it was among the earliest Christians.

In fact, the Qur'an does mention the cross, but only in passing, and only in an unaffirmative way. This mention, which led to disputes between Muslims and Christians for centuries, occurs in a Qur'anic passage that condemns a group of Jews that was apparently present in Medina. They are cursed, because "they disbelieved and uttered a terrible slander against Mary." Furthermore:

> And [they] said, "We have killed the Messiah, Jesus, son of Mary, the Messenger of God."
> They did not kill him, nor did they crucify him, but it was made to appear like that to them. Those that disagreed about him are full of doubt, with no knowledge to follow, only supposition.
> They certainly did not kill him. God raised him up to Himself. God is almighty and wise.[63]

The key statement here, "it was made to appear like that to them," or *shubbiha la-hum*, has led to endless speculations. Most Muslim exegetes, both in the classic era and the modern age, inferred from this phrase a theory of "substitution." Accordingly, Jesus was not crucified, but somebody was "substituted" in his place—perhaps one of his disciples, or Judas Iscariot who betrayed him, or Simon of Cyrene who helped him carry the cross.

Yet this "substitution" theory, which is still almost the standard view among Muslims today, raises lots of questions. Fakhraddin al-Razi, the medieval scholar, addressed some of them frankly in his major exegesis of the Qur'an. "God was no doubt capable of delivering Jesus from the hands of his enemies by simply taking him up to heaven," he first reminded. "What then," he asked, "is the purpose of casting his likeness on another man, except to condemn an innocent man to death to no purpose?" He also made the following observation, which is in fact a good reminder for all religious believers that their arguments against the rival tradition can turn back on themselves:

> All Christians in the world, with all their great love for Jesus and their extremist beliefs concerning him, have reported that they witnessed him being crucified and killed. If we were to deny this, we would cast doubt on the principle of *tawatur* [universally accepted transmission]. Casting doubt on this principle would also necessitate casting doubt on the prophethood of Muhammad and Jesus, and even on their very existence, as well as the existence of all other prophets, and that would be untenable.[64]

Other Muslim commentators took a second and less radically rejectionist interpretation of "appearance," arguing that Jesus was indeed crucified but he did not die on the cross. He rather secretly survived his execution, they suggested, despite his "appearance" of death. Ahmadiyya Muslims, an unorthodox sect of Islam, take this line. They even believe that after surviving the cross, Jesus moved to Kashmir, an area in the northern Indian subcontinent, to live there and ultimately to die a natural death.[65] Hence in the Kashmirian city of Srinagar, there is still a highly revered "tomb of Jesus."

Yet there is a third and radically different interpretation of the Qur'an's verdict on the cross—a road much less taken. It begins by noting the context of the statement "They did not kill him, nor did they crucify him." The context is a polemic against certain Jews—not Christians—who, apparently, both slandered Mary and also took pride in claiming "We killed the Messiah." (No wonder in Talmudic literature there is a narrative which "proudly proclaims Jewish responsibility for Jesus' execution."[66]) To these people the Qur'an says, no, "They did not kill him, nor did they crucify him, but it was made to appear like that to them."

In other words, the Qur'an is only telling us that *Jews* did not crucify and kill Jesus. It does not say nobody did that. It does not say, for example, that Romans did not crucify and kill Jesus, which was, of course, what really happened according to the canonical gospels.

Some scholars think that this third interpretation of the Qur'an's interpretation of the cross may be compatible with the Christian version of the story. One was the late William Montgomery Watt, one of the most eminent Western scholars of Islam. He argued that a Christian could in fact accept the Qur'an's statement on the crucifixion, "since the crucifixion was the work of Roman soldiers . . . [and] since the crucifixion was not a victory for the Jews in view of [Jesus'] resurrection."[67]

However, while this third interpretation makes it possible to reconcile the Qur'an with the *story* of the cross related in the canonical gospels, it probably cannot be reconciled with the *theology* of the cross related in Paul's letters. Accordingly, the crucifixion was a cosmic event in which Jesus suffered as an atonement for the sins of all humankind. This theology not only has no trace in the whole Qur'an, it also goes against some of its core doctrines—such as that sin is strictly personal, and "no burden-bearer can bear another's burden."[68] It also is theologically unnecessary, for the Qur'an does not share the theology of the Fall as well, which according to Christianity made every human being inherently sinful and thus in need of a savior.

QUR'ANIC DOCETISM?

There is one more point to consider regarding the Qur'an's take on the cross: its possible precedents in the Christian tradition.

In fact, those who are familiar with this tradition might have already seen a precedent for the Qur'anic statement "it was made to *appear* like that to them"—the early Christian "heresy" called docetism. The term comes from the Greek word *dokesis,* which literally means "appearance." It designated the doctrine that Christ did not really suffer on the cross, but it only seemed to be that way. It was quite popular in the second and third centuries of Christianity, and died out only after being condemned in the Council of Nicaea in AD 325.

However, there is an aspect of docetism which puts it at odds with the Qur'anic understanding of Jesus: For most docetics, the reason for denying the suffering of Christ was that they considered him to be too divine. The doctrine was most favored among Gnostics, for whom Christ was nothing but God—not "fully human and fully God." Hence, since God could not have suffered or died, Jesus could not have suffered or died. The theological background of docetism, in other words, was not close to Islam. It was rather quite antithetical to it.

Yet, well, the Lord works in mysterious ways. A closer look into early Christian sources reveals that there were also docetics of a whole different theological persuasion. We learn this from "Pseudo-Cyril," the seventh-century Christian author we mentioned before. This gentleman was a passionate preacher of mainstream Christian truth and also a chronicler of the different heretics he faced. One of the latter was a Samaritan living in Palestine, who believed "the son of Mary was a prophet of God" and also explained the Crucifixion in a docetic way: For him, the man crucified instead of "true Jesus" was rather "a prophet also called Jesus." True Jesus went up "a certain mountain," and it was not known what happened to him.[69]

Moreover, from the same Pseudo-Cyril, we also learn about another interesting personality: a monk named Annarichos, who lived in the Gaza area and who followed the "Gospel of the Hebrews," a lost Jewish Christian text mentioned earlier. This monk was reportedly a follower of "Ebion," implying that he was Ebionite. But he also had an unusual view of the Crucifixion. "When he [Jesus] was put on the wood of the cross," he believed, "his Father saved him from their hands and brought him up to heaven, beside him in glory."[70]

This quote not only sounds remarkably similar to the Qur'anic statement "They certainly did not kill him. God raised him up to Himself." It also comes from a source which was, reportedly, both Jewish Christian *and* docetic. So, one can think that if the Qur'an's take on the cross is explained as docetic, it can also fit in the overall continuity between Jewish Christianity and Islam.

This continuity is also visible in the fact that just like the Qur'an, Jewish Christian sources seem unfocused on the cross as a theological matter. Crucifixion never appears in basic Jewish Christian texts that we know of—the Epistle of James, the *Didache*, or the Q Gospel. "Of course the Q people knew of Jesus' death," notes James M. Robinson, the expert on the Q Gospel. "But they saw it more as the inevitable culmination of the activity of God's Wisdom, who had sent messengers to Israel down through the course of biblical history, prophets who had often been required to give their lives for God's cause."[71] Later Jewish Christians, such as the Ebionites, were no different. They were more interested in Jesus' teachings than in the meaning of his death. "Ebionites' Christ," in other words, "did not come to the world to sacrifice himself or to give his life for the ransom for many. Instead, he had a prophetic task."[72]

But was this prophet just like any other prophet in the history of Abrahamic faiths? Did his miraculous birth from a virgin or his unusual miracles hint that he was somehow special? And what did it exactly mean that "God raised him up to Himself," as the Qur'an says about the ending of his life on this earth? Does this mean he died? Or what?

These are questions that open some more interesting discussions, which I will explore in the next two chapters.

CHAPTER SEVEN

ISLAMIC CHRISTOLOGY

*Islam recognized the particular function of Christ, which . . .
differed from that of other prophets who usually brought a
law or reformed a previous one, by acknowledging his particular nature as the "Spirit of God."*

—Seyyed Hossein Nasr, Islamic philosopher[1]

ONCE UPON TIME, DAMASCUS, NOW THE CAPITAL OF THE MUCH-
troubled Syrian Arab Republic, was a Roman city and a Christian
citadel. It was home to a plenitude of denominations and churches,
along with a beautiful cathedral that had been converted in the late
fourth century from what used to be a temple of Jupiter. By the sixth
century, Christians of the city also began to believe that the head
of John the Baptist, severed in the first century on the orders of
Herod Antipas, was buried there. Hence a small shrine was built
within the cathedral—the shrine of John the Baptist.

Today, that shrine is still there, and is still venerated, but the
magnificent building is a mosque because Muslim armies conquered
Damascus, along with the rest of Syria, in the mid-630s, just a few
years after the passing of the Prophet Muhammad. Soon, after being shared for a while by Muslims and Christians, the cathedral
was converted into a mosque, as Damascus became the capital of
the Muslim empire ruled by the Umayyad Dynasty.

Yet Christians, and their creed, remained in the city. "The Christians were commonly given very fair treatment," a Christian author noted almost a century ago. "And, especially in the early days, many of them were employed in government offices."[2] One of these employees was Yuḥanna al-Dimashqi, or, as he is known in the West, John of Damascus. Besides being a Christian priest and theologian, John was also an erudite polymath, producing works on law, philosophy, and music. "Apparently his adhesion to Christian truth constituted no offence in the eyes of his Saracen countrymen," the *Catholic Encyclopedia* observes, "Saracen" being an archaic Christian term for Muslims. "For he seems to have enjoyed their esteem in an eminent degree."[3]

This eminent degree was none other than being the chief administrator at the court of caliph Abd al-Malik—the ruler who built the magnificent Dome of the Rock in Jerusalem. This official job in a Muslim empire did not keep John of Damascus from engaging in theological debates, however, as he had written extensive polemics against rival Christians—such as iconoclasts, a major current at the time—and Muslims. Against the latter, whose faith he had a good chance to examine, he wrote informed polemics. Unlike the Byzantine theologians, whose knowledge of Islam was much more indirect, John connected Islam not to diabolical forces, but to the Arian and Nestorian heresies.[4] He even devoted some ink to use the Muslims' own scripture to prove the divinity of Christ. On this particular matter, he also gave a bit of advice to his fellow Christians, in his *Disputatio Saraceni et Christiani*:

> If a Saracen asks you saying, "Who do you say Christ is," reply to him, "The Word of God"... Then you ask him in your turn, "What is Christ called in your Scripture?" It may be that the Saracen will want to ask you something else, but do not answer him until he has replied to your question. When he is absolutely compelled, he will reply to you, "In My Scripture, Christ is called the Spirit and the Word of God."[5]

And this was the moment that the Christian could say, "Aha, now I've got you!" John of Damascus, naturally, put this in more formal terms, and also gave us an important insight about the historical context of the discussion:

> Then ask him [the Saracen]: "Are the Spirit and Word of God called in your Scripture uncreated or created?" And if he tells you, "created," say to him: "And who created the Spirit and Word of God?" And, if compelled by necessity, he tells you that God created them, say, "Before God created the Word and the Spirit, did He not have either Spirit or Word?"
>
> And he will flee from you, nothing to answer. Because these, according to Saracens, are heretics, and therefore very much despised and rejected. And if you want to report him to the other Saracens, he will be very much afraid of you.[6]

The "heretics" John of Damascus noted here, who insisted that the Word of God is *created* by God, were the forerunners of the Mu'tazila. This was one of the early schools of Islamic theology, which had made its name by passionately defending three interrelated doctrines: humans act through free will, not through divine predestination; human reason is capable of finding truth, alongside revelation; and the Qur'an is a "created" book, not a preexistent one. The Umayyad Empire, under which these disputes began, disliked the Mu'tazila doctrines, for cynically political reasons, and suppressed them eagerly.[7] That is why the "Saracen" in the rhetorical conversation above would be "very much afraid" to say his views out loud.

Yet the Mu'tazila scholars had some good reasons to hold the doctrines they did. If free will is denied, they realized, then God's justice cannot be sustained; he appears as a capricious God who rewards or punishes his helpless creatures at will. If reason is denied, they noted, then the Greek wisdom they admired would be discarded and Islamic thought would become self-referential. And, finally, if the Qur'an is taken to be "uncreated," a preexistent being just like God Himself, they reasoned, then the Unity of God could be compromised.

Moreover, this third doctrine was necessary to deal with an argument that thinking Muslims had to deal with—the very argument that John of Damascus pinned down in his *Disputatio*: if Muslims believe that God's Word is "uncreated," then how can they deny the preexistence of Christ while their own scripture calls him "the Word of God"?[8]

THE WORD AND SPIRIT OF GOD

The term "word," or *kalima*, is used three times in the Qur'an for Jesus. In the first, he is called "a Word from God" who will be "confirmed" by Yahya, or John the Baptist.[9] In the second, we hear angels, during the Annunciation, telling Mary:

> Mary, God gives you news of *a Word from Him*, whose name will be the Messiah, Jesus, son of Mary, who will be held in honor in this world and the next, who will be one of those brought near [to God].[10]

The third is a verse that calls Christians to stop saying God is "Three"—to acknowledge "God is only One God." It then explains the nature of the Messiah: "The Messiah, Jesus son of Mary, was only the Messenger of God and *His Word, which He cast into Mary, and a Spirit from Him*."[11]

The title "messenger of God," or *rasulullah*, is very common in the Qur'an, as it is used for all prophets, from Abraham to Moses to Muhammad. However, Jesus, as we can see, is not only a prophet. He is also "Word *from* God," even "Word *of* God," and also a "Spirit from God."

Since both of these terms—"Word" and "Spirit"—are never used for any other human being in the Qur'an, they have generated curiosity for centuries. Christians such as John of Damascus, who read the Qur'an carefully, saw in them a reflection of their Word christology, based on the famous opening lines of the Fourth Gospel: "In the beginning was the Word, and the Word was with God, and the Word was God . . . And the Word became flesh, and dwelt among us." A modern-day Christian scholar even wrote about "the Christian potential of the Qur'an," based on this apparent parallelism.[12]

Islamic scholars, however, have traditionally given a more modest meaning to Jesus' being the divine Word. This term, they reasoned, only referred to the miraculous creation of Jesus, without a biological father, and with God's *creative word*, "Be!"[13] We see this creative word in the Qur'anic conversation between Mary and Gabriel, which takes place during the Annunciation. Accordingly, Mary asks, "How can I have a son when no man has ever touched me?" And Gabriel responds: "It will be so. God creates whatever He wills. When He decides on something, He just says to it, 'Be!' and it is."[14]

Another Qur'anic verse that gives weight to this view—that Jesus is the divine Word only in the sense of being created by the creative word "Be!"—is the one that compares him to Adam: "The likeness of Jesus in God's sight is the same as Adam. He created him from earth and then He said to him, 'Be!' and he was."[15]

Notably, such a modest meaning to "Word" was given in a much-forgotten ancient Christian text as well, *The Armenian Book of Infancy*, yet another apocryphal gospel that was popular among early Eastern Christians but did not make its way into the New Testament. In its narration of the Annunciation, this gospel reads: "The Word of God penetrated into [Mary] by her ear." As noted by a Catholic scholar, this sounds very similar to the Qur'anic statement, "He cast it [a Word] into Mary," and seems to suggest only a "creative Word."[16]

However, in the Islamic tradition, there are also some hints, and some overt comments, that Jesus was the Word of God in a more elevated sense as well. These hints come first of all from the Qur'an,

which suggests that Jesus had an unusual nature not merely in terms
of his birth, but also other miraculous aspects of his life. He spoke
in his cradle—and perhaps even in his mother's womb, depending
on how one reads the passage about Mary's birth pains.[17] He also
gave life to inanimate matter, by raising the dead or breathing into
clay figures and making them alive.[18] Especially the latter miracle
puzzled some Muslim exegetes, for creating life is a power ascribed
only to God. One of them, al-Razi, asked:

> Is it that God had deposited a special power in Jesus, so that when-
> ever he breathed into a thing it became alive, or is it that God
> created life in that thing when Jesus breathed into it in order for
> God to manifest His miracles?[19]

Al-Razi then opted for the second option, but added that since
"Jesus was generated from the breath of Gabriel into Mary . . . It is
not improbable that the breath of Jesus could infuse life and spirit."[20]

In the overall Qur'anic story of Jesus, there is something else
that is curious. When the Qur'an narrates the stories of prophets in
detail, it often mentions their flaws, which the Islamic tradition con-
ceptualized as *zalla*, or "lapse." Adam ate the fruit of the forbidden
tree, for example; Moses hit a man and killed him; and Muhammad
neglected a blind man searching for wisdom, which led to his cen-
sure by the Qur'an.[21] The Jesus of the Qur'an, however, has no *zalla*,
no mistake, no lapse. He is simply flawless. No wonder Mary was
heralded with "a faultless son."[22] And Jesus himself said, "God . . .
has made me blessed, wherever I am."[23]

Besides the Qur'an, a hadith found in the collection of Imam
Bukhari also implies an exceptional nature for Jesus. "When any
human being is born, Satan touches him at both sides of the body
with his two fingers," the Prophet Muhammad reportedly says here.
"Except Jesus, the son of Mary."[24]

Based on such clues, some Muslim commentators, including Ibn
Abbas, the cousin of the Prophet Muhammad, have suggested that

Jesus was the Word of God in a higher sense than the mere "creative Word" in his generation.[25] But in exactly what sense? Nishapuri, a Persian Shiite scholar of the fourteenth century, has offered an answer, first by defining a "perfect man" in union with God, and then noting, "Jesus was specially favored, among all other prophets and saints, by being called 'word' because he was created with the inherent capacity for this perfection."[26]

Two centuries earlier, another Shiite scholar, Shaykh Tabarsi, had discussed the meaning of Jesus' speech in the cradle and suggested that "God had perfected his reason even at that age . . . revealing to him what he uttered."[27] Accordingly, Jesus was not merely receiving occasional revelations like other prophets; every word of his was revelation by God.

While various Shiites and Sufis have been interested in such speculations about the nature of Jesus, orthodox Sunni commentators have often been more cautious on this delicate matter of theology. One notable twentieth-century figure, Sayyid Qutb, whose radical political views are only a part of his exegetical work, pondered the meaning of "Word of God," only to conclude: "This, like other such matters, belongs to the unseen which cannot be exactly known."[28] Human reason, he argued, in a typical traditionalist Sunni line of thought, was not created with the capacity to comprehending such mysteries, which could only lead to "pointless speculations."[29]

Among contemporary Muslim thinkers, one who ventured into such territory of mysteries to offer a notably higher version of Islamic christology is Hajj Muhammad Legenhausen, an American philosopher, a convert to Islam, and a professor at the Imam Khomeini Education and Research Institute in Iran. Legenhausen apparently builds upon the tradition started by Tabarsi that Jesus may be the Word of God not as "merely a creative word, but also a word of revelation." In this view, unlike the Prophet Muhammad, who was a normal human being who just occasionally received God's revelation, Jesus becomes the revelation itself. The parallel to Jesus in Islam thus becomes not the Prophet Muhammad, but the Qur'an.[30]

When one recalls that some key Muslim defenders of the "uncreated Qur'an" doctrine also saw the Torah and the Gospel as "uncreated" as well—the latter of which, in this interpretation, would be Jesus himself—one gets an Islamic christology not extremely far from Christian christology: Here you have a Jesus as the uncreated, preexisting Word.[31] Add to this that the same doctrine saw God's "attributes," including His Word, as "not He, [but] not other than He," and there emerges an interesting theological bridge between Islam and Christianity.[32]

Yet still, this higher Qur'anic Word theology would not make Jesus divine in the sense of making him an object of worship, as some Christians have suggested since the time of John of Damascus.[33] Muslims, after all, do not worship the Qur'an, even if they consider it as the uncreated Word of God. That is why, as the Muslim academic Mahmoud Ayoub once rightly observed, Muslims may agree with the opening statement of the Gospel of John: "In the beginning was the Word, and the Word was with God." But they can not agree with what follows next: "And the Word *was* God."[34]

Nevertheless, a higher Qur'anic Word theology puts Jesus somewhere between human beings and God—somewhere, one could suggest, on the same level with the angels. It is therefore perhaps telling that in its rejection of the Christian doctrine of the divinity of Christ, the Qur'an mentions him in the same breath with the angels near to God:

> The Messiah would never disdain to be a servant to God nor would the angels near to Him. If any do disdain to worship Him, and grow arrogant, He will in any case gather them all to Him.[35]

The Messiah was likened to an angel also by the great twelfth-century Sufi master Ibn al-Arabi, who wrote poems concerning Jesus. Ibn al-Arabi pondered the meaning of Jesus being "the Spirit of God," and interpreted it as Jesus' power to breathe life into the dead, with God's permission, just as Angel Gabriel breathed life into his mother:

Jesus came forth raising the dead because he was a divine spirit. In this the quickening was of God, while the blowing itself came from Jesus, just as the blowing was from Gabriel, while the Word was of God.[36]

In light of the theme of this book, it is perhaps also telling that the image of Jesus as an angel was present in another religious tradition, which was, of course, Jewish Christianity. Various sources show that among Jewish Christians there was an "angelomorphic christology." That is why the church father Tertullian disparaged the Ebionites for making Christ a mere man, "though more glorious than the prophets, in that they say an angel was in him." Epiphanius also wrote, "they say that he [Christ] was not begotten of God the Father, but created as one of the arch-angels . . . that he rules over the angels and all the creatures of the Almighty." In the "Pseudo-Clementine Writings," too, which reflect Jewish Christianity, Christ is presented as a great archangel that rules over seventy angels.[37] No wonder the Epistle to the Hebrews, one of the most sophisticated pro-Pauline letters in the New Testament, seems to be written partly as an argument against an "angelomorphic christology of Jewish origin."[38]

Hence, it seems fair to say that the Qur'an may be in line with Jewish Christianity in terms of its christology, as well: that the Messiah is no God, but also no ordinary mortal.

Finally, it is worth noting that the Islamic christology we have mapped so far would be quite parallel to some of the more metaphorical christologies offered by some progressive Christian thinkers, such as the late John Hick. "Jesus was so open to divine inspiration, so responsive to the divine spirit, so obedient to God's will, that God was able to act on earth in and through him," he wrote. "This, I believe, is the true Christian doctrine of the incarnation."[39] And *that*, I believe, is a doctrine of incarnation that Islam can wholeheartedly accept.

"THE SON OF GOD"

While the term "Word of God" may help build a theological bridge between Christianity and Islam, another key term in Christianity has certainly opened a theological rift: "Son of God." Beginning with the Qur'an, Islam has emphatically denied that Jesus could be called as such.

That is probably why the Qur'an repeatedly calls Jesus the "Son of Mary"—twenty-three times. In contrast, in the New Testament, the same title is found only once, in the Gospel of Mark. It is when people of Nazareth ask, "Is not this the carpenter, *the son of Mary,* and brother of James and Joses and Judas and Simon?"[40]

The Qur'an rejects the title "Son of God" not only for Jesus, but for anybody. For it finds the very idea of divine begetting deeply disrespectful to God. "God has no son and there is no other god accompanying Him," declares one of the Qur'anic verses that condemn the notion.[41] Another passage explains just how outrageous the idea is:

> They say, "The All-Merciful has a son." They have devised a monstrous thing.
>
> The heavens are all but rent apart and the earth split open and the mountains brought crashing down, at their ascription of a son to the All-Merciful!
>
> It is not fitting for the All-Merciful to have a son. There is no one in the heavens and earth who will not come to the All-Merciful as a servant.[42]

But what does it mean exactly to be a Son of God? Since the Qur'an finds it so scandalous, it must have a very scandalous meaning.

No wonder, when we look at the Arabic word the Qur'an uses for sonship: we see that it is, with one exception, *walad,* which means "son" in the physical sense. In other words, a god with a *walad* can only be understood as a deity who had sexual intercourse with a female counterpart. This was, of course, utterly disrespectful to, and absolutely incompatible with, the Abrahamic conceptualization of God. It was, on the other hand, the typical way gods were envisioned in many pagan societies, including Greeks, Romans, and, most importantly, pre-Islamic Arabs. The Arab gods represented by the idols in the Ka'aba had plenty of "sons" and "daughters," whom they begot through intercourse with their "wives."

This suggests that the Qur'an's very strong condemnation of the idea of divine sonship might have something to do with the pagan Arab context—the very "ignorance" Islam was determined to wipe out. In other words, the condemnation was not rooted in the suggested fact that Muslims "are carnal, [so] they can think only of what is flesh and blood," as Thomas Aquinas once argued.[43] It was rather rooted in the fact that Islam emerged in a cultural context in which people believed in deities having carnal relations.

In contrast, however, sonship to God in the monotheist Hebrew context—in the Old Testament sense of being chosen and beloved by God—would not be offensive to Islam.[44]

Hence some prominent Islamic scholars pointed to these two different meanings of sonship—the first one pagan and carnal, the second Hebrew and metaphorical—and argued that the latter can be acceptable. They include the Mu'tazila theologian Ibrahim al-Nazzam (d. 845), the Asharite theologian al-Sharastani (d. 1153), and the towering Sunni scholar al-Ghazali (d. 1111).[45] The great exegete of the Qur'an, al-Razi, also brought nuance to the meaning of Son of God, making a distinction between *walad*, a literal son, and *ibn*, which can be a metaphorical son. The latter term is used only once in the Qur'an to refer to the Christian view of Jesus, but it is the standard term in Arab Christian literature. "I believe," al-Razi therefore wrote,

it to be nearer to the truth to say that perhaps the word *ibn* [son] occurs in the Gospel to denote high honor, as the word *khalil*

[intimate friend of God, a Qur'anic term for Abraham] denotes
high honor.[46]

Al-Razi then criticized Christians only for "interpreting the word
'son' literally, to signify actual sonship."[47] In fact, of course, Christians do not imply any physical sonship to Jesus, in the sense of
projecting a sexual nature to God the Father. In that sense, Christianity is actually in agreement with Islam and Judaism and at
odds with Greek and Arab paganism. Yet still, mainstream Christians move on from the term "Son of God" to proclaim faith in *God
the Son*, defining Jesus as divine, as a part of a triune godhead. That
is unacceptable to Islam—as it is to Judaism.

However, this theological tension between Islam and mainstream Christianity does not necessarily exist between Islam and
the New Testament gospels. For in the gospels, Jesus is repeatedly
called Son of God, but never God the Son. The latter term was established in church councils, as an interpretation of the New Testament, and at the expense of the various "heretics" who had differing
interpretations.

Finally, we should note that the New Testament has various
passages that define Jesus as a "servant of God," and that can only
be music to Muslim ears. "Here is my servant whom I have chosen," Matthew reads for Jesus, quoting Isaiah.[48] Similarly, the
Qur'an reads for Jesus: "He is only a servant on whom We bestowed
Our blessing."[49]

THE HOLY SPIRIT

Christians who read the Qur'an may be repeatedly surprised to
come across some familiar terms that have powerful meanings in
their own theology. If one of these is "Word of God," as we saw,
another one is "Holy Spirit"—or *Ruh al-Qudus* in its Arabic original.

This term is used four times in the Qur'an, three of which are in
direct relation to Jesus. In all these three instances, we read that

God "strengthened" Jesus with the Holy Spirit.[50] In the fourth instance, however, "Holy Spirit" appears in the context of not Jesus but the Prophet Muhammad. We hear him saying, apparently in reference to the Qur'an, "The Holy Spirit has brought it down from your Lord with truth."[51]

So, the Holy Spirit is an agent that both "strengthened" Jesus and also brought down the Qur'an. Hence most Muslim commentators identified this force as the Angel Gabriel. Of course, the term has a whole different meaning in Christianity, where the Holy Spirit is conceived as the third person of the Trinity. Naturally that is not what the Qur'an means. In fact, as a scholar noted, "One might see a corrective, even a polemical intent in the Qur'an's use of the phrase."[52] Yes, there is a Holy Spirit, the polemic implies, but it is not a part of a triune God, it is only the Angel Gabriel.

Yet what does the Qur'an exactly mean by emphasizing that the Holy Spirit "strengthened" Jesus? Gabriel is believed to have occasional encounters with the Prophet Muhammad as well, to reveal to him verses of the Qur'an, but the Qur'an does not state that Gabriel "strengthened" Muhammad—or any other prophet. That is why al-Razi offered the possibility that "God commanded Gabriel to be with Jesus in all his circumstances."[53] This can also be a way of understanding how Jesus could be the Word of God in the sense of always speaking the words of God: the transmitter of the revelation was with him all the time.

THE PROBLEM WITH THE TRINITY

If there is one single concept in Christian theology that will never be accepted by Muslims, it is the doctrine of the Trinity—that God consists of the Father, the Son, and the Holy Spirit. To Islam, this is a very un-Abrahamic idea that violates the absolute oneness of God. Hence the Qur'an explicitly condemns the Trinity in two explicit passages. The first of them, quoted earlier, is a call to Christians:

People of the Book! Do not go to excess in your religion. Say nothing but the truth about God. The Messiah, Jesus son of Mary, was only the Messenger of God and His Word, which He cast into Mary, and a Spirit from Him. So have faith in God and His Messengers. Do not say, "Three." It is better that you stop. God is only One God. He is too Glorious to have a son! Everything in the heavens and in the earth belongs to Him. God suffices as a Guardian.[54]

This passage leaves little doubt that calling God "three" and defining Jesus as "son of God" is antithetical to Islam. Even if we recall that "son" in the Arabic context meant physical son, and that is not what Christianity implies for Jesus, the deification of the "son," which would make God "three," is clearly rejected.

The second Qur'anic passage addressing the Trinity has raised some questions, though. For it describes the Trinity that it condemns, which seems to be an unusual formulation of the doctrine. It reads:

Those who say that God is the third of three are unbelievers. There is no god but One God. If they do not stop saying what they say, a painful punishment will afflict those among them who are unbelievers.[55]

The unusualness here is in the phrase "God is the third of three." Although this may sound like the doctrine of the Trinity at first sight, it is not exactly applicable. A mainstream Christian would not claim "God is the third of three," but rather he would claim that there is one God with three "expressions." That is why it has been long suggested that what the Qur'an condemns here is not Trinity as we know it, but a deviant version of it—a kind of tritheism, or belief in three separate Gods, that mainstream Christians would also reject. That may be a possible interpretation of this verse. Yet it is also possible to read the "God is the third of three" phrase as an "intentional simplification" to expose the "weakness" of the Trinity "when analyzed from the strictly monotheistic perspective of the Qur'an."[56]

That is why, while some Christian authors have argued that the Qur'an can be reconciled with the Trinity, once both are properly understood, Muslims have almost universally disagreed with that notion, thinking that there is no way that the idea of a triune God can be compatible with Muslim scripture, which emphatically states: "He is God, Absolute Oneness."[57] This has in fact been established as the core theological principle in Islam, *tawhid*, meaning "attributing oneness." In contrast, Muslims point out, Christians believe in the opposite principle, *taslis*, meaning "attributing triuneness."

Of course, Islam is not alone in its rejection of the doctrine of the Trinity. Judaism, too, has the exact same position on the unity of God. No wonder that Jewish scholars, especially in the Middle Ages, engaged in many polemics with their Christian counterparts, refuting both the doctrine of the Trinity and also the prefigurations Christians found for it in the Old Testament, often with stretches of the imagination. As early as the third century, Rabbi Simlai, a Talmudic sage, had to explain that the Hebrew words *El*, *Elohim*, and *YHWH* used for God do not hint at any trinity, but rather connote one and the same person, as one could say "king, emperor, Augustus."[58]

Naturally, Jewish Christians rejected the doctrine of the Trinity as well. Although their documents show that they called Jesus Son of God, they apparently understood this term in the Hebrew sense, which did not imply any divinity for Jesus. A passage in the "Pseudo-Clementine" *Homilies* gives a remarkable glimpse of this view, in an imaginary dialogue between Peter the apostle, with whom the author identifies, and Simon, who is presented as having erroneous views about Christ. Peter says: "Our Lord neither asserted that there were gods except the Creator of all, nor did He proclaim Himself to be God." In response, Simon asks, "Does it not seem to you, then, that he who comes from God is God?" And Peter replies: "Tell us how this is possible; for we cannot affirm this, because we did not hear it from Him."[59] The passage also has the notable title: "Christ Not God, But the Son of God."

The evolution from this more modest christology to the doctrine of the Trinity had two major stages. First, Christ was defined as divine. Then, a triune godhead was formalized, involving God the Father, God the Son, and God the Holy Sprit. The formula was first schematized by the church father Tertullian at the beginning of the third century, or some 170 years after the passing of Jesus. But it did not go unchallenged. Within Gentile Christianity itself, there emerged various "heresies" in the second, third, and fourth centuries, all of which denied the divinity of Christ. They insisted that he was "subordinate" to God, or that he was "adopted" by him at the time of his baptism or resurrection. Known under names such as Anomeanism, Dynamic Montanism, or Priscillianism, these currents had slight differences, but they all rejected the Trinity.

The most influential of these heresies was Arianism, named after Arius (d. 336), a priest of Alexandria, who insisted that Christ was created—that "there was a time when he was not." Christ was therefore Son of God, not divine by nature, but only by grace and adoption. This was a theology not too far from Jewish Christianity, and no wonder the Arians were accused of being "Judaizers."[60] As a response to Arianism, orthodoxy, now under the aegis of the Roman Emperor Constantine, was established at the Council of Nicaea (325). At Nicaea, it was decreed that Jesus is "begotten, not made" and of "one substance with the Father"—a doctrine to which all Catholics and most Protestants still adhere. The full doctrine of the Trinity was established only half a century later, in 381, at the Council of Constantinople.

Yet the Arian tendency would never fully die out. As the "archetypal heresy," it would rather come back again and again.[61]

"RESTORATION OF CHRISTIANITY"

On October 27, 1553, on a beautiful hilltop near Geneva called Le Plateau de Champel, which is today an upscale neighborhood, something terrible happened. A heretic, who had been put under arrest about ten weeks previously, was brought in chains and tied to a stake. Soon, the wood under his feet was set on fire and the poor man was burned alive. Some say that John Calvin, a prominent theologian of the time, had asked that the kindling in this particular execution should be all chosen from green wood, so that the suffering of the victim would be prolonged.

Calvin is still quite famous today as the founder of Calvinism, one of the main branches of Protestant Christianity. Yet the victim, who is a bit less famous, was also an important Protestant leader: Michael Servetus. Born in Aragon, Spain, he had lived in various parts of Europe. He was a Renaissance polymath, who produced various works on mathematics, astronomy, and human anatomy—he was the first Westerner, in fact, to map out minor blood circulation.

Yet it was Servetus's work as a theologian that would seal his terrible fate. Like other Protestant reformers, such as Luther and Calvin, he had bravely challenged the Catholic Church's monopoly on Christianity. But Servetus's reform went further than these two, as he opposed two key doctrines accepted by both Catholics and other Protestants: the doctrine of predestination and, even more shockingly, the doctrine of the Trinity, which Servetus saw as a later invention in Christian thought that had no basis in the Bible.

This was not because Servetus lacked devotion to Christ. In fact, he was "in love with the figure of Christ."[62] When flames began burning him alive at the stake, his last words reportedly were: "Jesus, Son of the Eternal God, have mercy on me."[63] But there was a christological nuance here: For Servetus, Jesus was "the Son of the *Eternal God*," not "the *Eternal Son* of God." For in his view, Christ had become "Son" only during the Incarnation, and he was a preexistent being only as the Word of God. This was not exactly "the Arian heresy," yet Arianism was what Servetus was accused of and executed for.

But besides his perceived Arianism, there was something else that made Servetus deviant. Unlike most Christians of his time, he was aware of the Qur'an, albeit only thanks to partial and imperfect translations into Latin. Hence in his early 1531 book, *De Trinitatis Erroribus*, or "The Errors of the Trinity," he had mentioned the Qur'an several times. In his final and most lethal book, *Christianismi Restitutio*, or "Restoration of Christianity," published in 1553 right before his execution, he also quoted certain verses from the Qur'an, quite positively, which Calvin would use against him as a proof of blasphemy. In one of his passages sympathetic to Islam, in which Islam's Prophet still appeared as the enemy, Servetus wrote:

> Hear as well what Muhammad says, for more faith is to be put in one truth confessed by an enemy, than in a hundred of our lies. For he says in his Quran that Christ was the greatest of the prophets, the spirit of God, the power of God, the breath of God, the very soul of God, the Word born of a perpetual virgin by the breath of God . . . He says, moreover, that the Apostles and Evangelists and the first Christians were the best of men, and had written the truth, without believing in the Trinity or in three Persons in the Divine Being. Rather he said that men in later times introduced this.[64]

For Servetus, in other words, Islamic christology was an echo of what he believed to be true Christianity. Yet underlying his interest in Islam, as well as his interest in Judaism, was not his betrayal of his own religion but, quite contrary, his passion to evangelize it in a more reasonable fashion. "While many Christian apologists defended their faith by explaining what was wrong with others' religions," a modern scholar observes, "Servetus chose to explore what was amiss in Christianity by finding out why Muslims and Jews could not abide it and did not willingly convert."[65] A key obstacle to Christianity, Servetus concluded, was "this tradition of the Trinity," which had become "laughing-stock" for Muslims and Jews.[66]

To the Christendom of the time, these ideas were not only theologically shocking but also politically annoying. The ever-expanding Ottoman Empire had reached the gates of Vienna, and any sympathetic view of Islam was seen as "the Trojan horse that preceded the Turkish conquest."[67] So, Servetus appeared to many not just as a heretic but also as a traitor. No wonder both his body and his books were eagerly burned. Only three original copies of his major work, *Christianismi Restitutio,* have survived to date, in libraries in Paris, Edinburgh, and Vienna.

THE "TURKISH CHRIST"

As is often the case with history, the killing of Servetus did not kill his ideas. An "antitrinitarian" movement grew in mid-sixteenth-century Europe, especially in remote areas without a strong national state and centralized authority, such Poland, Hungary, and Ottoman-ruled Transylvania.[68] In all of them, new Christian churches emerged with "Judaizing" or "Islamizing" tendencies, which were often nothing more than a rejection of the doctrine of the Trinity.

The most notable element in this current was probably the Polish Brethren, a Protestant church founded in Poland in 1565 by the Italian theologian Fausto Paolo Sozzini. *Socinianism,* the doctrine derived from his name, quickly turned into a scandalous heresy in the eyes of both the Catholic Church and the Lutheran and Calvinist Protestants. In Socinian theology, Christ was the Logos, or Word of God, but only in the sense of being the *interpres divinae voluntatis,* or "interpreter of God's will." So Jesus, who was miraculously born of a virgin, was to be adored, but not worshiped as God. The Socinians also upheld human reason, denied the doctrine of original sin, and shunned infant baptism.[69] They did not have a single idea, I would suggest, that would contradict Islamic theology.

This parallelism was noticed as well by other antitrinitarians, who sought alliances in the Muslim world, partly in order to escape religious persecution. In Germany, Adam Neuser, a Protestant pastor, and his associate Johann Sylvan found themselves in trouble in 1570 as the result of an antitrinitarian manifesto written by Sylvan. Sylvan was captured, tortured, and ultimately beheaded with a sword in the marketplace of Heidelberg, a southwestern German town. Neuser managed to escape, and he soon wrote a letter to the Ottoman Sultan Selim II, in which he said:

> I am firmly persuaded that my retreat from among the idolatrous Christians will engage many Persons of Consideration to embrace your belief and your religion, especially since many of the most learned and most considerable amongst them are herein of the same Sentiments with me, as I shall inform your majesty by word of mouth.[70]

Neuser eventually was able to find his way to Constantinople (present-day Istanbul) in 1572, where he settled, converted to Islam, and even served the sultan as a translator at the palace. He also became the leader of a large circle of converts to Islam. When he died in 1576 after a serious illness, some Christians said that he must have been punished by God for his apostasy.[71] Neuser's abandonment of Christianity was a rare exception, to be sure, but it was enough to help discredit the antitrinitarian movement. Peter Melius Juhasz, the Calvinist bishop of Transylvania, had declared in 1568 that antitrinitarians were preaching nothing but a perverted "Turkish Christ."[72]

Back in Poland, the Socinian movement experienced its own drama in 1600, when a new Catholic king banned and crushed them. Hence many members of the church moved to the Netherlands, and soon had an influence in England as well. During this period of the early Enlightenment, some exponents, partly in their desire to find unorthodox ways to think about religion, became inspired by Socinian ideas, which were now also called Unitarian.

One of these thinkers was John Locke (d. 1704), the godfather of political liberalism. He had no interest in becoming a Muslim, but his antitrinitarian views led some people to accuse him of wanting to do so. In his passionate rebuttal of Locke, the Anglican cleric John Edwards argued that "this lank faith of his is in a manner no other than the faith of a Turk."[73] A parallel charge was that Locke seemed to "have consulted the Mahometan bible," which then was a scandalous thing to do.[74]

Another Englishman born in the same year as Locke, 1632, was Henry Stubbe, a less famous yet no less erudite Enlightenment writer. As a noted Latin and Greek scholar, mathematician, and historian, he too was attracted to antitrinitarian Christian theology and to sympathy for Islam. In 1671 he wrote *The Rise and Progress of Mahometanism*, a subversive work that portrayed the Prophet Muhammad as a wise legislator who reinstituted the inclinations of primitive Christianity. Stubbe even suggested that those inclinations were rooted in "Judaizing Christians," which he saw as the inspirers of Islam. The book was too provocative to be published in seventeenth-century England and was only circulated privately.[75]

THE MAHOMETAN CONSPIRACY

In August 1682 the Unitarian-Mahometan connection took a more coherent form in England with a new controversy. Two "single Philosophers," who "come as Orators of those Unitarians," presented a letter to Ahmet Ben Ahmet, the Moroccan ambassador, who was on a visit to London. They praised the ambassador, the emperor of Morocco, and the Muslim world in general, while describing themselves as "your nearest fellow champions." The Unitarians and Muslims are "fellow worshippers of that sole supreme Deity of the Almighty Father and Creator," they argued, suggesting an alliance against "those backsliding Christians named Trinitarians." Yet the Moroccan ambassador rejected the letter, which was soon

exposed, causing a public uproar against Unitarians and only helping to strengthen "Anglican suspicions about a Muslim-dissenter
conspiracy."[76]

In fact, there was no conspiracy. For one thing, the Muslim world
had really no idea about, let alone a hand in, intra-Christian theological rifts. Second, the Unitarians were actually hoping to convert
Muslims to their kind of true Christianity, rather than becoming
their spies. And third, their "treason" was an understandable outcome of their persecution. According to the inaptly named Tolera-
tion Act of 1689, Unitarians were not treated as English citizens:
They could not hold any public office, teach in schools, graduate from
Oxford or Cambridge, or receive a legacy or deed or gift.[77] It was
a typical case of a suppressed minority hopelessly looking for alliances abroad, only to be despised more as the enemy within—
a vicious cycle that is still very common today, not in the liberal
West, this time, but in the illiberal East, including the Muslim World.

About a century later, another English polymath, Joseph Priestley, who is often credited with the discovery of oxygen, gave rise to
another controversy by his antitrinitarian preaching—along with
his "anarchism," which was evident in his support for the American and French Revolutions. He too was accused of being "a disguised Mahometan who seeks to overthrow church and state," a
charge which he forcefully denied by emphasizing his dislike of Islam as a false religion.[78] But his affirmations of his faith could not
avert public anger, as an angry mob raided his home in Birming-
ham, England, in 1791. Soon, seeking religious freedom, Priestley
moved to the United States and settled in Pennsylvania, where he
founded the First Unitarian Church of Philadelphia. Thanks to pioneers like him, Unitarianism would further develop in nineteenth-
century America. It would have some influence even in the birth of
the Seventh-Day Adventist Church, which initially had nontrinitarian inclinations and which notably revived the "Judaizing" tendency of observing the Mosaic Law.[79]

Back in England, the obsession with the Unitarian-Muslim conspiracy continued for a while. A book published in London in 1830, titled *The Trial of the Unitarians, For a Libel on the Christian Religion*, presented an interesting example. This was a hypothetical mock trial of Priestley and two other Unitarian ministers of the time. They were prosecuted by the Anglican attorney general, for the attempt "by these mistaken men to melt down the Christian religion into the dross of Mahomedanism."[80] The proof was that these Christian heretics and the Mahometans "have come to these common terms," which were:

> That they both believe Christ to have been the Messiah, and the revealer of God to man; that he was a true prophet; that he gave sight to the blind, healed the lame, and raised the dead; and that what he taught was truth.[81]

These commonalities were making Unitarians favorable to Muslims, the attorney general warned, pointing to the scandalous apostasy of Neuser, who "finished his career by turning Mahomedan." Yet he added, in a stronger contempt for Unitarianism than for Islam:

> This result is not, perhaps, so much to be deprecated, since, of the two systems, the Mahomedan is the nearest to Christianity, for it embraces the belief that Christ was the Word of God; that He is the intercessor between God and man; and that He was conceived and miraculously born of a virgin . . . Gentlemen, if any of you have ever taken up the volume of the Alcoran [Qur'an], you will have found, in the early parts of it, that none are to be accounted true Mussulmans who do not believe the Scriptures of the Old and New Testament to be the word of God. Now, in all these several points of Mahomedan belief, the disciples of the Impostor excel the Unitarians, and out-run them in the nearness of their approach to Christianity.[82]

The word *Imposter* was used here, as common in premodern Christian literature, irreverently for the Prophet Muhammad. Besides that subjective comment, the attorney general of this hypothetical trial was objectively right: Islam was the nearest religion to Christianity. Its christology had unmistakable parallels with the gospels. And its teachings resonated with those of Christian "heretics"—whether they be Jewish Christians or Arians of the ancient past or the Unitarians of the modern era.

In other words, the rebirth of a nontrinitarian strain within Christianity in the midst of the Protestant Reformation was not due to the conspiratorial encroachment of Islamic beliefs in Christian minds. It was rather due to the critical reading of the religious traditions of Christianity itself. Some of those who engaged in this reading discovered a less divine and more prophetic Jesus. They discovered, one could say, a lost archetype.

CHAPTER EIGHT

A SECOND COMING?

God will not disgrace a community of which I am the beginning and Jesus the end.

—Prophet Muhammad[1]

LIKE ITS ABRAHAMIC SISTER FAITHS, ISLAM HAS A TRADITION OF eschatology—a narrative about how the world will come to an end. In this vision, the world we know, in fact the whole universe, will collapse one day, at "the Hour" as the Qur'an calls it, in a terrifying way. The sun will go black, the stars will be dimmed, and the mountains will move. In one of the vivid descriptions of the Hour, in the aptly named Qur'anic chapter "Ripped Apart" we read:

When the sky is ripped apart, obeying its Lord as it rightly must; when the earth is leveled out, casts out its contents, and becomes empty, obeying its Lord as it rightly must; You humans, toiling laboriously towards your Lord, will meet Him.[2]

As told here, the Hour will be only the beginning of the afterlife, where we humans will all "meet" our Maker. First, all the dead will arise from their graves, asking, "Alas for us! Who has raised us from our resting-place?"[3] Then all souls who were ever created and who ever lived will gather at a scene of the Great Reckoning, where God will judge each individual according to his or her deeds on earth. The good will be welcomed to paradise, an abode of pleasure and bliss, whereas the wicked will be thrown into hell, an abode of humiliation and torment. All these scenes of the afterlife are narrated in the Qur'an in detail—especially in the short chapters, which were early in the revelation but were placed toward the end of the text during the compilation of the Qur'an.

What will happen *before* the Hour, on the other hand, does not seem to be a great concern for Islam's scripture, which includes hardly anything about it. However, the Islamic tradition has developed a major extra-Qur'anic literature on this matter, mainly as a result of the hadiths, or sayings attributed to Muhammad. These were originally oral traditions, which were only canonized almost two centuries after the death of the Prophet. So they have never been considered as reliable as the Qur'an itself, and their "soundness" has always been a matter of controversy. Nonetheless, in both Sunni and Shiite Islam, a hadith-based literature developed that gives us a detailed scenario of the times before the Hour, or the "end of times."

Accordingly, decades before the coming of the Hour, the world will go through a major final confrontation between the forces of good and evil. In the earliest stage of this confrontation, humanity will be corrupted with sin, injustice will reign supreme, and Muslims will be divided, misguided, and oppressed. Then God will send a savior to Muslims, who will revive their faith, resolve their disputes, and empower them against their enemies. This savior will be called the *Mahdi*, or "the guided one." He will not be a prophet—someone who receives revelation from God—but he will still be the greatest figure in Islam since the last prophet—the Prophet Muhammad. He will actually be, one could say, Islam's own version of the Jewish Messiah.

Yet, according to the same narrative, the Mahdi will accomplish only a part of the mission of putting the world in order. For the greater task, he will need the help of a long-bygone prophet who will miraculously come back to earth to join forces with him. For an outsider to Islam, it would make sense to assume that this prophet must be none other than Islam's own—the Prophet Muhammad. Remarkably, however, he is none other than Jesus Christ.

QUR'ANIC ADVENT

Indeed, it may be news to Christians that, just like many among themselves, many Muslims are also anticipating a Second Coming of Jesus—*Nuzul Isa*, or "Descent of Jesus." It is a serious anticipation, though, and quite a powerful one. A 2012 poll conducted by the Washington-based Pew Research Center showed that roughly half of the populations in twenty-two Muslim-majority countries believe not only that Jesus will return, but also that his return is "imminent"—that it will happen in their lifetime. Those who shared this belief turned out to be 65 percent of the population in Turkey, 67 percent in Tunisia, 64 percent in Iraq, and 55 percent in Pakistan.[4]

Where exactly does this widespread belief come from? Most traditional Muslim sources would argue that it comes from both the Qur'an and the hadiths. It might be more accurate to say, however, that the Second Coming of Jesus is explicitly announced only in the hadith literature, whereas the Qur'an has only a few, and disputed, hints about it.

Let's first look at the Qur'an. There is certainly no passage that unambiguously states that Jesus will come back to earth at the end of times. Rather, Qur'anic exegetes have inferred that promise from a few ambiguous verses.

The first of these is the statement that denies that the Jews crucified and killed Jesus. After noting "they certainly did not kill him," the verse reads: "God raised him up to Himself."[5] Since the Qur'an never says "God raised him up to Himself" for anyone other than Jesus, many exegetes have thought that there is something unusual here. Moreover, in another Qur'anic verse, God speaks to Jesus and says: "Jesus, I will take you and raise you up to Me."[6] The expression "take you," or *mutawaffika*, has been interpreted in various ways, and while some suggested that it means "I will take you to your death," others opted for "I will gather you," or even "make you sleep."[7] As a result, an interpretation developed asserting that Jesus never died, went up to heaven alive, and continued living in a metaphysical realm—in fact, in the same realm with the angels.[8]

If this is really the case, and Jesus really never died, then what are we supposed to make of the statement that the Qur'an ascribes to him: "Peace be upon me the day I was born, and the day I die, and the day I am raised up again alive."[9] The exegetes found the solution in the Second Coming: Jesus will come back to earth again, to live the second part of his life and then to die a natural death at old age. A legend even grew up that after his Second Coming, Jesus would live for forty years, get married and have children, and ultimately be buried by Muslims next to Muhammad. Hence, to this day, in the very tomb of Islam's prophet in Medina, there is an empty space reserved for Jesus.

There are two other verses of the Qur'an that have been taken as evidence for the Second Coming of Jesus. The first one is in a passage that, after speaking of Jesus, plainly states: "He is a Sign of the Hour"—the Hour that will bring the end of the world.[10] This may, indeed, be taken as a hint that Jesus will appear again at the end of times. But it also may have a more modest meaning, such as that Jesus' miraculous birth is a sign of God's omnipotence, which will be even more visible at the Hour.

The other verse of the Qur'an related to this discussion is one that has puzzled exegetes for centuries. It comes right after the statement "God raised [Jesus] up to Himself," and makes a very perplexing claim: "There is not one of the People of the Book who will not believe in him before he dies."[11]

This is perplexing, because it is hard to understand what it exactly foretells. To begin with, it is unclear who is "he" in the clause "before he dies." Each and every individual Jew and Christian? Or Jesus himself?

Both options have been considered by Muslim exegetes—and rulers. In a chilling story, al-Hajjaj ibn Yusuf (d. 714), the heavy-handed governor of Iraq during the Umayyad Empire, opted for the former interpretation—that each and every individual in the People of the Book will believe in Jesus before *they* die. That would be all fine had he not also put this interpretation to a cruel test. As he told Shahr ibn Hawshab, an Islamic scholar who began to work under his auspices, he would "give orders for a Jew or Christian to be decapitated and watch him with my own eyes." He was hoping to see a testimony to faith in Jesus—faith as the way Islam describes. "But I do not see them move their lips," al-Hajjaj added with dismay, "before they are extinguished!" In return, Shahr ibn Hawshab told al-Hajjaj that he was executing these poor people for no reason: "O Emir," he cried, "it is not in accordance with how you have interpreted it!"[12] The "before he dies" clause is not about the death of individual Jews and Christians, the scholar explained, but about the death of Jesus.

This latter interpretation has been the more common one in Islamic tradition—that all Jews and Christians will believe in Jesus before *he* dies.[13] In this interpretation, the verse becomes a hint for the Second Coming of Jesus. It also hints at a prophecy concerning the end of times: When Jesus will come again, he will unite all monotheists under his banner, for all three Abrahamic faiths will recognize him as the Messiah.

Yet neither this verse nor others that are taken as evidence for Jesus' descent during the end of times are explicit. They all depend on how you interpret them. Therefore, it is not possible to say that the Qur'an is clear cut on this issue. No wonder some modernist interpreters of Islam, especially those who rely on the Qur'an but remain skeptical of the hadiths, have seen the Second Coming as a myth incorporated from Christianity.

PROPHECIES OF ARMAGEDDON

When we look at the hadith literature, we see no doubt that the Second Coming of Jesus is an article of faith. There are dozens of hadiths in core collections such as *Sahih Bukhari, Sahih Muslim*, and *Sunan Abu Dawood*—all named after their compilers—that tell us that the Prophet Muhammad, with God's gift, foresaw the end of times and narrated it to his contemporaries. "By the One whose hands my life is in," we hear from Muhammad, "surely the Son of Mary will descend amongst you as a just ruler."[14]

What will this "just ruler" do? Well, he is certainly not envisioned as the divine Savior of Christianity, but as a prophet who will confirm the truth of Islam—and in fact call on Christians to accept the truth by giving up their erroneous beliefs. An oft-repeated line in the hadith collections about Jesus reads: "He will break the cross, kill the swine, and abolish the *jizyah*," the latter being the poll tax levied on non-Muslims.[15] Muslim interpreters have often understood "breaking the cross" as disestablishing Christianity as a separate religion from Islam; and "killing the swine" as reestablishing the Mosaic Law with rules such as abstaining from pork. Meanwhile "abolishing the *jizyah*" was taken as a hint that either Christians will be given the grim choice, convert or die, or, more upliftingly, that the world will become so prosperous that there will be no need to collect taxes.

The hadiths, and commentaries written on them by scholars of the classical age of Islam, in fact present us with a colorful scenario of how events will proceed regarding the Second Coming of Jesus and its background. To give a brief summary, the scenario begins with the Mahdi, a progeny of the Prophet Mohammad, emerging at a time "when Muslims are killed everywhere." This great leader will reestablish the righteous Caliphate, unite all Muslims under his banner, and uplift the *umma*, the global community of Islam, from its malaise. However, soon the forces of evil will have their answer to the coming of the Mahdi: the rise of *al-Masih ad-Dajjal*, or "the Deceiving Messiah," which is Islam's version of the Antichrist. This will be an evil man who will enchant many people with his sorcery and will make them worship Satan. He will also gather a huge army that will crush the Muslims and encircle them in Jerusalem, which is envisioned in the hadiths as a Muslim city.

At this point, as the story goes on, God will send the only person on earth who can defeat the False Messiah—the True Messiah. Jesus, who is alive in heaven, will descend to earth, literally from the sky, first to Damascus and then to Jerusalem. In the latter city, he will meet the Mahdi, and will even modestly ask him to lead the prayer—recalling the New Testament story of Jesus being baptized by John the Baptist, although being superior to him. With the glorious coming of Jesus, the empowered Muslims will be able to defeat the army of the False Messiah, in the epic *al-Malahim ul-Uzma*, or "the Great Battle," which seems to be Islam's own version of the biblical Armageddon.

After all that turmoil, an era of peace, prosperity, and bliss will begin. The Mahdi will die at some point, but Jesus will continue to rule, as Jews, Christians, and Muslims will be united under his leadership. The entire earth will be filled with justice, "just as it were filled with injustice and oppression." Yet after the passing of Jesus, humanity will go down the path of corruption again—only until the Hour comes and finishes everybody and everything off.

This is a very condensed summary of the scenarios of Islamic eschatology, whereas the hadiths and their commentaries give us vivid details of almost every stage. Even the physical aspects of Jesus are related. "When you see him, recognize him," says a hadith, describing him as "a man of medium height, reddish fair, wearing two light yellow garments, looking as if drops were falling down from his head though it will not be wet."[16] It seems to describe a Jesus with an anointed head, fitting his title as the Messiah, or "the anointed."

In another hadith, we read not just about the physical appearance of Jesus but also how he will physically appear on earth:

At that moment God sends Jesus, the son of Mary, from heaven. He descends on the top of the white minaret at the east of Damascus, putting his hands on the wings of two angels. [He is so handsome that] when he bows his head, it is as if water drops, and when he lifts his head his hair shines like pearls. Any nonbeliever who receives his breath will die; his breath reaches as far as his sight. He pursues the Antichrist and finds him at the gate of Lod; then he kills him. Then certain people who were saved in the trial of the Antichrist come to Jesus. He touches their faces [to remove dust] and tells them about their place in paradise.[17]

While it may be already a bit hard for the modern mind to put faith in such a miraculous story, there is an additional reason to be suspicious about its accuracy: the mention of "the white minaret at the east of Damascus." When the Prophet Muhammad was alive, there certainly was no "white minaret" in Damascus, for it was a Christian city that Islam had not reached yet. In fact, there was no minaret anywhere, for Islamic architecture was still at a very simple stage. The very first known minaret was built in Basra, Iraq, around 655, or at least three decades after the passing of the Prophet.[18] So, the Prophet could not possibly have spoken about a "white minaret" in Damascus, at least to his contemporaries, who would not have known what he was taking about.

Such anachronisms in the hadith literature have led many experts to think that they were later legends put in circulation decades after the Prophet, according to the needs and fantasies of the early Muslim community. No wonder almost all the events in these narratives take place around Syria and Palestine—the very areas that these hadiths emerged from. We also know that many among the earliest generations of Muslims saw the end of times as imminent, so it is very possible that they read the Prophet's references to it, if there were any, by placing them into their own contexts. In particular, the Shiites, or "supporters of Ali," were most interested in awaiting the Mahdi, because they were persecuted by the Umayyad

Empire. Hence the belief in the Mahdi became a more powerful element in Shia Islam as compared to Sunnism.

That is why many modern scholars of Islam look at the eschatological literature with skepticism. They see it as introducing Jewish and Christian lore into Islam. They also rightly point out that the belief in awaited saviors has bred fatalism among Muslims and created fertile soil for charlatans. They are not wrong on that point, for the history of Islam, including the contemporary Muslim world, has no shortage of fake mahdis and messiahs.

Yet still, eschatology remains a powerful theme in Muslim culture, shared most profoundly by two bitterly opposed groups: Shiites, on the one hand, and Salafis, or ultraconservative Sunnis, on the other. In popular culture, including the Internet, there are endless speculations on whether the "end of times" has already begun and, if it has, how current world events fit into ancient prophesies.

As discomforting as it is, some of the groups that read current events in eschatological terms are those commonly called "extremist." When they read the hadiths telling that the world will be filled with "injustice" in the end of times, they see this as oppression by Zionism or Western imperialism, real or perceived. When they read in the same hadiths that a victorious "army of Mahdi" will arise against these forces, they think of current-day jihadists. In a sermon preserved and popularized on YouTube, Musa Cerantonio, an Australian convert to Islam and a preacher of militant jihad, explains how contemporary events fulfill ancient prophesies:

> The Prophet [Muhammad] said an army will march from Khorasan carrying black banners, and they will march unto Al-Quds [Jerusalem] defeating those in their way . . . They will give victory, they will give support and assistance—to who? To Imam Mahdi.
>
> Where is Khorasan today? In Iran, Afghanistan. We find that an army has appeared in the land of Khorasan, and what banner they carry? Do they carry the banner of nationalism or Arabism? No . . . All the mujahiddeen [jihadist] forces; be it Jabhat-an Nusra

in Syria! Be it Al-Qa'eda in Yemen! Be it ash-Shabab in Somalia! Be it at-Taliban in Afghanistan; they all carry the black banner of Tawheed! [Unity of God].[19]

The short list of the jihadist groups above does not include ISIS, the notorious Islamic State of Iraq and Syria, which was declared in 2013 and which became the world's most violent and repugnant terror group. Yet ISIS is just the latest in a series of militant groups that carry "black banners" and that see themselves as key actors in the end of times. In fact, reports about ISIS show that the group wanted to capture certain parts of Syria, in order to fulfill the "end of times" prophecies about them and to hasten the coming of the Mahdi and the descent of Jesus.[20] In July 2016, *Dabiq*, the monthly ISIS magazine, even came out with a cover story titled "Break the Cross," presenting a militant of the group who literally broke a cross, implying that the prophecies are being realized—by ISIS itself.

Of course, there is no doubt that ISIS, with all its barbaric violence, is too extremist for all other Muslims—in fact, even for other jihadists.[21] In that sense, its reference to Jesus must be taken as a perverted one—like the perverted reference the torturers of the Inquisition found in Jesus several centuries ago in the midst of Christendom. Yet still, it is one of the many signs showing how eschatology, including the Second Coming of Jesus, is a powerful theme in the contemporary Muslim world—a powerful theme that needs to be recognized and addressed.

ALLEGORICAL JESUS

So far, we have noted two opposite views among Muslims about the Second Coming of Jesus. The first is that it is a promise of the Qur'an and the Prophet Muhammad that will certainly take place at the end of times. Jesus, in this traditional view, will literally come down to earth from the sky and will change the world forever. The other, more modern, view is that it is a post-Qur'anic myth that should not be taken seriously.

Yet there is a third view as well: to accept the Second Coming of Jesus not literally but allegorically, not as a supernatural miracle, but as a natural transformation in the world—and within the world of Islam.

This allegorical interpretation goes back to Sa'd al-Din al-Taftazani (d. 1390), a Persian polymath and exegete of the Qur'an. In his commentary about the end of times, he suggested that the awaited Messiah and the Deceiving Messiah were perhaps not actual persons but symbols. While the Deceiving Messiah symbolized the dominance of evil and corruption, he argued, the coming of the Messiah meant the dominance of "the good and wholesomeness."[22]

This nonliteral approach to the matter would have a wider appeal in the nineteenth century, when some Muslim scholars, influenced by modern ideas, began to look at their tradition with a more critical mind. The most important name in this new trend was probably Muhammad Abduh (d. 1905), the Egyptian scholar who criticized the rigidity and dogmatism he saw in Islamic tradition and argued for a more flexible and rational interpretation of the core texts. Today he is either praised or condemned, depending on whom you ask, as the key pioneer of "Islamic modernism."

Abduh had plenty of reformist ideas, one of which was his interesting interpretation of Jesus' Second Coming. First, like al-Taftazani, he took this event not as a literal reference to a supernatural miracle but as an allegory of a transformation in the natural world we know. More importantly, he saw this transformation not as an Islamic victory over the infidels but as a reform within Islam itself. "The descent of Jesus and his ruling on earth," he wrote, "can be interpreted as the dominance of his spirit and his enigmatic message to people. This is what dominates Jesus' teachings of commanding mercy, love, and peace, which also emphasize the purposes of the law, rather than what is readily apparent and the shell of it but what does not penetrate into the kernel of the law."[23]

Here, Abduh was referring to a distinction made by some of his medieval predecessors between the literal injunctions of law and the "purposes" behind it, which was all about protecting human life and dignity. So, for Abduh, the details of the Shariah were the "shell," while its purposes made up the "kernel." And the Second Coming of Jesus could be a reference to none other than rediscovering the kernel.

Why? Because this was exactly what Jesus had done before, with regard to Judaism. Abduh went on to explain:

> Jesus, peace be upon him, did not bring to Jews a new law, but he brought for them something that would move them from being frozen on the literal meaning of the law of Moses, peace be upon him, and lead them to the understanding and the purpose of the law. He also commanded them to follow those purposes, and commanded them with something that attracts them to the realm of spirits through the search for perfect behavior.[24]

For those who still didn't get the point, Abduh also noted how Islam in the modern era needed the exact reform that Judaism needed at the time of Jesus:

> That is to say, when the people of the last divine law [Islam] became frozen on the literal meaning of the law, furthermore on the literal meanings of those who wrote their own opinions about the law, opinions that were killing the spirit of the law and removing its wisdom, it became necessary for them to undergo a Messiah-oriented renewal that would reveal to them the mysteries of the law, the spirit of the religion, and the true practice of it.[25]

Abduh's ideas opened a way. One of his prominent students, the relatively more conservative Rashid Rida (d. 1935), also argued: "the descent of Jesus means that people will return to the Qur'an and submit to the spirit of Islamic shari'a."[26] Another modernist Muslim thinker, Tantawi Jawhari (d. 1940), dismissed all the narratives about Armageddon and envisioned the Second Coming of Jesus as global "peace and cooperation of nations."[27]

Meanwhile, in Turkey, an Islamic scholar of Kurdish origin, Said Nursi (d. 1960), added a new dimension to the discussion. Like Rida, he suggested that Jesus might return not as a bodily person but as a "spiritual person," implying a new spiritual and intellectual trend in the world. Yet for him, this trend would not only amount to a renewal in Islam, but something even more ambitious—dialogue and cooperation between Muslims and Christians.[28]

Nursi's approach was partly a product of the world he lived in. In the late Ottoman Empire and early Turkish Republic, he had faced the spread of atheist philosophy, which he had countered by writing treatises defending faith in God with rational arguments. He also witnessed the rise of Soviet communism, which he saw as a bitter enemy of the faith—and, in fact, the very Antichrist prophesized in the Islamic tradition.[29]

In the face of this "terrifying current of irreligiosity," Nursi saw Islam and Christianity as allies. The return of Jesus, he further believed, was an allegory of this alliance and the rapprochement between the followers of these two faiths. For his part, he sent a collection of his works to Pope Pius XII in Rome, and in February 1951 received a personal letter of thanks. In 1953 he visited the Ecumenical Patriarch in Istanbul, Athenagoras, to pledge friendship and seek cooperation between Muslims and Christians in facing the challenges of the modern age.[30]

This was about a decade before the historic Second Vatican Council (1962–65) of the Catholic Church, at the end of which the council issued *Nostra Aetate*, or the Declaration on the Relation of the Church to Non-Christian Religions. "The Church regards with esteem also the Moslems," the groundbreaking document noted, continuing:

They adore the one God, living and subsisting in Himself; merciful and all-powerful, the Creator of heaven and earth, who has spoken to men; they take pains to submit wholeheartedly to even His inscrutable decrees, just as Abraham, with whom the faith of Islam takes pleasure in linking itself, submitted to God. Though they do not acknowledge Jesus as God, they revere Him as a prophet. They also honor Mary, His virgin Mother; at times they even call on her with devotion. In addition, they await the day of judgment when God will render their deserts to all those who have been raised up from the dead. Finally, they value the moral life and worship God especially through prayer, almsgiving and fasting.[31]

Regretting that for centuries "quarrels and hostilities have arisen between Christians and Moslems," the declaration called both sides "to work sincerely for mutual understanding" and to promote "social justice and moral welfare, as well as peace and freedom."

Nursi did not live long enough to see the publication of *Nostra Aetate*. Had he seen it, he probably would have been moved by it. Probably, he would also think that Jesus must be on his way.

CHAPTER NINE

WHAT JESUS CAN TEACH
MUSLIMS TODAY

*[Muslims] should not become like those to whom was given
Revelation aforetime, but long ages passed over them, and
their hearts grew hard.*

—The Qur'an 57:16[1]

"MARINES WITH CHARLIE COMPANY, 1ST BATTALION, 8TH
Marine Regiment, rest inside Fallujah Khulafah Rashid mosque
after driving insurgents from the building." That was the caption I
read under a photo that fell into my email inbox sometime in late
2004. It was a scene of almost two dozen American soldiers sitting
nonchalantly in the Iraqi mosque that they captured from their
Iraqi foes. It was published in the American press, as just one of the
many scenes from the war, and probably neither the publishers nor
most of their readers saw anything extraordinary in it.

Yet in the photo there *was* something extraordinary—something
shocking, actually. The soldiers were stepping on the carpets of
the mosque with their boots! This was, as it always is, a major affront to any Muslim place of worship—as stressed by my friend, a
devout Muslim, who emailed me the photo. "This is what they are
doing to our mosques with their filthy boots," his short note read.
"O believers, wake up!"

As you could guess, I was not the only fellow believer alarmed by this message. "The picture," as observed later by a journalist, "developed a life of its own." It moved from website to website, got published in paper after paper, and was shared over the Internet maybe a million times "to become part of a solid wall of hatred against America among Muslims."[2]

Yet there was something ironic in this cross-cultural drama. The marines of Charlie Company, who provoked this mass reaction in the Muslim world with a single photo, probably had no idea that they were doing anything offensive. As Americans who walk into their churches or even homes with their shoes on, they probably did not know what it means to enter a mosque with their boots on. Even if they had been told that it was inappropriate, they probably could not have comprehended how deep a sensitivity they were treading on.

In other words, the problem was not that these American soldiers intentionally insulted Muslims. It was that they were conquerors of a people whom they did not know and whose profound sense of the sacred they did not understand. Here was a "clash of civilizations," or, more accurately, the intrusion of a powerful civilization into a weaker one, where the former had ample might to defeat, but little empathy and insight to understand.

Notably, this was not the first time that our aged planet was witnessing such a dramatic encounter between two foreign civilizations. A quite similar one had taken place exactly two millennia ago, in a story at which we took a look in the first chapter of this book: the intrusion of the mighty Roman Empire into Judaea—into the world of the materially weak, yet religiously self-assured Jews.

To put it in more graphic terms, the incident of the marines of Charlie Company, the conquerors of Fallujah, was somewhat similar to the incident of the Roman commander Pompey, the conqueror of Jerusalem. As the Jewish historian Josephus noted, Pompey was in fact willing to show respect to the strange religion of the unfamiliar people he had militarily subdued. He just wanted to pay a visit to the Holy of Holies, to see their God with his own eyes. Yet the very fact that he defiled the holy ground with his filthy sandals would be enough of an affront to outrage pious Jews—and to unwittingly provoke new Jewish insurgencies.

THE TOYNBEE INSIGHT

No less than the late Arnold Toynbee (d. 1975), one of the intellectual giants of the past century, first pointed to the similarity between the modern encounter between the Muslim world and the West and the historic encounter between the Jews and the Roman Empire. In his 1948 book, *Civilization on Trial*, in an essay titled "Islam, the West, and the Future," the British historian drew parallels between the two cases, focusing especially on how Muslim responses to the West looked similar to the Jewish responses to Rome.

Toynbee began his argument by recalling the several waves of confrontation between Islam and the West—the early Muslim conquests, the Western Crusades, the Ottoman advances in Europe. In none of these old conflicts, Toynbee noted, were either Muslims or Westerners able to dominate each other, for neither was able to decisively disrupt the balance of power. In the modern era, however, the West grew incomparably more powerful and engaged in an effort to "Westernize the world." The Muslim world suffered its share of this ambitious expansion, which came in military, political, and cultural terms. "Islam is once more facing the West with her back to the wall," Toynbee observed,

> but this time the odds are more heavily against her than they were even at the most critical moment of the Crusades, for the modern West is superior to her not only in arms but also in the technique of economic life, on which military science ultimately depends, and above all in spiritual culture—the inward force which alone creates and sustains the outward manifestations of what is called civilization.[3]

Whenever civilizations face such dramatic challenges, Toynbee then explained, they develop two opposite responses. Just like the Jews who were challenged by Roman might and Hellenistic glamour, they divide into two parties: some become "Zealots," others become "Herodians." The first party clings strictly to its religious tradition, whereas the latter party decides to imitate the dominant aliens.

"The 'Zealot' is the man who takes refuge from the unknown in the familiar," Toynbee wrote, defining Zealotism as "archaism evoked by foreign pressure." He saw this trend in the "puritans" of his time, who were "the North African Sanusis and the Central Arabian Wahhabis."[4] Had he lived today, he would probably speak of Salafis and jihadists as well.

The other trend, Herodianism, was the opposite of Zealotism. "The 'Herodian' is the man who acts on the principle that the most effective way to guard against the danger of the unknown is to master its secret," Toynbee argued. "If 'Zealotism' is a form of archaism evoked by foreign pressure, 'Herodianism' is a form of cosmopolitanism evoked by the self-same external agency."[5]

Toynbee identified the iconic Herodians of the Muslim world as authoritarian Westernizers, such as Muhammad Ali of Egypt and Mustafa Kemal Ataturk of Turkey. A Westerner himself, he naturally sympathized with their efforts, but also acknowledged their shortcomings. He argued:

> The rare "Zealot" who escapes extermination becomes the fossil of a civilization which is extinct as a living force; the rather less infrequent "Herodian" who escapes submergence becomes a mimic of the living civilization to which he assimilates himself. Neither the one nor the other is in a position to make any creative contribution to this living civilization's further growth.[6]

Far worse, Herodians of the Muslim world have often oppressed the Zealots, Toynbee observed, "much more ruthlessly than the

Westerner would have the heart to do."[7] This, not surprisingly, only toughened up the Zealots. As a result, Herodians and Zealots too often "collided with each other and to some extent cancelled each other out."[8] A vicious cycle emerged, in other words, between Westernist-secularist Muslims and their nativist-Islamist rivals.

One thing Toynbee put his hope in was that the Zealots would always be weak, for they lacked the sophistication to use Western technology. "Steamships, railways, telegraphs, telephones, aeroplanes, motor-cars, newspapers, and the rest," he listed: "the use of these instruments is beyond the compass of the Islamic 'Zealot's' ability."[9] Had he lived today, and observed how the most ferocious Zealots such as al-Qaeda and ISIS excel in using modern weaponry and telecommunications, he would probably change his mind.

Toynbee also argued, again a bit too optimistically for his standpoint, that the West could have easily found a military solution if the Zealots went too far:

> As the Romans overthrew the Jewish "Zealots" in the first and second centuries of the Christian era, so some great power of the Western world of today—let us say, the United States—could overthrow the Wahhabis now any time it chose if the Wahhabis' "Zealotism" became a sufficient nuisance to make the trouble.[10]

Today, after the ambitious yet inconclusive "war on terror" that the United States carried out since September 11, 2001, we can conclude that things are not that simple. Zealotry among Muslims, in other words, cannot be wiped out by the West's military expeditions. In fact, if the latter has any impact, it is to fuel more zealotry, by deepening the sense of beleaguerment and of humiliation that sparked it in the first place. The more modern-day Pompeys come and tread on sacred Muslims ground, one could say, the more insurgents they provoke.

Yet still, Toynbee gave us an important insight by pointing out the Zealots-versus-Herodians dilemma in the Muslim world. It is an insight that deserves a bit more thought—and, for the purposes of this book, some theology as well.

BEYOND ZEALOTS AND HERODIANS

We know that the Jewish world during the time of Roman occupation was more diverse than represented by a mere dichotomy between the Zealots and the Herodians. There were in fact more parties among the Jews: the Sadducees, the Pharisees, and the Essenes. Yet still, a key issue dividing them was their approach to Rome. The Herodians, or the close circle of King Herod, were secularized and Hellenized Jews who saw their political interest in collaborating with Roman rule. The Sadducees were more religious, in fact a priestly class, but they were also collaborators with the Romans.

On the opposite side, the most important party was the Pharisees. Unlike the aristocratic Sadducees, they were more with the common people, whose respect they gained because of their strict adherence to the Halakha, the Jewish Law. Zealots, in fact, were an offshoot of the Pharisees, who agreed with the Pharisees on religious matters only to take a more actively militant stance against Rome. Among them, some even became *Sicarii*, or "daggermen," who were given this name because they assassinated Roman officials or their Jewish collaborators with daggers hidden under cloaks at public gatherings.

Then, as a third way, there were the much smaller sect of Essenes, who just turned their backs to this political turmoil and devoted themselves to an ascetic life of piety.

It is really remarkable that when we look at the contemporary Muslim world, we can see reflections of all of these ancient Jewish parties. If Herodians are represented by the Westernized secular ruling elite, as Toynbee argued, then the Sadducees are revived as conformist Islamic institutions and scholars who support and legitimize Herodian rule. On the opposition side, there are revived Pharisees, who are often called "conservatives" or "Islamists," and who stand out by their devotion to the Islamic version of religious law—the Shariah. The militant offshoots of these revived Pharisees are modern-day Zealots and *Sicarii*, who are typically known as jihadists and terrorists. Even the Essenes have their Muslim counterparts in the modern Sufi orders that focus on mysticism and godliness, refraining from any political action.

Of course, all these various Muslim parties believe that what they are doing is the right thing, but they often conflict with each other and, as Toynbee put it, "cancel each other out." Islamic civilization, therefore, keeps struggling with itself in an ever-deepening crisis. The modern West, arguably, is less crushing and more approachable than Rome, yet still the trauma of being dramatically outdone by an alien civilization, despite the very high opinion you have of your own, is a heavy one.

If the modern Muslim world is ever going to get itself out of this crisis, it will be the result of some new input—new ideas, new visions. Yet these new ideas should also resonate with the time-honored values of Islam. They cannot be merely secular ideas, for the very thing that defines Muslim civilization is its religion. Yet they cannot be the mere repetitions of old religious ideas, for all those old ideas developed at a time when Muslims were not yet in this modern-day crisis.

So how can Muslims develop religious ideas that may help them move on from their modern crisis? The typical answer is to go back to the Qur'an and the Sunna, the "example" of the Prophet Muhammad, and to reread them in the light of our times. This answer, of course, cannot be disputed for it refers to the very sources of Islam. But Muslims also need to see that there is something missing here: that we are living in a context very different from the context of the Qur'an and the Prophet Muhammad. These two sources—the divine message and the divinely ordained messenger—established a whole new religion called Islam and brought it to quick victory. We in the twenty-first century, however, are not supposed to establish a whole new religion. Quite the contrary, we are rather living within a religious tradition that has existed for more than fourteen centuries and which is carrying the burden of all that long history. And we are going through internal turmoil exacerbated by external pressure.

In other words, we Muslims are not living in the context of seventh-century Mecca and Medina. We are rather living in the context of first-century Nazareth and Jerusalem. Therefore, we need a "prophetic example" fit for the first-century drama. We need the method, and the message, of Jesus.

Isn't it none other than Jesus, after all, whose very "return" is promised in our tradition?

BACK TO ISRA'ILIYAT

The idea that a prophet other than Muhammad can offer any guide to Muslims is not as unorthodox as it may first sound. Quite the contrary, both the Islamic tradition and contemporary Muslim culture have plenty of references to the examples of other prophets. In particular, Moses has been referenced quite frequently in modern Muslim literature, especially with regard to his bravery against the pharaoh, with which secular dictators of the Middle East have often been equated.[11]

Reference to the example of Jesus, however, is relatively rare in Muslim culture. This might have something to do with the political biases of the contemporary Muslim world, such as anger at the "Christian West" for its foreign policy or the concern with the spread of Christianity through missionary work. These two real issues, Seyyed Hossein Nasr critically notes, bred among Muslims a misguided aversion "not only to Christianity . . . but even to the Islamic conception of Christ and Mary."[12] But this is a problem to be corrected, not a normality to be accepted.

Meanwhile, there is also a more innocent reason for the scarcity of the example of Jesus in Muslim culture: The Qur'an really does not tell us much about the context, the message, and the mission of Jesus. It certainly has some key insights that we have examined in previous chapters, but when compared to the more detailed story of Moses, the Qur'anic story of Jesus is quite concise.

Yet even more concise are the Qur'anic stories of Job (Ayub), who is narrated only briefly, or Elijah (Ilyas), Elisha (Alyasa), and Ezekiel (Zul-Kifl), who are mentioned merely in passing.[13] The earliest generations of Islamic scholars noticed this limitation, but they also found a solution that was hinted at by none other than the Qur'an itself: learning more from the pre-Qur'anic scriptures—the Torah, the Psalms, and the Gospel. For the Qur'an repeatedly confirms and praises these former books of God. Moreover, it commands the Prophet Muhammad, and by extension all Muslims, to "ask those who were reciting the Book before you."[14]

This Qur'anic insight led some early scholars of Islam to study Jewish and Christian texts, partly to explore the details of the prophetic stories that the Qur'an merely alludes to. Hence there developed a whole body of scholarship called *Isra'iliyyat*, which literally means "of the Israelites." Although the term explicitly refers to Jewish sources, Christian texts were also a strong source of this intellectual influence, which was transmitted partly through converts to Islam from Judaism and Christianity. Especially in the Umayyad and early Abbasid era, Isra'iliyyat added a lot to Muslim literature and culture, "flow[ing] into the Muslim lands like a river" as a Turkish scholar poetically notes, "triggering new crops to grow."[15]

One of the significant names in this tradition was Ahmad al-Ya'qubi (d. 897), a famed scholar of the early Abbasid era. He wrote *Ta'rikh ibn Wadih*, an ambitious work on world history, divided into two main volumes, the first devoted to pre-Islamic antiquity and the latter to the story of Islam. The section he devoted to Jesus was especially notable, not merely because of its length but also because of its in-depth borrowing from all the four canonical gospels, as well as from some early Christian exegetical traditions. Al-Ya'qubi, a pious Muslim, apparently saw no problem in learning the story of Jesus from Christian sources—only to add "an Islamic corrective at appropriate junctures."[16]

However, al-Ya'qubi belonged to one of the last generations that would show an interest in pre-Qur'anic scriptures. For as Islamic orthodoxy established itself, all other "foreign" sources of wisdom were marginalized. Isra'iliyyat increasingly turned into a deviation that needed to be rejected and cleansed, similar to the way that *falsafah*, or philosophy, was delegitimized.

Consequently, Islamic thought turned insular and self-referential. Inevitably, it stagnated. This stagnation was realized, and challenged significantly, only in the late nineteenth century, as critical Muslims recognized their underdevelopment in the face of the modern West and began to look for intellectual sources for reform. Reviving *falsafah*, or rational thought, was often seen as the way forward—and rightly so. Yet Isra'iliyyat could also open new horizons for Muslims, although this fact was only rarely noted—a gap this book, as one of its several aspirations, aims to point out.

Among the nineteenth-century reformers, there was actually one who took a notable step in that direction: the Egyptian scholar Muhammad Abduh, whose allegorical interpretation of Jesus' Second Coming I noted in the previous chapter. Abduh was in fact critical of Isra'iliyat in the sense that it incorporated noncanonical Jewish and Christian myths. Yet he was sympathetic to the Bible, arguing that the texts of the previous scriptures were not "corrupted," as the traditional view understood the Qur'an's statements on this issue. The Qur'an merely claims, Abduh argued, that Jews and Christians "corrupted" the *interpretation* of their scriptures, not their texts.[17] He even added that some Muslims "corrupt" the interpretation of their own scripture, the Qur'an, as well.[18]

Abduh died in 1905. One of the many young Egyptians he inspired was Abbas Mahmud al-Aqqad (d. 1964), who would become nationally famous as a journalist, a critic of Nazism and communism, and a biographer of fourteen important men—including his mentor Abduh, but more significantly Abraham, Muhammad, and Jesus. On Jesus, in 1953 he published *Abqariyat al-Masih*, or "The

Genius of the Messiah," which became a bestseller in Egypt among both Muslims and Christians. It was significant not only for its beautiful prose, but also as the first modern Muslim-authored story of Jesus that relied on not only the Qur'an but also the New Testament gospels.

One of al-Aqqad's insights was that Jesus had come into a traumatized Jewish world divided into sects, none of which, in his view, offered Jews the religious revival they needed. Jesus came with a "call," or *da'wah*, inviting his coreligionists to focus on the spirit of their tradition rather than on its dry legalism. "Jesus relocated ethics to a more humane center," al-Aqqad argued, "where the focus was a person's motives rather than meticulous compliance to the law."[19] Yet when most Jews did not accept this call, it moved on to the Gentile world to give rise to Christianity, for it was a universal message that could appeal to all humankind.

Al-Aqqad was certainly aware of the similarity of that ancient Jewish crisis to the Muslim crisis of his time. As a man with a "genuine commitment to Islam," he saw its better future in reform—reform toward reason, free will, and spirituality rather than legalism. And just like his mentor Abduh, who had envisioned "a Jesus-centered renewal of Islamic law and Muslims' behaviors," al-Aqqad as well saw Jesus as a source of inspiration for this reform.[20]

Sharing the same persuasion, I believe that the teachings of Jesus to his fellow Jews can today give us Muslims reformist guidance especially in two key matters. The first is the Kingdom of God, which Muslims would call the Caliphate. The second is religious law, which Muslims would call the Shariah.

THE CALIPHATE IS WITHIN YOU

As we have seen before, many Jews at the time of Jesus were eager to see the coming of *Malkuta de-Adonai*, or the Kingdom of God. This would have been a sovereign polity of Israel ruled by the divinely guided Messiah, who would defeat and expel the much-despised Empire of Rome. Native theocracy, in other words, would defeat foreign occupation.

The Pharisees were eagerly awaiting and praying for the Kingdom of God. Their radical offshoot, the Zealots, had taken the more active step of fighting for the same goal—by rebellions and assassinations, or, as we would call it today, insurgency and terrorism. Jesus, however, brought a new interpretation to the notion of the Kingdom of God. As we read in the Gospel of Luke:

> When he was demanded of the Pharisees, when the kingdom of God should come, he answered them and said, The kingdom of God cometh not with observation: Neither shall they say, Lo here! or, lo there! for, behold, the kingdom of God is within you.[21]

This famous passage in the New Testament has become the basis of one of the key themes of Christianity: the transformation of the political kingdom into a spiritual kingdom. The latter, as a Christian commentator put it, was a kingdom that would be "erected in the hearts of men, consisting in the subjection of their wills to the will of God, and in the conformity of their minds to his laws."[22]

Such a depoliticized kingdom probably looked too submissive to the Pharisees and especially to the Zealots. Yet Jesus did not declare, "We have no King but the Caesar," as some of his Jewish foes reportedly did.[23] In other words, the fact that he did not seek a confrontation with Rome did not mean that he submitted or defected to Rome. Moreover, future history proved his method right. The Zealots' militant quest for a political kingdom brought only more destruction to Jews, by provoking a brutal Roman backlash. In contrast, the peaceful quest for a spiritual kingdom, in the form of Christianity, not only survived but even won many hearts and minds within Rome itself.

Now, if we move on from the Judaea of the first century to the Muslim world of today, we will see that the latter also harbors a powerful anticipation for the Kingdom of God—it is called rather the Caliphate. This native theocracy, some Muslims believe, will defeat and expel the modern-day Romans and their collaborators, and bring glory to the *umma*.

Some Muslims are merely hoping to see the Caliphate established as a distant utopia, and they can be classified as "conservatives." Others are more engaged and actively work for the utopia through political action, which earns them the label "Islamists." Then there is a small minority that opts for armed struggle, which makes them "jihadists." And among these jihadists, only the most radical fringe, ISIS, declared a "Caliphate" in 2014, something that looks too militant for the overwhelming majority of Muslims.

But is a Caliphate really necessary for Muslims? For most Islamists and jihadists, the answer is absolutely yes. In fact, they see the reestablishment of the Caliphate not only as a hope to anticipate, but a duty to fulfill. "The establishment of a *Khaleefah* is an obligation upon all Muslims in the world," asserts a contemporary Islamist source. "Performing this duty, like any of the duties prescribed by Allah upon the Muslims, is an urgent obligation in which there can be no choice or complacency."[24]

However, other Muslims think that the Caliphate—a term implying the "successorship" to the Prophet Muhammad for the political leadership of Muslims—was merely a historical experience of the Muslim community, not an integral tenet of Islam. This argument was powerfully made in the early twentieth century by the Egyptian scholar Ali Abdel Raziq and the Turkish scholar Seyyid Bey, and has been advanced by reformist thinkers since then. Islamic energy, according to these reformists, should be focused not on establishing a specific form of state, but rather on advancing Islamic values under any state that grants Muslims security, dignity, and freedom. And Muslim societies should be governed by democratically elected leaders and parliaments.[25]

This reformist argument may be at odds with certain texts of the Islamic tradition, but it has a basis in Islam's most fundamental text—the Qur'an. Here, the term "caliph," which is often translated as "vicegerent," is used nine times in different verses, but not as the definition of a political entity among Muslims.[26] It is rather used, most significantly, to define the nature of human beings. In a memorable passage of the Qur'an, God himself decrees this onto-logical "caliphate" during a rhetorical conversation with angels:

> When your Lord said to the angels, "I am putting a *khalif* on the earth," they said, "Why put on it one who will cause corruption on it and shed blood when we glorify You with praise and pro-claim Your purity?" He said, "I know what you do not know."
>
> He taught Adam the names of all things. Then He arrayed them before the angels and said, "Tell me the names of these if you are telling the truth."
>
> They said, "Glory be to You! We have no knowledge except what You have taught us. You are the All-Knowing, the All-Wise."
>
> He said, "Adam, tell them their names." When he had told them their names, He said, "Did I not tell you that I know the Unseen of the heavens and the earth, and I know what you make known and what you hide?"[27]

In this fascinating story about the origin of man, Adam, the first human, appears as God's *khalif*, or vicegerent, because he is taught "the names of all things" and also bears the potential to "cause cor-ruption on [earth] and shed blood." Some Muslim thinkers have interpreted these as man's faculty to learn and reason, and his free-dom to chose between good and evil.

Yet Adam is not the only vicegerent—all his children, in other words, the whole human race—also are. "It is He who appointed you khalifs on the earth and raised some of you above others in rank," a Qur'anic verse reads, "so He could test you regarding what He has given you."[28] Another verse declares: "It is He who made you khalifs on the earth. So whoever is an unbeliever, his disbelief is against himself."[29] So, unbelievers are vicegerents as well, for they have the God-given faculties of reason and free will, which they just use in the wrong way.

In short, the Qur'anic concept of *khalifa* is a metaphysical notion that puts humankind in a special place within God's creation. No wonder the early Muslim exegetes saw no connection between this metaphysical notion and the political institution called the Caliphate, which was first led by the Prophet's close companions but was soon dominated by hereditary monarchy.[30]

Hence it is possible for Muslims today to abandon the commitment to the Caliphate as a political entity, but strive to be better caliphs on earth—as individuals with God-given faculties and responsibilities. It is possible for Muslims to think, in other words, that the Caliphate is not here or there, but within themselves.

THE SHARIAH IS MADE FOR MAN

The other passion of Jews at the time of Jesus was for the Jewish Law, or Halakha, which literally means "the path." Rooted in the detailed injunctions of the Torah, Halakha was an extensive set of rules that regulated every aspect of Jewish life from prayers to dietary laws to the penal code. The latter, from the perspective of our modern standards, included some pretty harsh measures, such as the stoning to death of adulterers or blasphemers.

As we can understand from the canonical gospels, Jesus brought a radically new interpretation to the Halakha. It is hard to think that this interpretation amounted to the near abandonment of the Law, at least for Jews themselves, as Paul and his Gentile followers later assumed. Yet it is safe to argue that Jesus called on his fellow Jews to realize and pursue the spirit of the Halakha rather than obsessing about its literal implementation.

Jesus initiated this emphasis, for he rightly realized the negative consequences of blind literalism. The first of these was the equation of piety with outwardly visible religious practice, which inevitably gave way to hypocrisy. This was especially true for the self-righteous clerical class, which included the priests, the scribes, and the Pharisees. "Beware of the teachers of the law," Jesus said:

> They like to walk around in flowing robes and love to be greeted with respect in the marketplaces and have the most important seats in the synagogues and the places of honor at banquets. They devour widows' houses and for a show make lengthy prayers. These men will be punished most severely.[31]

The very fact that the clerics looked down upon the sinners testified to their arrogance, which was a greater sin than most. Jesus explained this by comparing an observant Pharisee with a tax collector, whose job was then seen by most Jews as a treacherous collaboration with Rome:

> Two men went up to the temple to pray, one a Pharisee and the other a tax collector. The Pharisee stood by himself and prayed: "God, I thank you that I am not like other people—robbers, evildoers, adulterers—or even like this tax collector. I fast twice a week and give a tenth of all I get."
>
> But the tax collector stood at a distance. He would not even look up to heaven, but beat his breast and said, "God, have mercy on me, a sinner."
>
> I tell you that this man, rather than the other, went home justified before God. For all those who exalt themselves will be humbled, and those who humble themselves will be exalted.[32]

Soulless legalism not only nurtured hypocrisy and arrogance, as seen in the above parable, but also caused injustice or cruelty in the name of law. The adulteress the Pharisees brought to Jesus was a case in point. The Halakha demanded that she should be stoned to death, but Jesus called for mercy. "Let any one of you who is without sin," he famously called, "be the first to throw a stone at her."[33] It was another case of defending humble sinners from the wrath of the self-righteous puritans.

Similarly, when Jesus was questioned on why his disciples collected grain for food on the Sabbath, during which Jews are forbidden from doing any work, he gave quite a reflective answer: "The Sabbath was made for man, not man for the Sabbath."[34] The law, in other words, did not exist for its own sake. It existed for the sake of humans—and could be reinterpreted for them.

Now, if we again move on from the Judaea of the first century to the Muslim world of today, we will find a very similar situation regarding religious law. The Muslim version of the Jewish Halakha is the Shariah. It not only has the same literal meaning—"the path"— but also has very similar injunctions covering all aspects of life, from prayers to dietary laws to the penal code. And while Jews have long abandoned implementing their Halakhic penal code, some modern-day Muslims are passionate about implementing the Shariah's penal code, with chilling aspects such as stoning adulterers and executing heretics and blasphemers.

The Muslim devotion to the Shariah often comes from a sense of justice, but its literalist nature may rather cause horrendous injustice. Such are the cases, for example, of Muslim women, including very young girls, who are first raped by men and then stoned to death by other men for "adultery." The pattern, which took place repeatedly in Nigeria, Somalia, and Afganistan, is that first the victim gets raped in secret. Consequently she gets pregnant, only to be questioned soon by her kinfolk and ultimately by a court. At the court, she can't prove that she was raped, because the Shariah demands "four eyewitnesses" to penalize any sexual offense. Yet the pregnancy itself proves that she somehow committed "adultery," so she is publicly stoned to death.[35]

Such appalling cases of judicial murder would not have occurred if the Shariah-imposers cared about the *intention* of the verdicts that they only literally carried out. The Qur'an, which has nothing to say about stoning, does indeed decree the requirement of "four eyewitnesses." However, it says this only in the context of *protecting* women from the libel of adultery. "Those who make accusations against chaste women and then do not produce four witnesses," a verse commands, "flog them with eighty lashes and never again accept them as witnesses."[36]

So, "four witnesses" are necessary, because the Qur'an intends to protect innocent women from false accusations. In the literalist practice, however, this noble intention can be utilized to serve a cruel pattern of misogyny. Add to this the self-righteousness of Shariah-imposers that comes from their dry legalism, the arrogance they derive from this to look down upon the sinners, and you get a picture very similar to what Jesus condemned two thousand years ago:

> Woe to you, teachers of the law and Pharisees, you hypocrites! You give a tenth of your spices—mint, dill and cumin. But you have neglected the more important matters of the law—justice, mercy and faithfulness. You should have practiced the latter, without neglecting the former. You blind guides! You strain out a gnat but swallow a camel.[37]

The way forward for Muslims is to understand that just like the Halakha, the Shariah is made for men—and women, of course— and not the other way around.

Luckily, such an interpretive approach to law exists in the Islamic tradition, only waiting to be rediscovered. Its origin goes back to medieval scholars such as Imam al-Shatibi (d. 1388), the Andalusian legalist who focused on the *maqasid*, or intentions, of Islamic law, and formulated them as the protection of five fundamental values: religion, life, intellect, lineage, and property. Only the realization of these intentions, al-Shatibi reasoned, could infuse "spirit into the dead body, and real substance into the external shell (of the law)."[38] In the modern era, pioneering Muslim think-ers such as Fazlur Rahman Malik (d. 1988) tried to revitalize this nonliteralist approach to Islamic law with admirable intellectual effort for reform, yet only with limited impact.

For more impact, perhaps we can recall that Jesus, a great prophet of Islam, called for the exact same kind of reform in Juda-ism at a time when Jews were exactly like us. Jesus can, in other words, become a source of inspiration for the much-sought trans-formation in Islam.

Notably, Jesus' call for reform in Judaism had an impact within that tradition—only much later than at his time. This is evi-dent in the *Haskalah*, or "the Jewish Enlightenment," which was developed in Europe in the eighteenth and nineteenth centuries by Jewish intellectuals inspired by rationalism and liberalism. The father of the movement, Moses Mendelssohn (d. 1786), noted that while Jews cannot accept certain aspects of Christian theology, such as the divinity of Jesus, they can see Jesus' teachings as a model for reinterpreting Jewish Law.[39] Mendelssohn also passionately argued that a reformed Judaism, which would go back to its found-ing principles, would be "devoid of coercive power and entirely compatible with freedom of conscience." In return, Christian skep-tics insisted that Judaism, a system of "armed ecclesiastical law," could "never be purified or modernized to become compatible with freedom of conscience."[40] It sounds very much like the pessi-mistic judgements about Islam in the West today.

Haskalah gave rise to the birth of Reform Judaism in the nine-teenth century, which took morality and ethics as the core of the religion, while accepting flexibility in law and ritual. Its pioneers, such as Rabbi Abraham Geiger (d. 1874) and Rabbi Samuel Hirsch (d. 1889), "fashioned an image of Jesus that could serve as a model for the contemporary Reform Jew."[41]

Another believer inspired by Jesus to reform his own tradition was the Egyptian Khalid Muhammad Khalid (d. 1996). Trained at the al-Azhar University of Cairo, Sunni Islam's most prestigious center of learning, he spent his life as an independent Muslim writer, with seminal books including his 1958 volume, *Muhammad and Christ: Together on the Road.* Accordingly, the two great prophets were the two pillars of Islam, with Muhammad emphasizing justice and using the sword, and Jesus emphasizing mercy and upholding peace. And it was quite meaningful that Muhammad, who opened the way, foretold that it would be closed by Jesus with his Second Coming. This meant, in Khalid's beautiful words:

> He is the love which knows no hatred, he is the peace that knows no disquiet, and he is the salvation that does not perish. And when all this is realized on earth, then at the same time, the return of Christ is realized. This is the Christ who will return, and whose return the Messenger prophesied: peace, love, truth, the good and beauty. With the truthful Messenger, we declare: "Christ, not Barabbas, the true not the false, love not hatred, peace not war, life not destruction."[42]

"Christ, not Barabbas" . . . This, of course, is the exact opposite of what a crowd in Jerusalem reportedly said some two millennia ago. Yet a lot has changed in the world since then. The mighty Roman Empire, which crucified Jesus, is long gone. Jews, who at times were persecuted as the "killers" of Jesus, have discovered his place in their own tradition and established friendship with his followers. And those followers, who were just a handful of people at the time of the crucifixion, now are numbered in billions. They follow Jesus, and they worship him.

As Muslims, who are latecomers to this scene, we have disagreements with both Jews and Christians. But we have major agreements as well. With Jews, we agree a lot on God. With Christians, we agree that Jesus was born of a virgin, that he was the Messiah, and that he is the Word of God. Surely, we do not worship Jesus, like Christians do. Yet still, we can follow him. In fact, given our grim malaise and his shining wisdom, we need to follow him.

ACKNOWLEDGMENTS

First, I am thankful to all those who made this book come to life: my unfailing agent Jeff Gerecke, my brilliant executive editor Karen Wolny, and others at St. Martin's Press—Alan Bradshaw, Stephen Wagley, Laura Apperson, Kelly Too, Adriana Coada—who all worked meticulously to make the book better and better.

I am also grateful to various friends, who are all experts in their academic fields, and who kindly took the time to read my drafts and to offer extremely helpful critiques and suggestions. In particular, I am very grateful to Asma Afsaruddin, professor of Islamic studies at Indiana University; John D. Barton, associate professor of religion and director for the Center for Faith and Learning at Pepperdine University; Zafer Duygu, associate professor of religion at the Department of Syriac Language and Literature at Mardin Artuklu University; Gabriel Said Reynolds, professor of Islamic studies and theology at the University of Notre Dame; and Jerald Whitehouse, the former director of the Seventh-day Adventist Church's Global Center for Adventist-Muslim Relations.

Then there are many other friends who encouraged, helped, or facilitated my research. They include the all-gracious Bernard Brandstater and his wonderful wife, Beverly, from Redlands, California; Omid Safi, the director of the Islamic Studies Center at Duke University; Burcak Kozat, associate director of the Abbasi Program in Islamic Studies at Stanford University; and Bruce Clark, the senior religion and public policy editor for *The Economist*. Also thanks to the libraries at Duke University, Loma Linda University, Hamilton College, Stanford University, and the Istanbul Center for Islamic Studies (ISAM).

Then there are people closer to my heart. My wife, Riada Asimovic Akyol, who herself is a brilliant writer and scholar, helped me hugely throughout my work with her spiritual and intellectual support, in addition to her amazing research skills. The strength I derived from my loving parents, Tulin and Taha Akyol, along with my young brother, Ertugrul, who is on his own promising path to scholarship, was invaluable. There was also the inspiration I derived from a very young fine gentleman, Levent Taha Akyol, who is just sixteen months old while I am writing these words. I was not a father yet when I began working on this book; but with his coming, now I blissfully am. And I know a lot more about life, its meaning, and its purpose than I ever knew before.

Finally, all my highest thanks and praise is for God, whom I believe created all that there is, including you and me. As we say in the Islamic tradition, all the achievements in this work are His blessings, whereas all the flaws are my shortcomings.

—Istanbul

NOTES

Unless otherwise noted, all Bible quotations are from either the New International Version or the Berean Study Bible.

INTRODUCTION

1. Jeffrey J. Bütz, *The Brother of Jesus and the Lost Teachings of Christianity* (Rochester, VT: Inner Traditions, 2005), p. 188.
2. Epistle of James 4:13–17.
3. Qur'an 18:23–24, *The Noble Qur'an: A New Rendering of Its Meaning in English*, trans. Aisha Bewley (Norwich, UK: Bookwork, 1999), with Arabic word *Allah* anglicized as "God."
4. From the gospels of Matthew and Luke, we know that Mary married a man named Joseph (Mark 1:18–25 and Luke 2:1–17). That they had children after Jesus is not explicitly noted in the New Testament, but it has been often inferred from the mention of Jesus' siblings: "Is not this the carpenter, the son of Mary, the brother of James, and Joses, and of Juda, and Simon? and are not his sisters here with us?" (Mark 6:3). Also see Matthew 13:55–56.
5. James D. Tabor, *Paul and Jesus: How the Apostle Transformed Christianity* (New York: Simon and Schuster, 2012), p. 39.
6. James Tabor, *The Jesus Dynasty: The Hidden History of Jesus, His Royal Family, and the Birth of Christianity* (New York: Simon and Schuster, 2006), p. 261.
7. The "New Perspective on Paul" was developed most significantly by three eminent scholars: E. P. Sanders, James D. G. Dunn, and N. T. Wright. Their starting

point is that Second Temple Judaism—the Judaism of the time of Jesus—was not "legalistic" in the negative sense that Christians, especially Protestants, later assumed: having no sense of God's "grace." The argument was followed by the proposition that Paul departed from Judaism not in the sense of introducing "grace," which was already there, but by expanding it outside of the People of Israel. See: Kent L. Yinger, *The New Perspective on Paul: An Introduction* (Eugene, OR: Cascade Books, 2011). Also see: Craig C. Hill, "On the Source of Paul's Problem with Judaism," in *Redefining First-Century Jewish and Christian Identities: Essays in Honor of Ed Parish Sanders*, ed. Fabian E. Udoh (Notre Dame, IN: University of Notre Dame Press, 2008), pp. 311–318.

8. These troubling aspects in Islamic law do indeed exist—yet not in the Qur'an, but in the post-Quranic jurisprudential tradition, which partly reflects the cultural and political context of the formative centuries of Islam. For more, see my previous book: *Islam without Extremes: A Muslim Case for Liberty* (New York: W.W. Norton, 2011), pp. 100–106.

9. Qur'an 61:14.

10. Tabor, *The Jesus Dynasty*, p. 315.

11. Robert Eisenman, *James the Brother of Jesus: The Key to Unlocking the Secrets of Early Christianity and the Dead Sea Scrolls* (New York: Penguin Books, 1998), p. 3.

12. Ibid.

CHAPTER ONE

1. John Hick, "Jesus and the World Religions," in *The Myth of God Incarnate*, ed. John Hick (London: SCM Press, 1977), p. 171.

2. Virtually all scholars believe that Jesus was crucified in the spring of either AD 30 or AD 33, with the majority opting for the former. In their 2014 book, *The Final Days of Jesus: The Most Important Week of the Most Important Person Who Ever Lived* (Wheaton, IL: Crossway, 2014), Andreas Köstenberger and Justin Taylor argue that the date of crucifixion must certainly be Friday, April 3, AD 33. They note, however, that "It is not an essential salvation truth." It is not essential for this book either.

3. John 19:17–22.

4. John 14:6.

5. *Judaea* is derived from a Hebrew term used to designate the southern, mountainous part of the Land of Israel, right around Jerusalem. Under their rule, the Romans created a larger province of Judaea that included the adjacent regions of Samaria and Idumea as well. The Roman term for Judaea was *Iudaea*, from which the word *Jew* originates.

6. Flavius Josephus, *Antiquities of the Jews, Book XIV, Chapter IV*, in *The Works of Flavius Josephus: The Learned and Authentic Jewish Historian and Celebrated*

Warrior, trans. William Whiston (Cincinnati: E. Morgan, 1841). Fully available on www.ultimatebiblereferencelibrary.com.

7. Flavius Josephus, *Antiquities of the Jews, Book XVIII, Chapter I* in *The Works of Flavius Josephus,* trans. William Whiston (London: Grigg & Elliot, 1841). Fully available on www.ultimatebiblereferencelibrary.com.

8. On the divisions among the Pharisees, see: John Bowker, *Jesus and the Pharisees* (New York: Cambridge University Press, 1973), pp. 29–39. Their image as dry legalists devoid of "grace" has also been powerfully challenged, first by E. P. Sanders in his groundbreaking book, *Paul and Palestinian Judaism* (Minneapolis: Fortress Press, 1977), and later by other scholars who came to espouse a "new perspective" on Paul, which itself was based on a new perspective on Second Temple Judaism. For a Muslim point of view on the Pharisees, emphasizing that they got some "unfairly bad press," see Ruqaiyyah Waris Maqsood, *The Separated Ones: Jesus, the Pharisees and Islam* (London: SCM Press, 1991). As for Sadducees, it has been argued that their image as elites might refer not to their economic class, but to their intellectualism. See: Martin Goodman, "The Place of the Sadducees in First-Century Judaism," in *Redefining First-Century Jewish and Christian Identities: Essays in Honor of Ed Parish Sanders,* ed. Fabian E. Udoh (Notre Dame, IN: University of Notre Dame Press, 2008), pp. 146–148. Also see: Jacob Neusner and Bruce D. Chilton, eds., *In Quest of the Historical Pharisees* (Waco, TX: Baylor University Press, 2007). The editor and one of the authors of the volume, Jacob Neusner, also brings a balanced and informed critique to Sanders, objecting to "his rich capacity to make up distinctions and definitions as he goes along, then to impose these distinctions and definitions on sources that, on the face of it, scarcely sustain them" (p. 395). The book's conclusion is that we actually have "a remarkably small core of hard historical evidence" about the Pharisees (p. 423), and it is hard to make a conclusive description of all their teachings and their overall stance on Jesus.

9. Acts 15:5.

10. Kaufmann Kohler, M. Seligsohn, s.v. "Judas the Galilean," *The Jewish Encyclopedia* (New York: Funk and Wagnalls Company, 1906), vol. 7, pp. 370–371.

11. The Qur'an has no hint of Jesus being a militant figure. Hence one of the prominent exegetes of the Qur'an, the twelfth-century scholar Shaykh Tabarsi, explicitly objected to the view that Jesus called on the disciples to wage armed struggle, arguing that Jesus was rather "sent with the mission to admonish and not to fight." See Mahmoud M. Ayoub, *The House of 'Imran,* vol. 2 of *The Qur'an and Its Interpreters* (Albany: State University of New York Press, 1984), p. 161.

12. James D. G. Dunn offers an important corrective to the excess of the "historical Jesus" research tradition, which he blames as being too biased against faith as a real factor in understanding Christian origins. The quotations are from Dunn, *A New Perspective on Jesus: What the Quest for the Historical Jesus Missed* (Grand Rapids, MI: Baker Academic, 2005), pp. 22–23.

13. Kyu Sam Han, *Jerusalem and the Early Jesus Movement: The Q Community's Attitude toward the Temple* (London: A & C Black, 2002), p. 96.

14. David deSilva and Emerson B. Powery, *Invitation to the New Testament* (Nashville, TN: Abingdon Press, 2005), p. 60.

15. Joseph L. Trafton, "What Would David Do? Messianic Expectation and Surprise in Psalm of Solomon 17," in *The Psalms of Solomon: Language, History, Theology,* ed. Eberhard Bons and Patrick Pouchelle (Atlanta, GA: SBL Press, 2015), p. 156.

16. For examples of these arguments, see: Hyam Maccoby, *Jesus the Pharisee* (London: SCM Press 2003); Harvey Falk, *Jesus the Pharisee: A New Look at the Jewishness of Jesus* (Eugene, OR: Wipf and Stock Publishers, 2003); Edmond Bordeaux Szekely, *The Essene Jesus: A Reevaluation from the Dead Sea Scrolls* (Cartago, Costa Rica: International Biogenic Society, 1977); Robert Feather, *The Secret Initiation of Jesus at Qumran: The Essene Mysteries of John the Baptist* (Rochester, VT: Bear & Company, 2005).

17. A. N. Wilson, *Jesus* (London: Sinclair-Stevenson, 1992), pp. 127–128.

18. John 1:43–47.

19. As noted by Roman Catholic scholar Raymond E. Brown, "the two narratives [in Matthew and Luke] are not only different—they are contrary to each other in a number of details." The examples he points out are: 1) In Luke, Mary lives in Nazareth and the census of Augustus is used to explain how the child was born in Bethlehem; but in Matthew, Mary is already placed in Bethlehem and "there is no *hint* of a coming to Bethlehem." 2) In Luke, we read that the family returned peaceably to Nazareth after the birth at Bethlehem; but in Matthew, Jesus was almost two years old when the family fled from Bethlehem to Egypt. See: E. Brow, *The Birth of the Messiah: A Commentary on the Infancy Narratives in the Gospels of Matthew and Luke,* The Anchor Yale Bible Reference Library (New Haven, CT: Yale University Press, 1999), p. 46.

20. Luke 2:1, 3.

21. Luke 2:4. The Reza Aslan quote is from *Zealot: The Life and Times of Jesus of Nazareth* (New York: Random House, 2013), chapter 3.

22. For a detailed evaluation of why Luke's census could not really have taken place as he narrates, that it "goes against all that we know of Roman economic history" and in fact is "all outside the plane of reality," see N. F. Gier, *God, Reason, and the Evangelicals* (Lanham, MD: University Press of America, 1987), pp. 145–149. The comment "preposterous," on the other hand, is from Aslan, *Zealot,* chapter 3.

23. Among early church fathers, Jerome put this argument most forcefully in his *Against Helvidius, on the Perpetual Virginity of the Virgin Mary,* dating from AD 383. According to Jerome, "Joseph was only putatively, not really, the husband of Mary," and "the 'brethren' of the Lord were his cousins, not his own brethren." Trans. W. H. Fremantle, G. Lewis, and W. G. Martley, in *Nicene*

and Post-Nicene Fathers, 2nd ser., vol. 6, ed. Philip Schaff and Henry Wace (Buffalo, NY: Christian Literature Publishing Co., 1893); revised and edited for New Advent by Kevin Knight, http://www.newadvent.org/fathers/3007 .htm.

24. Matthew 4:17.
25. Mark 10:52.
26. Matthew 9:22.
27. Matthew 16:14.
28. Wilson, *Jesus,* p. 106.
29. Matthew 5:17.
30. John P. Meier, *A Marginal Jew: Rethinking the Historical Jesus,* vol. 4 (New Haven, CT: Yale University Press, 2009), p. 648.
31. Kenneth L. Carroll, "The Place of James in the Early Church," *John Rylands University Library Bulletin* 44, no. 1 (1961): 58.
32. Luke 11:42–46.
33. Joseph Jacobs, Kaufmann Kohler, Richard Gottheil, and Samuel Krauss, s.v. "Jesus of Nazareth," *The Jewish Encyclopedia* (New York: Funk and Wagnalls Company, 1906), vol 7, p. 163.
34. In the words of the *Jewish Encyclopedia:* "This was by no means a novelty in Jewish religious development: the Prophets and Rabbis had continuously and consistently insisted upon the inner motive with which pious deeds should be performed, as the well-known passages in Isa. i. and Micah vi. sufficiently indicate." (Ibid.).
35. See the Parable of the Good Samaritan in Luke 10:25–37.
36. F. E. Peters, *Jesus and Muhammed: Parallel Tracks, Parallel Lives* (Oxford: Oxford University Press, 2011), pp. 101–102.
37. Ibid.
38. Mark 8:27–31.
39. John 19:15.
40. Geza Vermes, *The Real Jesus: Then and Now* (Minneapolis, MN: Fortress Press, 2010), chapter 8.
41. "The Messianic Idea in Judaism," *Judaism 101,* http://www.jewfaq.org /mashiach.htm.
42. Luke 19:38. In Mark, the same passage reads: "Hosanna! Blessed is he who comes in the name of the Lord!" (Mark 11:10).
43. Mark 11:10.
44. Mark 14:53–72.
45. Leviticus 24:16.
46. Acts 7:59.
47. As Reza Aslan puts it: "[Jesus] has been in Jerusalem only a few days but already he has caused a riot at the Court of Gentiles, violently disrupting the Temple's financial transactions. He has replaced the costly blood and flesh

sacrifice mandated by the Temple with his free healings and exorcisms. For three years he has raged against the Temple priesthood, threatening their primacy and power. He has condemned the scribes and the elders as 'a brood of vipers' and promised that the Kingdom of God would sweep away the entire priestly class. His very ministry is founded upon the destruction of the present order and the removal from power of every single person who now stands in judgment of him." Excerpt from Aslan, *Zealot,* chapter 12.

48. The quote comes from *Kitab al-'Unwan,* written by Agapius of Manbij in northern Syria in the tenth century and discovered by Western scholarship thanks to the work of Shlomo Pines. See Pines, *An Arabic Version of the Testimonium Flavianum and Its Implications* (Jerusalem: Israel Academy of Sciences and Humanities, 1971), p. 16.

CHAPTER TWO

1. Edwin K. Broadhead, *Jewish Ways of Following Jesus: Redrawing the Religious Map of Antiquity* (Tübingen, Germany: Mohr Siebeck, 2010), p. 172.
2. John 21:1–3.
3. In fact, we do have evidence from the New Testament itself that the early Jesus movement used the term "synagogue." The people at Capernaum commend to Jesus a centurion who "loves our nation and has built our synagogue" (Luke 7:5). At the Jerusalem council, James notes, "Moses has been preached in every city from the earliest times and is read in the synagogues on every Sabbath" (Acts 15:21). More importantly, in his letter addressing fellow Jewish Christians, James refers to their gathering places as "synagogues" (James 2:2).
4. James Tabor makes this suggestion in *Paul and Jesus: How the Apostle Transformed Christianity* (New York: Simon and Schuster, 2012), p. 8.
5. For the prominence of James in the early church, see: Burnett Hillman Streeter, *The Primitive Church* (London: Macmillan, 1929), p. 42–47.
6. As we understand from Acts 15, it was up to James to decide what part of the Mosaic Law the Gentile Christians were obliged to follow or not.
7. R. Newton Flew, *Jesus and His Church: A Study of the Idea of the Ecclesia in the New Testament* (London: Epworth Press, 1938), p. 184.
8. Eusebius, *Historia Ecclesiastica,* 2. 23, in *Ante-Nicene Fathers: The Twelve Patriarchs, Excerpts and Epistles, the Clementia, Apocrypha, Decretals, Memoirs of Edessa and Syriac Documents, Remains of the First Ages,* ed. Philip Schaff, online at Christian Classics Etheral Library, http://www.ccel.org.
9. John Painter, *Just James: The Brother of Jesus in History and Tradition,* Studies on Personalities of the New Testament Series (Columbia, SC: University of South Carolina Press, 2004), p. 125. For Roman baths and promiscuity, see: Flavio Conti, *A Profile of Ancient Rome* (Los Angeles: Getty Publications, 2003), p. 195. In fact, Roman baths were not rejected by most Jews. Yet, "some

Jews may have had reservations about the nudity and licentious atmosphere that pervaded the mixed baths . . . just as others . . . including the Church Fathers." (Catherine Hezser, *Jewish Daily Life in Roman Palestine* [London: Oxford University Press, 2010], p. 617.)

10. Wesley Hiram Wachob, *The Voice of Jesus in the Social Rhetoric of James* (Cambridge, UK: Cambridge University Press, 2000), p. 27.

11. "Seen from a historical perspective, the author is almost certainly not the brother of Jesus, the work likely responds to Pauline ideas, and the book is probably known by the writer of Jude. The most plausible location, then, is somewhere in the late first or early second centuries in an area influenced by a hellenized Judaism. [Yet] This literary history should not be confused with its more primitive tradition history. The connection to the teaching of Jesus, the articulation of Jewish ethical instruction, and the eschatological urgency all suggest the book reflects a tradition of Jewish Christian thought and practice." Broadhead, *Jewish Ways of Following Jesus*, p. 134.

12. The comment is from "The Bible-Teaching Ministry of Charles R. Swindoll," https://www.insight.org/resources/bible/the-general-epistles/james. Accessed on July 4, 2016.

13. William R. Baker, "Christology in the Epistle of James," *Evangelical Quarterly* 74, no. 1 (January–March 2002): 51.

14. James 2:1–4.

15. Kenneth L. Carroll, "The Place of James in the Early Church," *John Rylands University Library Bulletin* 44, no. 1 (1961): 52–53.

16. A. N. Wilson, *Jesus* (London: Sinclair-Stevenson, 1992), p. 38.

17. See Karen Armstrong, *The First Christian: St. Paul's Impact on Christianity* (London: Pan, 1983).

18. Acts 1:21–23.

19. Galatians 1:11–12.

20. On the "Arabia" at the time of Paul, see: Arthur Segal, "Roman Cities in the Province of Arabia," *Journal of the Society of Architectural Historians* 40, no. 2 (May 1981): 108–121.

21. Galatians 1:17.

22. Galatians 1:19–20.

23. Acts 15:1.

24. Acts 15:29.

25. Acts 21:21.

26. This persecution narrative has recently been challenged. See: Brent D. Shaw, "The Myth of the Neronian Persecution," *Journal of Roman Studies* 105 (2015): 73–100.

27. Ferdinand Christian Baur, *Paul the Apostle of Jesus Christ: His Life and Works, His Epistles and Teachings* (Ada, MI: Baker Academic, 2010). This two-volume work was originally published in German in 1845. For the tension

between Paul and James, see especially chapter 5. Baur's views have been widely criticized in the twentieth century, but his designation of Jewish Christianity as a separate type of early Christianity has endured. For a recent argument that defends Baur's thesis, see: Abel Mordechai Bibliowicz, *Jews and Gentiles in the Early Jesus Movement: An Unintended Journey* (New York: Palgrave Macmillan, 2013). Bibliowicz argues: "Paul and later Pauline-Lukan believer authors were not fending off 'Judaizers,' they were de-Judaizing the Jesus tradition" (p. 203). Also see: Annette Yoshiko Reed, "'Jewish Christianity' after the 'Parting of the Ways,'" in *The Ways That Never Parted: Jews and Christians in Late Antiquity and the Early Middle Ages*, ed. Adam H. Becker and Annette Yoshiko Reed (Minneapolis, MN: Fortress Press, 2007), pp. 361–372.

28. Galatians 2:11–13.

29. 2 Corinthians 11:22.

30. See Tabor, *Paul and Jesus*, "The Battle of the Apostles," pp. 203–226.

31. Philippians 3:2–3.

32. Samuel Zinner offers a similar yet somewhat slightly different explanation—that the difference over christology grew after the dispute on law and only gradually. In his words, "At first, the sole area of contention between the two Christian variants, Jacobean and Pauline, was the question of Torah observance, not the question of Christological dogma, since at the beginning of Christianity the Jerusalem church's Christology was the only available model. But regarding the later Christological crises, the Gentile Christians' demand that Jewish Christians adopt Greek philosophical concepts and terminology to express the nature of Christ and the trinity proved disastrous from the point of view of ecclesiastical history." Zinner, *The Abrahamic Archetype: Conceptual and Historical Relationships between Judaism, Christianity, and Islam* (Bartlow, UK: Archetype Books, 2011), p. 5.

33. Robert B. Sloan, "The Christology of James," *Criswell Theological Review* 1, no. 1 (1986): 29. While Sloan, an Evangelical Christian, admits this gap between the "theocentric" James and the "christocentric" Paul, he also argues it is only "apparent."

34. Neil Richardson notes that Paul's thought and writings are in fact "both theocentric and Christocentric," but he also observes a "shift" in Paul's writing over time, with "a trend towards a more Christocentric perspective" (Richardson, *Paul's Language about God* [Sheffield, UK: Bloomsbury Publishing, 1994], p. 321). James Dunn also characterizes "Paul's Gospel" as "Christocentric." (Dunn, "In Quest of Paul's Theology: Retrospect and Prospect," in *Pauline Theology, Volume IV: Looking Back, Pressing On*, ed. E. Elizabeth Johnson and David M. Hay [Atlanta, GA: Scholars, 1997], p. 111.)

35. Epistle of James 2:20–24.

36. Epistle of James 2:26.

37. Wilson, *Jesus*, p. 37.

38. The phrase is from Mark 13:27.
39. Acts 24:4.
40. See Richard Bauckham, "James and the Jerusalem Community," in *Jewish Believers in Jesus*, ed. Oskar Skarsaune and Reidar Hvalvik (Peabody, MA: Hendrickson, 2007), pp. 58–59.
41. Flavius Josephus, *Antiquities of the Jews*, 20.9.1, in *The Works of Flavius Josephus: The Learned and Authentic Jewish Historian and Celebrated Warrior*, trans. William Whiston (Cincinnati: E. Morgan, 1841).
42. Hegesippus, "Fragments from His Five Books of Commentaries on the Acts of the Church," in *Historical Jesus Theories*, ed. Peter Kirby (Early Christian Writings, 2016), http://www.earlychristianwritings.com/text/1clement-hoole.html.
43. See Bruce Chilton and Jacob Neusner, *The Brother of Jesus: James the Just and His Mission* (Louisville, KY: Westminster John Knox Press, 2001), pp. 49–50. They, too, note that "James and the Jerusalem church supported a mission to other Jews based on the continuing validity of the law including circumcision. The execution of James by Ananus does nothing to undermine this understanding."
44. P. H. R. van Houwelingen, "Fleeing Forward: The Departure of Christians from Jerusalem to Pella," *Westminster Theological Journal* 65, no. 2 (2003): 181–200.
45. See: Patricia Crone, "Jewish Christianity and the Qur'ān (Part One)," *Journal of Near Eastern Studies* 74, no. 2 (October 2015): 226.
46. For example, the role of Pilate in the crucifixion of Jesus is increasingly marginalized from Mark to John, and the real blame is put on the Jews. See Reza Aslan, *Zealot: The Life and Times of Jesus of Nazareth* (New York: Random House, 2013), chapter 12.
47. Acts 14:11–12.
48. *Jewish Encyclopedia*, s.v. "Son of God."
49. N. T. Right and Marcus J. Borg, *The Meaning of Jesus: Two Visions* (New York: HarperCollins, 2007), p. 162.
50. Psalms 89:26–27.
51. Geza Vermes, *The Real Jesus: Then and Now* (Minneapolis, MN: Fortress Press, 2010), chapter 8.
52. *Jewish Encyclopedia*, s.v. "Son of Man."
53. An Evangelical author who is pleased that Paul indeed saw Jesus as divine through these definitions also notes, "Paul's views on Jesus were without precedent in the Judaism of his time." Ryan Turner, "Did Paul Think Jesus Was God?," https://carm.org/paul-think-jesus-was-god. Accessed on July 4, 2016.
54. This comment is from Douglas R. A. Hare, *The Son of Man Tradition* (Minneapolis, MN: Fortress Press, 1990), p. 1.
55. Richard N. Longenecker, *The Christology of Early Jewish Christianity* (Naperville, IL: Alec R. Allenson, 1970), p. 151.

56. For a detailed analysis, see James D. G. Dunn, *Christology in the Making: A New Testament Inquiry into the Origins of the Doctrine of the Incarnation* (London: SCM Press, 1980), pp. 46–61.

57. As for the dates of the gospel's composition, I refer to the dates suggested by Geza Vermes: Mark, AD 70; Matthew and Luke, AD 80–100; John, AD 100–110.

58. Matthew 16:17.

59. Mark 15:34 and Luke 23:46. For a comparison of the crucifixion passages in Mark and Luke, see: Bart D. Ehrman, *Misquoting Jesus: The Story Behind Who Changed the Bible and Why* (San Francisco: HarperSanFrancisco, 2005), pp. 142–143. It is also very interesting that in Matthew, we hear from Jesus the same call as the one in Mark: "Eli, Eli, lema sabachthani?" But then we read: "When some of those standing there heard this, they said, 'He is calling Elijah.'" It is as if Matthew is trying to offer an alternative sense of why Jesus cried to "My God" (Matthew 27:47–48).

60. Luke 23:47 and Matthew 27:54.

61. "Jesus and the Hidden Contradictions of the Gospels," NPR interview with Bart D. Ehrman, March 12, 2010, http://www.npr.org/templates/story/story .php?storyId=124572693, accessed on February 1, 2016.

62. Bart D. Ehrman, *How Jesus Became God: The Exaltation of a Jewish Preacher from Galilee* (New York: HarperOne Reprint, 2015), p. 345.

63. This comment is from Larry Hurtado, whose works have been an important defense of the view that the divinity of Christ was an early realization within Christianity. (Hurtado, *How on Earth Did Jesus Become a God: Historical Questions about Earliest Devotion to Jesus* [Cambridge, UK: Wm. B. Eerdmans, 2005], p. 205.) Also see the much more detailed work by Hurtado: *Lord Jesus Christ: Devotion to Jesus in Earliest Christianity* (Cambridge, UK: Wm. B. Eerdmans, 2003).

64. Richard Bauckham, *God Crucified: Monotheism and Christology in the New Testament* (Grand Rapids, MI: Wm. B. Eerdmans, 1999), p. viii.

65. The famous hadith "my community will never agree on error" reflects a trust in the historical evolution of the Muslim community, disregarding the cultural, political, and economic contexts that may have played a definitive role in the formation of Sunni orthodoxy. It is thus not an accident that reformist trends in modern-day Islam often begin questioning those mundane historical dynamics in the making of the Sunni orthodoxy. In contrast, in Shiite Islam, the providential wisdom is sought within the "imam." These conflicting doctrines are in fact very reflective of the fact that Sunni Muslims have almost always constituted the majority in the *umma*, whereas Shiites have constituted the minority. (Also see: Norman O. Brown, Jerome Neu, and Jay Cantor, *The Challenge of Islam: The Prophetic Tradition* [Berkeley, CA: North Atlantic Books, 2009], p. 74).

66. Romans 11:26.

67. Justin Martyr, *Dialogue with Trypho,* Chapter XLVIII, fully available at: http://www.earlychristianwritings.com/text/justinmartyr-dialoguetrypho .html. Accessed on July 4, 2016.

68. Irenaeus, *Against Heresies* 1.26, available at: http://www.newadvent.org/fathers /0103.htm. Accessed on July 4, 2016.

69. Matthew 5:3. For the term "the poor" being an "honorific self-designation deriving from the Bible," see James Carleton Paget, *Jews, Christians, and Jewish Christians in Antiquity* (Tübingen, Germany: Mohr Siebeck, 2010), pp. 344–348.

70. Eusebius Pamphilius, "The Heresy of the Ebionites," in *Church History, Life of Constantine, Oration in Praise of Constantine* 27, trans. Philip Schaff, available online at: Christian Classics Ethereal Library, http://www.ccel.org, accessed on July 4, 2016.

71. Ibid.

72. Ibid.

73. Epiphanius, *Panarion* 29.9.1 and 29.9.2, quoted in Edwin K. Broadhead, *Jewish Ways of Following Jesus: Redrawing the Religious Map of Antiquity* (Tübingen, Germany: Mohr Siebeck, 2010), p. 176.

74. All the summaries of Jerome's views and quotes from his work are from Broadhead, *Jewish Ways of Following Jesus,* pp. 164–174.

75. Ibid., p. 172.

76. Ibid.

77. James R. Edwards, *The Hebrew Gospel and the Development of the Synoptic Tradition* (Grand Rapids, MI: Wm. B. Eerdmans, 2009), p. 38.

78. John Chapman, "Didache," *The Catholic Encyclopedia* (New York: Robert Appleton, 1908).

79. Stephan Finlan, "Identity in the Didache Community," in *The Didache: A Missing Piece of the Puzzle in Early Christianity,* ed. Jonathan A. Draper and Clayton N. Jefford (Atlanta, GA: SBL Press, 2015), pp. 29–31. The author notes that the Jesus of the Didache is "life-giver, teacher, and revealer, but not . . . sacrificial victim" (p. 30).

80. Geza Vermes, *Christian Beginnings: From Nazareth to Nicaea, AD 30–325* (London: Penguin Books, 2013).

81. Aaron Milavec, *The Didache: Faith, Hope, & Life of the Earliest Christian Communities, 50–70 C.E.* (Mahwah, NJ: Paulist Press, 2003), pp. 270–272.

82. In fact, according to some scholars, "There can be no doubt at all that behind the mask of Simon Magus stands Paul." (Graham Stanton, *Studies in Matthew and Early Christianity* [Tübingen, Germany: Mohr Siebeck, 2013], p. 430.)

83. *Clementine Homilies,* Homily XVI, Chapter XIX, "Opposition to Peter Unreasonable," in James Donaldson and Alexander Roberts, *Ante-Nicene Fathers, Vol. VIII: e Twelve Patriarchs, Excerpts and Epistles, e Clementina, Apocrypha,*

Decretals, Memoirs of Edessa and Syriac Documents, Remains of the First Ages, Amazon Digital Services LLC, 2012 (originally published by Edinburgh, UK: T. & T. Clark, between 1867 and 1873), p. 323.

84. Ibid., Book IV, Chapter XXXV, "False Apostles," p. 142

85. See: Samuel Zinner, *The Abrahamic Archetype,* p. 124, ff. 18.

86. For the view that Jewish Christianity is a myth, see: Joan E. Taylor, "The Phenomenon of Early Jewish-Christianity: Reality or Scholarly Invention?," *Vigiliae Christianae* 44, no. 4 (December 1990): 313–334.

87. James D. G. Dunn, *Unity and Diversity in the New Testament: An Inquiry into the Character of Earliest Christianity* (London: SCM Press, 2006), pp. 263, 264.

88. For Muslim polemics against Paul, see: Patrick Gray, *Paul as a Problem in History and Culture* (Grand Rapids, MI: Baker Academic, 2016), pp. 41–47. Among classical Muslim polemicists, the one who understood Paul relatively better than others was the eleventh-century Mutazila scholar Abd al-Jabbar, who blamed Paul for "entering the religions of the Romans." (Ibid., p. 44).

89. If Paul was really a figure as described by the "New Perspective" scholars such as James Dunn, however, even this "abandoning Judaism too much" criticism would somewhat vanish. For Dunn argues that Paul did not abandon the Judaic law, as Protestants such as Luther later understood, but only abandoned the salvific nationalism among the Jews. The issue, Dunn argues, was "Whether God's grace is *to* Israel exclusive of Greek or is rather *through* Israel with Greek also in view" (Dunn, *New Perspective on Paul* [Grand Rapids, MI: Wm. B. Eerdmans 2005], p. 170). In this case, Paul's universalism would only resonate with that of Islam.

90. This comment on Paul comes from a critic, Abel Mordechai Bibliowicz, who, among other things, criticized the "anti-Judaic strand in Paul," while acknowledging that he "pioneered the rich and fruitful universe of personal belief." This was crucial, because before Paul, "for first-century Romans, belief (i.e., the beliefs of individuals) was to a large extent an unknown and unappreciated dimension of the human cognitive and religious experience. Individual belief was of no concern to the Roman authorities, religious or secular." In such a conceptual universe, "Paul's emphasis on belief must have been revolutionary. The notion that the beliefs of each and every individual were the arena where the drama of salvation unfolded must have been exhilarating in a society where individual freedom, regardless of class, was very limited." (Abel Mordechai Bibliowicz, *Jews and Gentiles in the Early Jesus Movement: An Unintended Journey* [New York: Palgrave Macmillan, 2013], pp. 35–36.)

91. After the disastrous revolt of AD 132–135, Jews became outcasts in the whole Roman world, as Emperor Hadrian banned Torah study, Sabbath observance, circumcision, Jewish courts, and even meeting in synagogues. Christianity

was then already a distinct faith that parted ways with Judaism, but it was accused by some Romans of "atheism," "cannibalism," and even "incest"—gross
misinterpretations of Christian refusal to worship visible gods, their practicing of
the eucharist, and their emphasis on "love." (T. D. Barnes, "Pagan Perceptions of
Christianity," in *Early Christianity: Origins and Evolution to A.D. 600*, ed.
Ian Hazlett [London: SPCK, 1991], pp. 233–234.)

92. The quote is from Tertullian, to Scapula 5; quoted here from Paul Hartog, "The
Maltreatment of Early Christians: Refinement and Response," *South Baptist
Theological Journal* 18, no. 1 (2014): 61.

CHAPTER THREE

1. The word *cube* is commonly accepted to have originated from the Greek word
kúbos, but that itself maybe connected to Arabic. In her glossary of terms,
Karen Armstrong confidently notes, "From Ka'aba we get our word 'cube,'"
Holy War: The Crusades and Their Impact on Today's World (New York: Anchor
Books, 2001), p. 591.

2. Qur'an 96:1–5, in *The Noble Qur'an: A New Rendering of Its Meaning in English*, trans. Aisha Bewley (Norwich, UK: Bookwork, 1999). Hereafter cited as
Bewley translation.

3. Muhammad Ibn Ishàq, *The Life of Muhammad*, trans. A. Guillaume (Oxford,
UK: Oxford University Press, 1955) p. 107.

4. Qur'an 68:2, Bewley translation.

5. Qur'an, 93:3, Bewley translation.

6. Qur'an 7:71, Bewley translation.

7. Qur'an 35:14, Bewley translation.

8. Qur'an 39:3, Bewley translation.

9. Qur'an 2:132–133.

10. Qur'an 2:47, Bewley translation.

11. In Qur'an 4:167, Bewley translation, we read: "And [We sent] messengers about
whom We have related [their stories] to you before and messengers about whom
We have not related to you."

12. Qur'an 46:9, Bewley translation.

13. Qur'an 28:46, Bewley translation.

14. For an interesting reading of world history through the lens of the global
conquest of "Abrahamism," see Walter Russell Mead, *God and Gold: Britain,
America, and the Making of the Modern World* (New York: Alfred A. Knopf,
2007), pp. 275–282.

15. Ernest Renan, "Mohammedanism," *Cyclopædia of Political Science, Political
Economy, and the Political History of the United States*, ed. John J. Lalor (New
York: Maynard, Merrill, 1889), Vol II: available online at "Online Library of
Liberty," http://oll.libertyfund.org. Accessed on July 14, 2016.

16. There are many examples of this narrative; one example is Elisabeth Sabaditsch-Wolff, "Islam Is a Political Ideology Disguised as a Religion," CBN (Christian Broadcasting Network), September 14, 2010.

17. Fred M. Donner, *Muhammad and the Believers: At the Origins of Islam* (Cambridge, MA: Belknap Press of Harvard University Press, 2010), p. xii.

18. Qur'an 90:7–18, Bewley translation.

19. *Didache*, in *The Apostolic Fathers*, trans. Kirsopp Lake, Loeb Classical Library (Cambridge, MA: Harvard University Press, 1912), available at: earlychristian-writings.com. Accessed on December 20, 2015.

20. Qur'an 19:96, Bewley translation.

21. As summarized by Donner, *Muhammad and the Believers*, p. 30.

22. More tragic than expulsion was the slaughter of the males of the third Jewish tribe in Medina, the Banu Qurayza. But there are unorthodox ways of reading this bitter story, as I explained in my previous book, *Islam without Extremes: A Muslim Case for Liberty* (New York: W.W. Norton, 2011), pp. 57–58.

23. Qur'an 3:3, Bewley translation.

24. Qur'an 5:47, Bewley translation.

25. Qur'an 2:62, Bewley translation.

26. Donner, *Muhammad and the Believers*, p. 75.

27. Zachary Karabell, *People of the Book: The Forgotten History of Islam and the West* (London: John Murray, 2007), pp. 19–20.

28. Narrated by Ibn Ishaq in his *Sira* (biography) of the Prophet, quoted here from F. E. Peters, *A Reader on Classical Islam* (Princeton, NJ: Princeton University Press, 1993), p. 62.

29. Qur'an 30: 2–5, Bewley translation.

30. Qur'an 3:64, in *The Qur'an: A New Translation*, trans. M. A. S. Abdel Haleem (Oxford, UK: Oxford University Press, 2004). Hereafter cited as Haleem translation.

31. For a detailed evaluation of the image of Heraclitus in Islam, see Nadia Maria El-Cheikh, "Muhammad and Heraclius: A Study in Legitimacy," *Studia Islamica* 89 (1999): 5–2.

32. *The Covenant of the Prophet Muhammad with the Christians of Najran*, trans. John Andrew Morrow (Tacoma, WA: Angelico Press, Sophia Perennis, 2013).

33. According to Donner, this is a post-Qur'anic development that crystalized under the Caliphate of the Ummayad Dynasty (661–744). The Ummayads, "more than anyone else helped the Believers attain a clear sense of their own distinct identity and of their legitimacy as a religious community." Donner, *Muhammad and the Believers*, p. xii.

34. Karen Armstrong, *A History of God* (New York: Ballantine Books, 1993), p. 395.

35. "Today all good things have been made permissible for you. And the food of those given the Book is also permissible for you and your food is permissible for them." Qur'an 5:5, Bewley translation.

36. The common view in Islamic tradition is that the Qur'an allows only Muslim *men* to marry Jews and Christian *women*, but not the other way around. But the Qur'anic verse that allows interfaith marriage does not explicitly ban Muslim women from marrying men of the People of the Book as well: "So are [permissible] chaste women from among the believers and chaste women of those given the Book before you, once you have given them their dowries in marriage, not in fornication or taking them as lovers" (5:5).

37. For a recent evaluation of Islamic conquests from within Christian sources, see Zafer Duygu, "The Projections of Islamic Conquests and Muslim Sovereignty in 7th Century on the Christian Historiography," *Journal of Artuklu Academia* 1, no. 1 (2014): 33–65.

38. Donner, *Muhammad and the Believers*, 107.

39. Michael Philip Penn, *When Christians First Met Muslims: A Sourcebook of the Earliest Syriac Writings on Islam* (Oakland, CA: University of California Press, 2015), p. 36.

40. Ibid., pp. 88–89, 92. One must note that there were also quite negative depictions of Islam by the eastern Christians who were conquered by early Muslim armies. Michael Philip Penn examines this "incredible diversity of Syriac depictions, ranging from overtly antagonistic to downright friendly," and underlines that this "belies a solely hostile reaction." In his view, "these texts remind us that Christians' and Muslims' first interactions were not characterized by unmitigated conflict" (ibid., p. 7).

41. For both the Jerome and the al-Qumisi quotes and the details of the impact of the Muslim conquest of Jerusalem on Jews, see: Moshe Gil, *A History of Palestine, 634–1099* (Cambridge, UK: Cambridge University Press, 1997), pp. 69–71.

42. Allan Harris Cutler and Helen Elmquist Cutler, *The Jew as Ally of the Muslim: Medieval Roots of Anti-Semitism* (Notre Dame, IN: University of Notre Dame Press, 1986), pp. 92–93.

43. Ibid., p. 89.

44. For an in-depth examination of the role of Moses in the Qur'an, see: Brannon M. Wheeler, *Moses in the Qur'an and Islamic Exegesis* (New York: Routledge, 2013).

45. "European Jewish-Muslim Group Formed to Protect Religious Freedoms," *Jewish News Online*, September 10, 2015, http://jewishnews.timesofisrael.com /european-jewish-muslim-group-formed-to-protect-religious-freedoms/. Accessed on July 14, 2016.

46. No wonder Rabbi Baruch Efrati, an Israeli rabbi based in the West Bank, decreed in 2011 that travelling Jews could use mosques for prayers, because in the Jewish tradition "there is no prohibition on praying in mosques." In contrast, the rabbi said, "praying in churches was completely and strictly forbidden. In fact, it is forbidden to step into a church." "Pray in Mosque, Rabbi

Rules," Ynetnews.com, November 2, 2011, http://www.ynetnews.com/articles
/0,7340,L-4016144,00.html. Accessed on July 14, 2016.

47. Sidney H. Griffith, *The Church in the Shadow of the Mosque: Christians and Muslims in the World of Islam* (Princeton, NJ: Princeton University Press, 2012), p. 70.

48. John C. Blair, *The Sources of Islam: An Inquiry into the Sources of the Faith and Practice of the Muhammadan Religion* (Madras: Christian Literature Society for India, 1925), p. 55.

49. Abraham I. Katsh, *Judaism in Islam: Biblical and Talmudic Backgrounds of the Koran and Its Commentaries* (New York: New York University Press, 1954); reviewed in Gerson D. Cohen, "Judaism in Islam, by Abraham I. Katsh," *Commentary* (February 1, 1955).

50. Qur'an 5:44, Bewley translation.

51. Qur'an 5:46, Bewley translation.

52. *The Encyclopaedia of Islam*, vol. 4 (Leiden, the Netherlands: Brill, 1960–2005), s.v. "'Isa," p. 81.

53. Qur'an 3:50, Bewley translation.

54. Qur'an 5:72, Bewley translation with the author's rewording.

55. These Median verses with references to the "Messiah" are 3:45, 4:157, 4:171, 4:172, 5:17, 5:72, 5:75, 9:30, and 9:31.

56. Qur'an, 4:171–172, Bewley translation with Arabic words anglicized.

57. Jacques Jomier, "Il Corano è contro la Biblia?," quoted here from the translation from the Italian original by Martiniano P. Roncaglia in "Éléments Ébionites et Elkésaïtes dans le Coran," *Proche Orient Chrétien* 21 (1971): 101–126. Translated by Susan Boyd-Bowman as a chapter of *Koranic Allusions: The Biblical, Qumranian, and Pre-Islamic Background to the Koran*, ed. Ibn Warraq (Amherst, NY: Prometheus Books, 2013), p. 358.

58. Hans Küng, *Islam: Past, Present, and Future* (Oxford, UK: Oneworld Publications, 2007), p. 44.

CHAPTER FOUR

1. John Toland, *Nazarenus: Or Jewish, Gentile, or Mahometan Christianity* (London: 1718), pp. iv–vi. The full text is available at: Archive.org as digitized by the Princeton Theological Seminary. Also see: F. Stanley Jones, *The Rediscovery of Jewish Christianity: From Toland to Baur*, Society of Biblical Literature (Leiden, the Netherlands: Koninklijke Brill, 2012).

2. Toland, *Nazarenus*, pp. 84–85.

3. After mentioning several sources for possible roots of "Mahometical Doctrines," Stubbe argued: "For my part I believe that [Mahomet] was a convert to the Judaizing Christians and formed his Religion as far as possible in resemblance of theirs." Henry Stubbe, *An Account of the Rise and Progress of Maho-*

metanism (London: Luzac and Company, 1911 reprint), p. 145. The book was orginally written and distributed in 1671.

4. Adolf von Harnack, "Islam," from an excerpt translated by Markus Gross from *Lehrbuch der Dogmengeschicte* (Tübingen, Germany: 1909), published in *Christmas in the Koran,* ed. Ibn Warraq (Amherst, NY: Prometheus Books, 2014), p. 246.

5. Ibid.

6. Hans-Joachim Schoeps, *Jewish Christianity: Factional Disputes in the Early Church,* trans. Douglas R. A. Hare (Philadelphia: Fortress Press, 1969), p. 140. The original German edition was published by A. Francke (Bern: AG Verlag, 1964).

7. Shlomo Pines, "The Jewish Christians of the Early Centuries of Christianity According to a New Source," *Proceedings of the Israel Academy of Sciences and Humanities* 2, no. 13 (1966): 1–74.

8. See: S. M. Stern, "New Light on Judaeo-Christianity?" *Encounter* 28, no. 5 (May 1967): 53–57; and S. Stern, "'Abd al-Jabbàr's Account of How Christ's Religion Was Falsified by the Adoption of Roman Customs," *Journal of Theological Studies* 19, no. 1 (April 1968): 128–185. Also, for a good evaluation of the controversy between Pines and Stern, and the very work which caused it, the book by the medieval Muslim writer Abd al-Jabbar, see: Gabriel Said Reynolds, *A Muslim Theologian in the Sectarian Milieu: Abd al-Jabbar and the Critique of Christian Origins* (Leiden, the Netherlands: Brill, 2004).

9. Published in English in *Koranic Allusions: The Biblical, Qumranian, and Pre-Islamic Background to the Koran,* ed. Ibn Warraq (Amherst, NY: Prometheus Books, 2013).

10. See François de Blois, "Naṣrānī (Ναζωραῖος) and Ḥanīf (ἐθνικός): Studies on the Religious Vocabulary of Christianity and of Islam," *Bulletin of the School of Oriental and African Studies* 65 (2002): 1–30; Edouard M. Gallez, *Le messie et son prophète: Aux origines de l'Islam,* vol. 1: *De Qumrân à Muhammad,* 2nd ed. (Paris: Éditions de Paris, 2005); Joseph Azzi, *The Priest and the Prophet: The Christian Priest, Waraqa Ibn Nawfal's, Profound Influence Upon Muhammad, the Prophet of Islam* (The Pen Publishers, 2005); and Joachim Gnilka, *Die Nazarener und der Koran: Eine Spurensuche* (Freiburg, Germany: Herder, 2007). The excerpt is from Sidney H. Griffith, *The Bible in Arabic: The Scriptures of the "People of the Book" in the Language of Islam* (Princeton, NJ: Princeton University Press, 2013), and in iBooks.

11. See Patricia Crone, "Islam, Judeo-Christianity, and Byzantine Iconoclasm," *Jerusalem Studies in Arabic and Islam* (Part Two) (1980): 59–95.

12. de Blois, "Naṣrānī (Ναζωραῖος) and Hanīf (ἐθνικός)," p. 25.

13. Hans Küng, *Islam: Past, Present, and Future* (Oxford, UK: Oneworld Publications, 2007), p. 496.

14. *Clementine Homilies,* Homily XVI, Chapter XIX, "Opposition to Peter

Unreasonable," in James Donaldson and Alexander Roberts, *Ante-Nicene Fathers, Vol. VIII: e Twelve Patriarchs, Excerpts and Epistles, e Clementina, Apocrypha, Decretals, Memoirs of Edessa and Syriac Documents, Remains of the First Ages,* Amazon Digital Services LLC, 2012 (originally published by Edinburgh, UK: T. & T. Clark, between 1867 and 1873), p. 31.

15. Qur'an 2:163, Bewley translation.

16. Gerard P. Luttikhuizen, *The Revelation of Elchasai: Investigations into the Evidence for a Mesopotamian Jewish Apocalypse of the Second Century and Its Reception by Judeo-Christian Propagandists* (Tübingen, Germany: Mohr Siebeck, 1985), pp. 3, 12, 27–28.

17. Qur'an 3:49, Bewley translation.

18. Patricia Crone, "Jewish Christianity and the Qur'ān (Part One)," *Journal of Near Eastern Studies* 74, no. 2 (October 2015): 230.

19. Ibid. Crone further explains: "This [Qur'anic conception] is in line with a famous passage in the Jewish Christian section of the "Pseudo-Clementine" *Recognitions* (probably composed in the mid-fourth century), in which we are told that the only difference between the authors and 'those of our people who do not believe' or, as the Latin version puts it, 'between us who believe in Jesus and the unbelieving Jews,' is that 'we' believe Jesus to be the prophet foretold by Moses and the eternal Christ whereas the unbelieving Jews do not. It is not easy to imagine Chalcedonian (Melkite), West Syrian (Monophysite or Jacobite), or East Syrian (Nestorian) Christians presenting Jesus as a prophet to the Israelites, nor have mainstream Christian parallels ever been adduced to my knowledge."

20. In "Jewish Christianity and the Qur'ān (Part One)," Crone cited only the "Pseudo-Clementine" *Recognitions.*

21. Ibid., p. 230.

22. Ibid., p. 237.

23. Notably, the Islamic tradition also elevates Moses as *Kalim Allah,* or "the Converser with God," along with five other "major prophets": Adam, "the Chosen of God"; Noah, "the Prophet of God"; Abraham, "the Friend of God"; Jesus, "the Spirit of God"; and Muhammad, "the Apostle of God."

24. Irenaeus, *Adversus Haereses* 5.1.3. The full text is available at: http://www.earlychristianwritings.com. Accessed on May 5, 2016.

25. Fragments of Hegesippus, http://www.earlychristianwritings.com/text/hegesippus.html. Accessed on May 5, 2016.

26. The Qur'anic word is *khamr,* and whether it refers to only wine or all intoxicating drinks has actually been discussed in the Islamic tradition. See: *Encyclopaedia of the Qur'an,* vol. 5 (Leiden, the Netherlands: Brill, 2001–2006), s.v. "Wine," p. 481.

27. For all the references, see John J. Gunther, *St. Paul's Opponents and Their Backgrounds: A Study of Apocalyptic and Jewish Sectarians Teachings* (Leiden, the Netherlands: Brill Archive, 1973), p. 139.

28. Epiphanius, *Panarion*, 30.7–9. Also see Petri Luomanen, *Recovering Jewish-Christian Sects and Gospels* (Leiden, the Netherlands: Brill, 2012), p. 35. The issue Epiphanius discusses here is why the Ebionites abstained from meat and wine, which is a restriction compared to Jewish Law and not liberality, but this practice might well have been merely one element of a broader reform and reinterpretation of Jewish Law that the Ebionites held and that they believed came from Jesus.

29. Qur'an 3:50–51, Bewley translation with Arabic words anglicized.

30. Ömer Faruk Harman, "Yahudi Hıristiyanlığı," in *İslam Ansiklopedisi*, vol. 43 (Ankara, Turkey: Türk Diyanet Vakfı, 2013), p. 186.

31. The same question is the headline of a long article on the same topic: "Did Jewish Christians See the Rise of Islam?" in *The Ways That Never Parted: Jews and Christians in Late Antiquity and the Early Middle Ages*, ed. Adam H. Becker and Annette Yoshiko Reed (Minneapolis, MN: Fortress Press, 2007), pp. 361–372. His answer tends to be positive. Meanwhile, one counterargument to our view that Jewish Christianity vanished by the end of the fifth century may come from John of Damascus (676–749), who condemns "the Cerinthians," "the Nazarenes," and "the Ebionites," but it seems that he was listing all the known heresies in the history of the church, rather than giving information about actually existing communities in his time. See John of Damascus, *Writings, The Fathers of the Church Patristic Series*, vol. 37 (Washington, DC: Catholic University of America Press, 1958, 1999), pp. 118–119.

32. Sidney H. Griffith, *The Bible in Arabic: The Scriptures of the "People of the Book" in the Language of Islam* (Princeton, NJ: Princeton University Press, 2013), pp. 36–37

33. This argument was put forward most passionately by the Lebanese scholar Joseph Azzi, in a book written in Arabic and translated first into French with the title *Le prêtre et le prophète: Aux sources du Coran* (Paris: Maisonneuve et Larose, 2001), and then into English with the title *The Priest and the Prophet: The Christian Priest, Waraqa Ibn Nawfal's Profound Influence upon Muhammad, the Prophet of Islam* (Los Angeles: The Pen Publishers, 2005). Once Waraqa can really be proved to be Ebionite, Azzi's argument would be really powerful, but one has to assume that about Waraqa in the first place. Gerhard Böwering, professor of religious studies at Yale University, finds Azzi's study "highly speculative and poorly documented" and defines it as "an audacious claim that has yet to be substantiated." Böwering, "Recent Research on the Construction of the Qur'an," in *The Qur'ān in Its Historical Context*, ed. Gabriel S. Reynolds (London: Routledge, 2008), p. 80.

34. This is suggested by de Blois, "Naṣrānī (Ναζωραῖος) and Hanīf (ἐθνικός)," p. 16.

35. Samir Khalil Samir, "The Theological Christian Influence on the Qur'an: A Reflection," in *The Qur'an in Its Historical Context*, ed. Gabriel Said Reynolds (London: Routledge, 2008), p. 160.

36. Ismail Faruqi makes this definition in *The Cultural Atlas of Islam* (New York: Macmillan, 1986). He does not go as far as defining the "Semitically oriented Christians" as Jewish Christians, but he seems to raise an important point. In his full words: ". . . the ascendancy of the Church of Rome backed by the Byzantine Empire had alienated these Semitically oriented Christians. When they were hereticated by the Church of Rome, and persecuted by the Byzantine Empire or its puppets on the scene, they took refuge in the desert. There, they swelled the ranks of Jewish refugees and reinforced the Abrahamic tradition with their monotheistic and spiritualizing version of Christianity. Both Jews and Christian immigrants to the desert found a ready welcome among those Arabs who upheld the Mesopotamian-Abrahamic tradition. Together, they consolidated that tradition in Peninsular Arabia which came to be known as *Hanifiyyah*. Its adherents, the *hanif(s)*, resisted every association of other gods with God, refused to participate in pagan rituals, and maintained a life of ethical purity above reproach. It was common knowledge that the *hanif* was a strict monotheist who paid no tribute to tribal religion, that he was of impeccable ethical character, and that he kept aloof from the cynicism and moral lasciviousness of other Arabs. The *hanifs* always stood above tribal disputes and hostilities. Everybody knew of their presence since they belonged to nearly all tribes. Moreover, they had the reputation of being the most learned in religion. The Prophet knew the *hunafa'* well enough to say: 'Islam is identical with Hanifiyah,' and above him stood the Qur'an's authoritative identification of Abraham as a *hanif*" (p. 61).

37. The name *Isawiyya* came from not Isa, or Jesus, but from the founder of the sect, Abu Isa al-Isfahani. Whether this is a Jewish Christian sect, or merely a Jewish sect respectful to Jesus as prophet to the Gentiles, is disputed. See Gabriel Said Reynolds, *A Muslim Theologian in the Sectarian Milieu: 'Abd Al-Jabbār and the Critique of Christian Origins* (Leiden, the Netherlands: Brill, 2004), p. 7, footnote 27.

38. Pines, "The Jewish Christians of the Early Centuries of Christianity According to a New Source," p. 45.

39. Reynolds, *A Muslim Theologian in the Sectarian Milieu*, p. 5.

40. Crone, "Islam, Judeo-Christianity, and Byzantine Iconoclasm," p. 74.

41. Qur'an 61:14, Bewley translation with Arabic words anglicized.

42. Qur'an 5:72–73, Bewley translation with Arabic words anglicized.

43. Qur'an 5:82, Haleem translation with the author's rewording.

44. Qur'an 5:83–85, Haleem translation.

45. Ernst Hammerschmidt, "Jewish Elements in the Cult of the Ethiopian Church," *Journal of Ethiopian Studies* 3, no. 2 (July 1965): 1.

46. Ibid., p. 12.

47. Samuel Zinner, *The Gospel of Thomas: In the Light of the Early Jewish, Christian and Islamic Esoteric Trajectories* (London: The Matheson Trust, 2011), p. 101.

48. "One could imagine a situation where there existed, presumably in Mecca, an isolated outpost of Nazoraean 'Jewish Christianity' and where Muhammad's acquaintance with Pauline teachings would have come." Blois, "Naṣrānī (Ναζωραῖος) and Hanīf (ἐθνικός)," p. 27.

49. Qur'an 5:5, Haleem translation.

50. Blois, "Naṣrānī (Ναζωραῖος) and Hanīf (ἐθνικός)," p. 16.

51. Qur'an 9:30. The same verse also condemns Jews for saying "Uzayr [Ezra] is the son of God." Admittedly, this is hard to explain, for there is no record of Jews venerating Ezra as the "Son of God," especially in the sense of ascribing divinity to him, which would make the situation similar to the case of Jesus in Christianity. Hence the prominent Muslim exegete Muhammad ibn Jarir al-Tabari (d. 923) had argued that, far from being a standard Jewish claim, this claim was made by a person called Pinhas, most probably a Medinan Jew, who also said, "God is poor and we are rich." Or, al-Tabari suggested, this claim may have been made by a number of Medinan Jews who visited the Prophet upon his arrival in Medina in the year 622 and asserted the divinity of Uzayr. See: *Encyclopedia of the Qur'an*, vol. 2, s.v. "Ezra," p. 156.

52. The verse is 5:82. Patricia Crone, too, takes this verse as indicating a problem with Blois's argument that al-Nasara are simply Jewish Christians. See: Crone, "Jewish Christianity and the Qur'ān (Part One)," p. 325, footnote 74.

53. Alphonse Mingana, "Syriac Influence on the Style of the Kur'ān," *Bulletin of the John Rylands Library* 11, no. 1 (1927): 96 .

54. Sidney H. Griffith, *The Bible in Arabic: The Scriptures of the 'People of the Book' in the Language of Islam* (Princeton, NJ: Princeton University Press, 2013), p. 37.

55. Gabriel Said Reynolds, "On the Presentation of Christianity in the Qur'ān and the Many Aspects of Qur'anic Rhetoric," *Al-Bayan: Journal of Qur'an and Hadith Studies* 12 (2014): 43, 46, 54.

56. See Fred M. Donner, *Muhammad and the Believers: At the Origins of Islam* (Cambridge, MA: Belknap Press of Harvard University Press, 2010), pp. 54–56. Also see Nicolai Sinai, who argues that if the Qur'an was "late," one would expect to see in it reflections of post-Muhammadan political phenomena, which do not appear in it: "If the Quranic *rasm* did not reach closure until c. 700, it does seem odd that it should nowhere engage with the major developments that defined Islamic history between 630 and 700, in particular the unprecedented speed with which an alliance of 'barbarian' tribes from the fringes of the Byzantine and Sasanian empires established themselves as the masters of an immense territory, and the bitter disputes and civil wars that soon wreaked havoc on the unity of the conquerors." Sinai, "When Did the Consonantal Skeleton of the Quran Reach Closure? Part II," *Bulletin of the School of Oriental and African Studies* 77 (2014): 516–517.

57. Behnam Sadeghi and Uwe Bergman, "The Codex of a Companion of the Prophet and the Qurān of the Prophet," *Arabica* 57, no. 4 (2010): 343–436. On

the facts against the "late Qur'an" hypothesis, also see: Asma Afsaruddin, *First Muslims: History and Memory* (Oxford, UK: Oneworld Publications, 2007), pp. xiv–xvi.

58. Yehuda D. Nevo, "Towards a Prehistory of the Qur'an," in *What the Koran Really Says*, ed. Ibn Warraq (Amherst, NY: Prometheus Books, 2002), pp. 131–170.

59. Facsimile 1.24, the last two sentences. Nevo himself used here the term "Lord of Creation," but I prefer the translation "Lord of the Worlds," as it is more precise regarding the Arabic *Rabb-ul alameen*. See: Nevo, "Towards a Prehistory of the Qur'an," pp. 135, 160.

60. Nevo, "Towards a Prehistory of the Qur'an," p. 148.

61. Ibid., p. 150.

62. Gerald Hawting, *Idea of Idolatry and the Emergence of Islam: From Polemic to History* (Cambridge, UK: Cambridge University Press, 2006), p. 40.

63. Both Pseudo-Cyril quotes are from Patricia Crone, "Jewish Christianity and the Qur'an (Part Two)" *Journal of Near Eastern Studies* (April 2016): 3.

64. Guillaume Dye, "Jewish Christianity, the Qur'ān, and Early Islam: Some Methodological Caveats," paper presented at the Eighth Annual ASMEA Conference Washington, October 29–31, 2015, at the workshop "Jewish Christianity and the Origins of Islam." Quoted with the author's permission.

65. Dye points to Neal Robinson, whose work seems to indicate a longer list of heresies that might have influenced Islam: Nestorianism, Monophysitism, Tritheism, Antideco-Marcianites, Ebionites, Elkasites, Manichaeism, Gnosticism, let alone Judaism. Robinson, *Christ in Islam and Christianity* (Albany: State University of New York Press, 1991), pp. 19–21.

66. The phrase "Jurassic Park for ancient 'heresies'" was coined by Jack Tannous in "Syria between Byzantium and Islam: Making Incommensurables Speak" (PhD dissertation, Princeton University, 2010), p. 396. I owe its usage here to Dye, who referred to Tannous in "Jewish Christianity, the Qur'ān, and Early Islam."

67. Samuel Zinner, *The Abrahamic Archetype: Conceptual and Historical Relationships between Judaism, Christianity and Islam* (Bartlow, UK: Archetype Books, 2011), p. vii.

68. The original article by Martiniano P. Roncaglia is "Éléments Ébionites et Elkésaïtes dans le Coran," *Proche Orient Chrétien* 21 (1971): 101–126. Translated by Susan Boyd-Bowman as a chapter of *Koranic Allusions: The Biblical, Qumranian, and Pre-Islamic Background to the Koran*, ed. Ibn Warraq (Amherst, NY: Prometheus Books, 2013), p. 367.

69. Ibid., p. 368.

70. Qur'an 5:47–48, Bewley translation with Arabic words anglicized.

71. For Murjia, see my book *Islam without Extremes* (New York: W.W. Norton, 2011), pp. 83–85. For the condemnation of Murjia by ISIS, the so-called Islamic State of Iraq and Syria, see my article "A Medieval Antidote to ISIS," *New York Times*, December 21, 2015.

CHAPTER FIVE

1. In fact, Muslim tradition apparently could not accept that Mary is "above all women," even in light of the Prophet's teaching. Hence came the hadith that made Khadija, the first wife of the Prophet Muhammad, equal with Mary. "The best of the women *of her time* was Mary daughter of 'Imran and the best of the women *of her time* was Khadija daughter of Khuwaylid" (emphases added). Abu alFida' Isma'il Ibn Kathir, *Tafsir al-Qur'an al-'Azim*, vol. 2 (Beirut: Dar al-Andalus, 1385), pp. 37ff.; quoted here from Neal Robinson, *Christ in Islam and Christianity* (Albany: State University of New York Press, 1991), p. 63. I personally find this hadith very doubtful because of its clear contradiction of the Qur'an and its apparent intention of overpraising the Prophet and his family, which is a post-Qur'anic trend.

2. Qur'an 3:42, Bewley translation.

3. For more on the Maryamiyya order, see *Against the Modern World: Traditionalism and the Secret Intellectual History of the Twentieth Century*, ed. Mark Sedgwick (Oxford, UK: Oxford University Press, 2009), pp. 147–160.

4. "God's Plan for Peace between Christianity and Islam," http://www.catholica pologetics.info/apologetics/islam/Godsplan.htm. Accessed on April 7, 2016.

5. Qur'an 19:2, Haleem translation.

6. Qur'an 19:2–6, Haleem translation with Arabic words anglicized.

7. Qur'an 19:7–9, Muhammad Habib Shakir translation. Hereafter cited as Shakir translation. Taken from Terry Kepner (ed.), *Three Translations of the Koran Side by Side: Hafiz Abdullah Yusuf Ali, Mohammed Marmaduke Pickthall, Muhammad Habib Shakir* (Bennington, NH: Flying Chipmunk Publishing, 2009).

8. One controversy over this Qur'anic passage is whether verse 19:7 defines *Yahya*, or John, as having "a name we have given to no one else before" (Bewley translation). This is a common translation, which has raised objections from Christian polemicists that it is a gross mistake, for there are other Johns in the Old Testament. However, the word translated as "with the same name," *samiy*, does not necessarily mean that. It occurs only twice in the Qur'an, in this verse and in 19:65. In both instances, the early and prominent Muslim exegete Ibn al'Abbas took it to mean "similar." Hence he wrote that what is meant here is that there had never before been a boy similar to John in the sense of being born to an aged father and a barren mother. See Robinson, *Christ in Islam and Christianity*, p. 65. I prefer that explanation, and hence opted here for the Shakir translation that relies on it.

9. Qur'an 19:10, Bewley translation. The same incident is also reported in chapter "Family of Imran," with some slight difference: "He said, 'My Lord, appoint a Sign for me.' He said, 'Your Sign is that you will not speak to people for three days, except by gesture. Remember your Lord much and glorify Him in the evening and after dawn'" (3:41).

10. Luke 1:20.

11. Qur'an 3:39, Haleem translation.

12. Qur'an 19:12–15, Haleem translation. It is worth noting that the Qur'an expression quoted from John here, "Peace was on him the day he was born, the day he died, and it will be on him the day he is raised to life again," is also quoted in the same chapter from Jesus almost verbatim: "Peace was on me the day I was born, and will be on me the day I die and the day I am raised to life again" (19:33).

13. Luke 1:15.

14. The origin of the names of Qur'anic suras, or chapters, is disputed among Muslims. Some believe that they were given by the Prophet Muhammad himself, even with the guidance of Angel Gabriel, but others think that the Muslim tradition later chose names for each sura by simply taking words from their contents. I accept this latter argument.

15. See pp. 119–122 in this book.

16. Qur'an 3:35–37, Haleem translation; I have changed the word *provisions* here to *food*, as preferred by most other translations.

17. Muslim exegetes have debated what this miraculous food Mary found in her sanctuary was like. Some suggested, "it was summer fruits in winter, and winter fruits in summer." According to others, it was grapes out of season. See Mahmoud M. Ayoub, *The House of 'Imran*, vol. 2 of *The Qur'an and Its Interpreters* (Albany: State University of New York Press, 1984), p. 100.

18. The first known work that highlighted the parallels between the Qur'an and the *Protoevangelium of James* is from the seventeenth century: Heinrich Sike, *Evangelium infantiae, vel liber apocryphus de infantia servatoris* (Trajecti ad Rhenum [Utrecht]: F. Halma et G. van de Water, 1697). Another, more recent pioneering work is Wilhelm Rudolph, *Die Abhängigkeit des Qorans von Judentum und Christentum* (Stuttgart, Germany: Kohlhammer, 1922). Since 1922, various academic articles have addressed the issue.

19. *The Protoevangelium of James* in *The Ante-Nicene Fathers: Translations of the Writings of the Fathers Down to A.D. 325*, vol. 8, ed. Alexander Roberts, Sir James Donaldson, Arthur Cleveland Coxe, and Allan Menzies (Buffalo, NY: Christian Literature Publishing Co., 1886), p. 362.

20. Qur'an 3:35, Haleem translation.

21. *The Protoevangelium of James*, p. 362.

22. Ibid., p. 363.

23. Qur'an 3:38, Haleem translation, only "provisions" is replaced with "food."

24. *The Protoevangelium of James*, p. 363.

25. Ibid.

26. Qur'an 3:44, Haleem translation.

27. Tabari, *Jami' al-bayan fi ta'wil al-Qur'an*, vol. 3, pp. 241, 244, and 246.

Taken here from Ömer Faruk Harman, "Meryem," in İslam Ansiklopedisi (Encyclopedia of Islam), vol. 29 (Ankara, Turkey: Türk Diyanet Vakfı, 2013), p. 240.

28. Gabriel Said Reynolds, *The Qur'an and Its Biblical Subtext* (London: Routledge, 2010), p. 144.

29. Sidney H. Griffith, "The Gospel, the Qur'ān, and the Presentation of Jesus in al-Ya'qūbī's Ta'rīkh," in *Bible and Quran: Essays in Scriptural Intertextuality*, ed. John C. Reeves (Boston: Brill, 2004), p. 136.

30. See: Megan Nutzman, "Mary in the Protevangelium of James: A Jewish Woman in the Temple?," *Greek, Roman, and Byzantine Studies* 53 (2013): 551–578. Nutzman argues: "The author of Prot. Jas., while demonstrably Christian in his presentation of Jesus, was also familiar with interpretations of the Torah circulating among his Jewish contemporaries." On the particular issue of Mary's presence at the Jewish Temple, which has been seen as historically improbable, she argues: "Rather than betraying an ignorance of Judaism, Mary's relationship to the temple artfully weaves together the unique position in the Jerusalem temple allotted to accused adulteresses, to girls who wove the temple curtains, and to female Nazirites" (p. 552).

31. Ibid., pp. 556ff. Bellarmino Bagatti, a Franciscan priest and archeologist, also argues that the *Protoevangelium* was "designed to promote Jewish Christianity in Palestine." Bagatti, *Excavations in Nazareth* (Jerusalem: Franciscan Printing Press, 1969), p. 11, quoted here from Edwin K. Broadhead, *Jewish Ways of Following Jesus: Redrawing the Religious Map of Antiquity* (Tübingen, Germany: Mohr Siebeck, 2010), p. 324.

32. Oscar Cullmann, "Infancy Gospels," in *New Testament Apocrypha: Gospels and Related Writings*, vol. 1, ed. Wilhelm Schneemelcher, trans. R. McL. Wilson (Cambridge, UK: J. Clarke, 1991), p. 425.

33. Luke 1:31.

34. Quote above: Qur'an 19:16–21. Quote here: Qur'an 21:91 and 66:12, Haleem translation.

35. See Robinson, *Christ in Islam and Christianity*, p. 162.

36. For an evaluation of the Qur'an's terminology on the creation of Jesus in Mary's womb, see: Crone, "Jewish Christianity and the Qur'an (Part Two)," p. 9.

37. Qur'an 19:16, Haleem translation.

38. In his popular 1930 translation of the Qur'an, *The Meaning of the Glorious Koran*, Marmaduke Pickthall in fact translated the word as "a chamber looking East." Taken from Terry Kepner (ed.), *Three Translations of the Koran Side by Side: Hafiz Abdullah Yusuf Ali, Mohammed Marmaduke Pickthall, Muhammad Habib Shakir* (Bennington, NH: Flying Chipmunk Publishing, 2009).

39. Barbara Freyer Stowasser, *Women in the Qur'an, Traditions, and Interpretation* (Oxford, UK: Oxford University Press, 1996), pp. 156ff.

40. Ezekiel 43:4.
41. Hesychius is quoted by Guillaume Dye, "The Qur'ān and Its Hypertextuality in Light of Redaction Criticism," paper for the Fourth Nangeroni Meeting, *Early Islam: The Sectarian Milieu of Late Antiquity?* Early Islamic Studies Seminar, Milan, June 15–19, 2015, p. 5.
42. Qur'an 19:22–27, Bewley translation.
43. Some give a date for Pseudo-Matthew between AD 600 and 625; Hans-Josef Klauck, *Apocryphal Gospels: An Introduction* (London: T. and T. Clark, 2003), p. 78. The New Testament scholar Dan Wallace dates it much later, to the eighth to ninth century AD (Daniel Wallace, Ed Komoszewski, and James Sawyer, *Reinventing Jesus* [Grand Rapids, MI: Kregel Publications, 2006], p. 156).
44. *The Gospel of Pseudo-Matthew*, trans. Alexander Roberts, in *The Ante-Nicene Fathers: The Writings of the Fathers Down to A.D. 325*, vol. 8 (New York: Cosimo, 2007), p. 377.
45. The quote is from Hosn Abboud, *Mary in the Qur'an: A Literary Reading* (London: Routledge, 2014), p. 56. Stephen J. Shoemaker makes the same observation in "Christmas in the Qur'an: The Qur'anic Account of Jesus' Nativity and Palestinian Local Tradition," *Jerusalem Studies in Arabic and Islam* 28 (2003): 19.
46. Shoemaker points to these narratives as the ancient traditions of the Virgin Mary's Dormition and Assumption, preserved by several Syriac fragments copied in the later fifth century, in "Christmas in the Qur'an," p. 19.
47. Dye, "The Qur'ān and Its Hypertextuality in Light of Redaction Criticism," p. 6.
48. Antoninus Placentius, *Itinerarium*, in *Itineraria et alia Geographica*, ed. P. Geyer, Corpus Christianorum, Corpus Latina 175 (Turnhout, Belgium: Brepols, 1965), p. 137; quoted here from Shoemaker, "Christmas in the Qur'an," p. 22.
49. Shoemaker, "Christmas in the Qur'an," pp. 33–34.
50. *Protoevangelium of James*, 17.
51. Shoemaker, "Christmas in the Qur'an," p. 27.
52. Ibid.
53. Ibid., p. 38.
54. Ibid.
55. Ibid., p. 36. Shoemaker uses all this data to offer a late-origins thesis for the Qur'an—that the Qur'an's narrative about Mary was written when its presumed authors went out of Arabia and encountered the Jerusalem-based traditions about Kathisma. However, he grants: "It must be admitted that we have not completely eliminated the possibility that these two Christian traditions were somehow known to Muhammad, who combined them independently in the Hijaz, as the traditional understanding would have it." Ibid., p. 39.
56. The most detailed criticism of Shoemaker's thesis on the Kathisma Church

comes, to my knowledge, from Patricia Crone's post-humorous article: "Jewish Christianity and The Qur'ān (Part Two)," pp. 16–19. First, Crone rejects the argument that "Muslims must have picked up the story of Mary and the palm tree after the conquests," reminding readers that Quraish, the tribe of the Prophet, could well be acquainted with the Kathisma traditions. She also reminds that there are two churches involved, so that Shoemaker's thesis about the "conflation" of two separate legends by the Qur'an does not have to be the case.

57. The relevant passage is Rev. 12:1–6. It is Patricia Crone's argument that the woman suffering birth pains here is "the main inspiration behind the Qur'ānic account" of Mary. (Ibid., p. 18.)

58. Qur'an, 23:50, Haleem translation.

59. Qur'an 19:28, Bewley translation, with Arabic words anglicized.

60. From which Jewish tribe Mary came has been disputed, but there are grounds to consider her a Levite, which would make her a descendant of Aaron. The Gospel of Luke 1:5 says that Mary was the cousin of Elizabeth, who was a descendant of Aaron the high priest. This suggests at least a possibility that Mary too was a Levite.

61. Suleiman A. Mourad, "Mary in the Qur'ān: A Reexamination of Her Presentation," in The Qur'ān in Its Historical Context, ed. Gabriel Said Reynolds (London: Routledge, 2008), pp. 163–174.

62. This comment comes from Guillaume Dye, of the Université Libre de Bruxelles, who adds, regarding the problem of the Qur'anic conflation of Mary and Miriam: "It is certainly fair to say that typology is one of the most widespread exegetical devices in Christianity. It can easily be combined with allegoric exegesis, which considers Biblical characters, places or episodes (i.e., concrete, material entities) as symbols of abstract or spiritual notions. So, when the Qur'ān states that Mary is Aaron's sister and 'Imrān's daughter, it does not state that Mary, the mother of Jesus, is Aaron's biological sister and 'Imrān's biological daughter, but it claims that she is prefigured, one way or another, by the 'family of 'Imrān,' especially Aaron and Miryam (obviously, the homonymy on Maryam plays a role, but it does not entail that the main parallel is between Mary and Miryam). In other words, it is not simply a connection to Aaron's lineage." Dye, "The Qur'ān and its Hypertextuality in Light of Redaction Criticism," p. 9.

63. Ibid., p. 13. Emphasis added.

64. Ibid., p. 14.

65. Patricia Crone makes this argument about the Qur'an's implicit reference to an "Aaronid Messiah" in her "Jewish Christianity and The Qur'ān (Part Two)," pp. 11–14. The direct quote here is from the same article, p. 13.

66. Ibid., p. 12.

67. Jonathan M. Reck, "The Annunciation to Mary: A Christian Echo in the Qur'ān," Vigiliae Christianae 68 (2014): 370.

68. Qur'an 19:22–27, Bewley translation.
69. Qur'an 19:29–34, Bewley translation with Arabic words anglicized.
70. The Catholic Christian view, as Neal Robinson puts it, was that, "despite their great number and the diversity of the countries in which they lived, [Christians] knew nothing of this miracle and had no record of it in their scriptures," *Christ in Islam and Christianity*, p. 9.
71. Mahmoud Ayoub, *The House of 'Imran*, pp. 137–138.
72. "The Arabic Gospel of the Infancy of the Saviour," trans. Alexander Walker, in *Ante-Nicene Fathers*, vol. 8, ed. Alexander Roberts, James Donaldson, and A. Cleveland Coxe (Buffalo, NY: Christian Literature Publishing Co., 1886). Full text available at: http://www.newadvent.org/fathers/0806.htm. Accessed on July 14, 2016.
73. Qur'an 3:45–46, Bewley translation with Arabic words anglicized.
74. Qur'an 5:110, Bewley translation with Arabic words anglicized.
75. Emir Fethi Caner and Ergun Mehmet Caner, *More Than a Prophet: An Insider's Response to Muslim Beliefs about Jesus and Christianity* (Grand Rapids, MI: Kregel Publications, 2003), p. 49.
76. One of the towering traditional exegetes of the Qur'an, Razi, with reference to other Muslim theologians, had argued that "Jesus's speaking in the cradle was only for the purpose of asserting his mother's innocence." See Ayoub, *The House of 'Imran*, p. 138.
77. The Qur'anic verse is 4:156, Bewley translation.
78. The earliest reference to Pantera is probably from the church father Origen, who mentions him regarding a Jewish polemic that was intended to discredit the virgin birth (*Contra Celsum* 1:32–33). Also, there are several Talmudic references to Jesus' attribution as "son of Pantera" (*Rab. Qoh* 1:8; Ḥul. 2:22f.) and polemical accusations of Mary's immorality (*Sanh.* 67a; Šabb. 104b). Meanwhile, it is also possible that the "monstrous slander against Mary" may have had other explanations. The Muslim traveler and chronicler Ali b. Husayn al-Mas'udi (d. 956) held that "Jews spread the rumor that Zechariah had sexual relations with Mary." Robinson, *Christ in Islam and Christianity*, p. 45.
79. Luke 11:27–28.
80. Luke 8:20–21.
81. John 2:4.
82. See: John 19:26–27.
83. One such scholar is James D. Tabor, in *The Jesus Dynasty: The Hidden History of Jesus, His Royal Family, and the Birth of Christianity* (New York: Simon and Schuster, 2006), p. 248.
84. The rest of the Qur'anic passage reads: "Then when [the child] achieves his full strength and reaches forty, he says, 'My Lord, keep me thankful for the blessing You bestowed on me and on my parents, and keep me acting rightly, pleas-

ing You. And make my descendants salihun. I have made tawba to You and I am truly one of the Muslims'" (46:15).

Disobedience to parents is commanded only when they try to pull their children away from God—even then, a "courteous" break is advised: "We have instructed man concerning his parents. Bearing him caused his mother great debility and the period of his weaning was two years: 'Give thanks to Me and to your parents. I am your final destination. But if they try to make you associate something with Me about which you have no knowledge, do not obey them. Keep company with them correctly and courteously in this world but follow the Way of him who turns to Me. Then you will return to Me and I will inform you about the things you did'" (31:14–15, Aisha Bewley translation).

Meanwhile, another type of intrafamily tension occurs when the parents call their child to God but the latter refuses. The Qur'an depicts such sons or daughters in a very negative light: "But what of him who says to his parents, 'Fie on you! Do you promise me that I will be resurrected when generations before me have passed away?' They both call on Allah for help: 'Woe to you! Have iman! Allah's promise is true.' But he says, 'This is nothing but the myths of previous peoples'" (46:17, Bewley translation).

85. The story is narrated in the hadith collection of Abu Dawud, "Al-Adab," in *Sunan Abu Dawud*, 64; here it is taken from Zeki Sarıtoprak, with his commentary included, *Islam's Jesus* (Gainesville: University Press of Florida Press, 2014), p. 8.

86. The exegete who made this comment is Sayyed Qutb, who has become somewhat notorious for this role in the making of a radical political Islam. Yet his scholarly work on the Qur'an *tafseer* (exegesis) should not be underestimated. The quote is from Qutb, *Fi Zilal al-Qur'an*, 4:2304–2306, quoted in Sarıtoprak, *Islam's Jesus*, p. 9.

87. Such modernist commentators include the Pakistanis Sayyid Ahmad Khan and Gulam Ahmed Parwez, the Egyptian Tawfiq Sidqi, and the Indian Muhammad Ali. Ahmad Khan argues that the statement that "Mary guarded her chastity" does not mean that she never had intercourse with any man, but "it means that she only had intercourse with her husband." He and others try to interpret the story without any supernatural element. Muhammad Ali interprets the medieval Muslim biographer of the Prophet Ibn Ishaq's saying that Jesus was formed in the womb like every other child of Adam to mean that "Jesus was conceived by a woman in the manner in which all women conceive. Then she was delivered of him as women are delivered of their children." He reaches the conclusion that Jesus was the legitimate child of Joseph and Mary, as against Jewish slanders of illegitimacy. See Geoffrey Parrinder, *Jesus in the Quran* (London: Oneworld Publications, 2013), chapter 7, "The Annunciation." In Turkey, too, a modernist/leftist exegete, İhsan Eliaçik, in his general approach of offering natural explanations for the apparent miracles in the

Qur'an, offers a self-admitted "speculation" on this matter: Mary might have had a sexual dream that might have triggered a biological reaction in her body that somehow led to her being "impregnated by herself," *Yaşayan Kur'an [The Living Qur'an]*, vol. 2 (Istanbul: İnşa Yayınları, 2007), pp. 143–144.

88. The comment is from Emir Fethi Caner and his brother Ergun Mehmet Caner. Both writers, converts from Islam and of Turkish origin, are quite critical of the Muslim faith. The quote is from their polemical book opposing Islam, *More Than a Prophet: An Insider's Response to Muslim Beliefs about Jesus and Christianity* (Grand Rapids, MI: Kregel Publications, 2003), p. 49.

89. Qur'an 5:17, Bewley translation with Arabic words anglicized.

90. In the words of biblical scholar Heikki Räisänen: "Many Western critics have accused Muhammad of inconsistency: since he rejects the divinity of Jesus, he ought not to have accepted the Virgin Birth either (or vice versa). This charge is groundless, however. Muhammad made it quite clear how the Virgin Birth, as he understood it, should be integrated into his uncompromisingly monotheistic view." "The Portrait of Jesus in the Qur'ān: Reflections of a Biblical Scholar," *The Muslim World* 70, no. 2 (April 1980): 126.

91. Eusebius Pamphilius (Eusebius of Caesarea), *Church History* 27, "The Heresy of the Ebionites," full text available at: http://biblehub.com/library/pamphilius /church_history/chapter_xxvii_the_heresy_of_the.htm/. Accessed on July 14, 2016.

92. J. Gresham Machen, *Virgin Birth of Christ* (Cambridge, UK: James Clarke, 1987), p. 21.

93. Ibid.

94. Ibid., p. 22.

95. Qur'an 5:116–118, Haleem translation.

96. Gabriel Said Reynolds points this out in his 2016 online lecture series titled "Introduction to the Quran: The Scripture of Islam." Available at https://www .my-mooc.com/en/mooc/introduction-quran-scripture-islam-notredamex -th120-2x/.

97. The verse that seems to target the doctrine of the Trinity reads: "Those who say that God is the third of three are unbelievers. There is no god but One God. If they do not stop saying what they say, a painful punishment will afflict those among them who are unbelievers" (5:73). But one curious detail here is that the word *Trinity* does not exactly suggest "God is the third of three." So there have been many discussions on this verse, on whether it presents the Trinity correctly, or whether it targets an unorthodox form of it that would be heretical for mainstream Christians as well.

98. Qur'an 9:31, Bewley translation with Arabic words anglicized.

99. The prominent Muslim exegete Ibn Kathir mentions this hadith in his *tasfeer* and specifically for this verse.

100. *Luther's Works*, vol. 47 (St. Louis, MN: Fortress Press and Concordia, 1957), pp. 45ff.
101. Robinson, *Christ in Islam and Christianity*, p. 20.
102. Epiphanius, *Panarion*, 78.23.10.
103. The suggestion is Geoffrey Ashe's; I refer to it via Michael P. Carroll, *The Cult of the Virgin Mary: Psychological Origins* (Princeton, NJ: Princeton University Press, 1992), p. 43.

CHAPTER SIX

1. Hekki Räisänen, "The Portrait of Jesus in the Qur'ān: Reflections of a Biblical Scholar," *The Muslim World* 70, no. 2 (April 1980): 129.
2. Qur'an 2:136, Bewley translation.
3. Qur'an 2:253, Haleem translation.
4. Geoffrey Parrinder, *Jesus in the Qur'an* (London: Oneworld Publications, 2013), p. 16.
5. Al-Tabari, *Jami' al-bayan*, 3:269–270, cited in Asma Afsaruddin, "The Messiah 'Isa, Son of Mary: Jesus in the Islamic Tradition," in *Nicholas of Cusa and Islam: Polemic and Dialogue in the Late Middle Ages*, ed. Ian Christopher Levy et al. (Leiden: Brill, 2014), p. 185.
6. Qur'an 3:49.
7. Qur'an 3:50–51, Bewley translation with Arabic words anglicized.
8. The occasions are 3:51, 5:72, 5:117, 19:36, and 43:64.
9. John 20:17, New International Version. Emphasis added.
10. Qur'an 43:63, Bewley translation.
11. Qur'an 2:253, Haleem translation.
12. Qur'an 17:101, Bewley translation. The Qur'an does not name these miracles one by one altogether, but they are mentioned in different verses of the Qur'an. See 7:133, 27:12, and 26:63. The full list here was given by the traditional Muslim exegete Tabari. *Encyclopaedia of the Qur'an*, vol. 3 (Leiden, the Netherlands: Brill, 2001–2006), s.v. "Moses," p. 422.
13. Qur'an 3:49, Bewley translation with Arabic words anglicized.
14. Qur'an 5:109–110, Bewley translation with Arabic words anglicized and "tribe of Israel" reworded as "Children of Israel."
15. On how Jesus' miracles have been interpreted by Muslim scholars, see: Kate Zebiri, "Contemporary Muslim Understanding of the Miracles of Jesus," *The Muslim World* 90, no. 1–2 (March 2000): 71–90.
16. Matthew 6:19.
17. One of the early scholars, Ismail ibn Abd al-Rahman Suddi, a famous *muhaddith* (transmitter of hadiths), wrote, "He [Jesus Son of Mary] used to tell the boys who were with him in school what their parents did and what they put

aside for them and what they ate. He said to a boy, 'hurry off.' 'Your family have put aside such and such for you and they are eating such and such.' So the boy hurried off and cried in front of his family until they gave him that thing. So they said, 'who informed you about this.' 'He said, 'Jesus.' That is the meaning of the saying of the Majestic and Almighty God: 'I declare to you what you eat and what you store up in your houses'" (3:49). Abū Jafar Muḥammad ibn Jarīr al-Ṭabarī, *Jami' al-Bayan 'an Ta'wil 'ay al-Qur'an*, part 3, p. 194. Quoted here from Neal Robinson, *Christ in Islam and Christianity* (Albany: State University of New York Press, 1991), p. 67.

18. For a more detailed analysis of these parallels, see Neal Robinson, "Creating Birds from Clay: A Miracle of Jesus in the Qur'ān and in Classical Muslim Exegesis," *The Muslim World* 79, no. 1 (January 1989): 1–11.

19. Razi is quoted and commented on by Robinson in "Creating Birds from Clay," p. 10.

20. Ibid., pp. 1–2.

21. Mona Siddiqui, *Christians, Muslims and Jesus* (Cornwall, UK: Yale University Press, 2013), p. 142.

22. Some have linked the birds out of clay to *Toledet Yeshu* as well, which is a medieval Jewish polemic against Christianity, or an "anti-gospel." In it, the story of Jesus making clay birds is indeed mentioned, but as a part of a very hostile interpretation of Jesus and Mary that Islam would never accept. Hence Gabriel Said Reynolds is right to note, "The Toledoth is unfailingly hostile to Mary and Jesus, portraying the former as a harlot and the latter as a sorcerer, whose power comes not from God but from his abuse of the mysterious letters of God's name. In its hostility to Mary and Jesus the text is not only anti-Christian but also anti-Islamic." Reynolds, *A Muslim Theologian in the Sectarian Milieu: 'Abd Al-Jabbār and the Critique of Christian Origins* (Leiden, the Netherlands: Brill, 2004), p. 234.

23. *Infancy Gospel of Thomas, section II, verses 1–5*, trans. M. R. James, in *The Apocryphal New Testament: Translation and Notes* (Oxford: Clarendon Press, 1924), available online at: http://gnosis.org/library/inftoma.htm. Accessed on July 14, 2016.

24. The Anglican bishop and scholar Kenneth Cragg has argued that the Qur'anic emphasis that Jesus' miracles were performed "by God's leave" is "potentially a mediating feature between the Qur'an and the New Testament," because the latter as well teaches that everything that Jesus said and did was by divine authority and leave. Cragg, *Jesus and the Muslim* (London: George Allen & Unwin, 1985), pp. 33ff.

25. There are other themes in the *Infancy Gospel of Thomas* that would sound bizarre, and unacceptable, not just to mainstream Christian but also to Muslim minds. The most notable examples are Jesus cursing a boy, who then becomes a

corpse, or Jesus cursing another boy, who falls dead and his parents become blind.

26. Andries van Aarde, "Ebionite Tendencies in the Jesus Tradition: The 'Infancy Gospel of Thomas' Interpreted from the Perspective of Ethnic Identity," *Neotestamentica* 40, no. 2 (2006).

27. Ibid., p. 362.

28. *Infancy Gospel of Thomas,* section XVI, verses 1–2.

29. Qur'an, 61:6, Bewley translation with Arabic words anglicized. This sura, or chapter, of the Qur'an is believed to be the 109th among the 114 suras of the Qur'an according to the chronology of revelation.

30. The references to Paraclete are in John 14:16; 14:26, 15:26, 16:7.

31. Geoffrey Parrinder, *Jesus in the Qur'an* (Oxford, UK: Oneworld Publications, 2003), pp. 96–98.

32. John 14:26.

33. W. Montgomery Watt, "His Name Is Ahmad," *The Muslim World* 43, no. 2 (April 1953): 110–113.

34. It is worth noting that this very dilemma weakens an Orientalist claim that the Ahmad prophecy is a "later interpolation" into the Qur'an by Muslims who wanted to praise their own prophet because it would be "difficult to understand why the name Muhammad had not been interpolated, since it was much more obvious." (It is Montgomery Watt who made this argument in "His Name Is Ahmad," p. 113. The quote here is from Geoffrey Parrinder, *Jesus in the Qur'an,* p. 98.) Yet the same dilemma is valid for the Muslim perspective as well: Since the Qur'an refers to Muhammad by name four times in other verses, why would it make Jesus refer to Ahmad, a name mentioned only in this particular verse?

35. Watt proposed this theory in "His Name Is Ahmad," p. 113.

36. The Qur'an's "Holy Spirit," which probably is a reference to Angel Gabriel, is mentioned in three different verses as an agent with which God "strengthened" Jesus: 2:87, 2:253, 5:110.

37. Qur'an 3:3, Bewley translation with Arabic words anglicized.

38. The Qur'anic term *zabur* for Psalms seems to come from the word *mizmar,* which is found in the Book of Psalms itself as *mizmor,* which refers to a single-pipe instrument resembling the oboe. Theologically, it seems to refer to the "songs" said to praise God. See: *Encyclopaedia of the Qur'an,* vol. 4, s.v. "Psalms," p. 314.

39. Qur'an 5:44, Haleem translation.

40. Qur'an 5:47, Haleem translation.

41. Tabataba'i quoted in Mahmoud, *The House of 'Imran,* vol. 2 of *The Qur'an and Its Interpreters* (Albany: State University of New York Press, 1984), pp. 140–141.

42. *Encyclopaedia of the Qur'an*, vol. 2, s.v. "Gospel," p. 342.

43. It is Epiphanius from whom we learn that Nazaraeans and Ebionites also used the *Diatessaron*. See: *Panarion* 29.9.4 and 30.3.7. *The Panarion*, trans. Frank Williams (Leiden: Brill, 1987).

44. As Claude Gilliot notes, the *Diatessaron* argument makes sense, but it is "not easy to know which Gospel text Muhammad could have been familiar with." Gilliot, "The Authorship of the Qur'an," in *The Qur'an in Its Historical Context*, ed. Gabriel Said Reynolds (London: Routledge, 2008), p. 99.

45. *Encyclopaedia of the Qur'an*, vol. 2, s.v. "Gospel," p. 341.

46. A fuller list of Q Gospel sayings would include: the certainty of the answer to prayer (ask, search, knock, for a caring Father does provide), the beatitudes, the love of enemies, turning the other cheek, giving the shirt off one's back, going the second mile, giving and expecting nothing in return, the golden rule, the tree known by its fruit, storing up treasures in heaven, freedom from anxiety like ravens and lilies, taking up one's cross, losing one's life to save it, parables of the mustard seed, the yeast, the invited dinner guests, the lost sheep, the lost coin, and the entrusted money.

47. James M. Robinson, ed., *The Sayings of Jesus: The Sayings Gospel Q in English* (Minneapolis, MN: Augsburg Books, 1979), p. 1.

48. Whether Paul has thirteen or fourteen letters in the New Testament is disputed, depending on whether the Letter to the Hebrews is considered as Paul's work or not.

49. A. H. Mathias Zahniser, *Encyclopaedia of the Qur'an*, vol. 1, s.v. "Apostle," p. 123.

50. Qur'an 3:52–53, Haleem translation.

51. Qur'an 61:14, Haleem translation.

52. Ibn Kathir makes this argument in his *tafseer*, or exegete of the Qur'an, as do some modern-day Muslim apologists. What is also interesting in Ibn Kathir's explanation for verse 61:14 is how he put the "Muslim party" among early Christians as a separate line stemming from two camps: the (Syrian) Jacobites, who believed that Jesus has one single nature, human and divine at the same time (monophysiticism), and the Nestorians, who believed that Jesus had two natures, human and divine but separate. In Ibn Kathir's words:

"They [Christians] divided into three groups. One group, Al-Ya'qubiyyah (the Jacobites), said, 'Allah remained with us as much as He willed and then ascended to heaven.' Another group, An-Nasturiyyah (the Nestorians), said, 'Allah's son remained with us as much as Allah willed and He then raised him up to heaven.' A third group said, 'Allah's servant and Messenger remained with us as much as Allah willed and then Allah raised him up to Him.' The last group was the Muslim group. The two disbelieving groups collaborated against the Muslim group and annihilated it. Islam remained unjustly concealed until Allah sent Muhammad." (Muhammad Saed Abdul-Rahman,

Tafsir Ibn Kathir, Juz' 6 (Part 6): An-Nisaa 148 to Al-Ma'idah 81 [London: MSA Publications Limited, 2009], p. 22.)

53. Qur'an 5:112–115, Bewley translation with Arabic words anglicized.

54. Michel Cuypers, *The Banquet: A Reading of the Fifth Sura of the Qur'an* (Miami, FL: Convivial Press, 2009), pp. 416–417, 419.

55. Gabriel Said Reynolds, "On the Qur'ān's Mā'ida Passage and the Wanderings of the Israelites," in *The Coming of the Comforter*, ed. B. Lourié, C. A. Segovia, and A. Bausi (Piscataway, NJ: Gorgias, 2011), p. 96.

56. Matthias Radscheit, *Encyclopaedia of the Qur'an*, vol. 5, s.v. "Table," p. 190.

57. Exodus 12:14.

58. Psalm 78:19. Gabriel Said Reynolds also points out that the word *table* here reads *ma'edd* in the Ethiopian Bible, which is remarkably similar to the *ma'ida* of the Qur'an. See: Reynolds, "On the Qur'an's Mā'ida Passage and the Wanderings of the Israelites," *The Coming of the Comforter*, ed. B. Lourié, C. A. Segovia, and A. Bausi (Piscataway, NJ: Gorgias, 2011), p. 103.

59. For both the Irenaeus quote and its interpretation, see Petri Luomanen, *Recovering Jewish-Christian Sects and Gospels* (Leiden, the Netherlands: Brill, 2012), pp. 21–22.

60. James D. Tabor, among other scholars, argues that the ceremony of bread and wine as a substitution for the body and blood of Jesus cannot be attributed to the historical Jesus and his setting. "The idea of eating the body and blood of one's god, even in a symbolic manner, fits nothing we know of Jesus or the Jewish culture from which he comes." In contrast, "in one of the magical papyri we read of a spell in which one drinks a cup of wine that has been ritually consecrated to represent the blood of the god Osiris, in order to participate in the spiritual power of love he had for his consort, Isis." Tabor, *Paul and Jesus: How the Apostle Transformed Christianity* (New York: Simon and Schuster, 2012), pp. 150–151 . It is also notable that the *Didache* 9 and 10, which is widely believed to be a Jewish Christian document, presents a ceremony of bread and wine, but includes no reference at all to them being the "body" and "blood" of the Messiah.

    A contrary argument to this view—that "eating" the body of the Messiah is alien to Judaism—was offered by Brant Pitre in a reference to a phrase in the Babylonian Talmud attributed to Rabbi Hillel that reads, "there will be no Messiah for Israel, since they have already eaten him during the reign of Hezekiah." Yet in my view this is a very vague reference and can be explained as idiomatic. See Pitre, "Jesus, the Messianic Banquet, and the Kingdom of God," *Letter & Spirit* 5 (2009): 156–157.

61. This comment on the Ebionite view of the Last Supper is from Hans Schwarz, *Christology* (Cambridge, UK: William B. Eerdmans, 1998), p. 149.

62. 1 Corinthians 15:14.

63. Qur'an 4:157–158, Haleem translation.

64. Razi also offered answers to this objection and several others he raised, but as Ayoub observes, "his answers to these objections are far less convincing than the objections themselves." Ayoub, *The House of 'Imran,* p. 177.

65. For a detailed example of this Ahmadiyya argument, see the book written by the founder of this sect, who is believed to be "the promised messiah and mahdi": Hadhrat Mirza Ghulam Ahmad, *Jesus in India: Jesus' Delivery from the Cross and Journey to India* (London: Islam International Publications, 2003). The original Urdu edition was published in 1908 in Qadian.

66. Peter Schäfer, *Jesus in the Talmud* (Princeton, NJ: Princeton University Press, 2007), p. 74.

67. The Watt quote is from W. M. Watt, *Muslim-Christian Encounters* (London: Routledge, 1991), p. 22. I owe this reference to Gabriel Said Reynolds, who quoted Watt in one of his articles, which also is a powerful argument for reconciling the Qur'an's take on the cross with the narrative of the gospels. See Reynolds, "The Muslim Jesus: Dead or Alive?," *Bulletin of SOAS* 72, no. 2 (2009): 254.

68. Qur'an 35:18 and 53:38—the exact same phrase is used in both verses. Bewley translation.

69. Patricia Crone, "Jewish Christianity and the Qur'an (Part Two)," *Journal of Near Eastern Studies* (April 2016): 8.

70. Ibid.

71. James M. Robinson, *Jesus: According to the Earliest Witness* (Philadelphia: Fortress Press, 2009), chapter 11.

72. Luomanen, *Recovering Jewish-Christian Sects and Gospels,* p. 45.

CHAPTER SEVEN

1. Seyyed Hossein Nasr, *Ideals and Realities of Islam* (Chicago: ABC International Group, 2000), p. 22. Fully available at: archive.org. Accessed on June 28, 2016.

2. James Robson, *Christ in Islâm* (London: John Murray, 1929), p. 16.

3. John Bonaventure O'Connor, "St. John Damascene," in *The Catholic Encyclopedia,* vol. 8 (New York: Robert Appleton Company, 1910).

4. The contrast here is underlined by Oddbjørn Leirvik, ed., *Images of Jesus Christ in Islam,* 2nd ed. (London: A & C Black, 2010), pp. 119–120.

5. Laurence E. Browne, *The Eclipse of Christianity in Asia* (Cambridge, UK: Cambridge University Press, 1933), pp. 110–111.

6. Daniel J. Sahas, *John of Damascus on Islam: The "Heresy of the Ishmaelites"* (Leiden, the Netherlands: Brill, 1972), p. 114. I took the second part of the quote from Sahas, which appeared to be a better translation.

7. For more on this matter, see my previous book, *Islam without Extremes: A Muslim Case for Liberty* (New York: W.W. Norton, 2011), pp. 83–92.

8. No wonder Christians who try to find a parallel between their own Logos theology and Jesus' definition as Word (*Kalima*) in the Qur'an sympathize not
with the Mu'tazila theology but with the rival Ashari school, which insisted on
the "uncreatedness" of the Qur'an. For an interesting work on this topic, see
the articles by Joseph L. Cumming, pastor of the International Church at Yale
University, "Kalām Allāh in Islam and in Christianity" (2004) and "Muslim
Theologian Abu al-Hasan al-Ash'ari's Doctrine of God, and Possible Christian
Parallels" (2014), http://www.josephcumming.com/links/index.html. Accessed
on July 4, 2016

9. Qur'an 3:39.

10. Qur'an 3:45, Haleem translation. Emphasis added.

11. Qur'an 4:171, Emphasis added. Bewley translation with Arabic words anglicized. Emphasis added.

12. Kenneth Cragg used this expression in "Islamic Theology: Limits and Bridges,"
in *The Gospel and Islam: A Compendium*, ed. Don M. McCurry (Monrovia,
CA: MARC, 1979), p. 31.

13. For example, Ibn Kathir writes, in his commentary on verse 4:171: "This incident [of the miraculous birth of Jesus] was in place of the normal conception
between man and woman that results in children. This is why 'Isa was a word
and a Ruh (spirit) created by Allah, as he had no father to conceive him. Rather,
he came to existence through the word that Allah uttered, 'Be,' and he was,
through the life that Allah sent with Jibril [Gabriel]."

14. Qur'an 3:47, Bewley translation with Arabic words anglicized.

15. Qur'an 3:59, Bewley translation.

16. Thomas J. O'Shaughnessy, *The Koranic Concept of the Word of God* (Rome:
Pontificio Istituto Biblico, 1948), pp. 45, 46, and 51.

17. The suggestion that Jesus might have spoken even in his mother's womb
comes from Qur'an 19:24, which reads: "A voice called out to [Mary] from
under her, 'Do not grieve! Your Lord has placed a small stream at your feet.'"
(Bewley translation.) The "voice" here has been often interpreted as an angel,
but it has also been interpreted as the baby Jesus who was right to be born.

18. That Jesus gave life to inanimate matter refers to the Qur'anic stories of Jesus
making a clay bird and breathing life into it, and to his raising of the dead (3:49
and 5:110).

19. Razi quoted in Mahmoud Ayoub, *The House of 'Imran*, vol. 2 of *The Qur'an
and Its Interpreters* (Albany: State University of New York Press, 1984), p. 145.

20. Ibid.

21. The admonition of Muhammad for neglecting a blind man searching for
wisdom is placed in the beginning of the Qur'anic chapter "*'Abasa*," or "He
Frowned," whose very title comes from this episode. For the sins of other
prophets in the Qur'an, there are Adam (7:23), Abraham (26:82), Moses (28:16),
Jonah (37:142), and Muhammad himself (47:19 and 48:2).

22. The Arabic term in this verse for Jesus is *ghulaaman-zakiyyan*, often translated as "a most-holy boy." The word *zakiyya*, meaning "blameless," appears only twice in the Qur'an. The other occasion is in the story about Moses in which he meets a young man who is described as being innocent (18:74). But in that case, the word only referred to the young man's innocence of any crime deserving of death. In Jesus' case, however, the angel seems to describe his whole being before he was even born.

23. Qur'an 19:31, Bewley translation.

24. *Sahih Bukhari*, vol. 4, book 54, no. 506, hadith narrated by Abu Huraira. Another version of the same hadith mentions not just Jesus but also Mary: "There is none born among the off-spring of Adam, but Satan touches it . . . except Mary and her child," vol. 4, book 55, no. 641, narrated by Said bin al-Musaiyab. However, it is possible that "Jesus, son of Mary" could have evolved into Jesus *and* Mary during transmission.

25. Ayoub, *The House of 'Imran*, p. 131.

26. Ibid., p. 133.

27. Ibid.

28. Ibid., p. 151.

29. I use the term "traditionalist Sunni" here in the sense of *Ahl al-Hadith*, the line in early Islam, best represented by Imam Hanbal, that emphasized the limits of human reason and discouraged all forms of rational philosophy. For more on this topic, see my *Islam without Extremes*, pp. 96–116. The summary of Qutb's position is from Ayoub, *The House of 'Imran*, pp. 35–36.

30. Legenhausen partly relies on the work of the twentieth-century Shiite scholar Muhammad Husayn Tabataba'i, who noted, "with regard to the Torah and the Qur'an, there are specific references in the Qur'an about how these books were revealed, being written on tablets and descending in plain Arabic language, respectively. With regard to the *Injil*, however, there is no such description." He adds to this the problem of the Qur'an referring to one "gospel," whereas the New Testament includes four "gospels." The solution he offers is that Jesus himself is the "gospel." In his words: "If the revelation given to Jesus was conveyed to his followers through his life, in word and deed, this would explain the use of the term *Injil* in the Qur'an for both the divine revelation and for the gospels used by the Christians." Hajj Muhammad Legenhausen, "Jesus as Kalimat Allah, the Word of God," at https://www.academia.edu/2516415/_Jesus _as_Kalimat_Allah_the_Word_of_God _. Accessed on February 18, 2016.

31. The view that not just the Qur'an but also the Torah (Tawrat) and the Gospel (Injil) are "uncreated" was defended by none other than Imam Ahmad Hanbal, the very founder of the "uncreated Qur'an" school. (Ibn Hanbal, *Aqida*, 302; quoted in Daniel Madigan, *The Qur'an's Self-Image: Writing and Authority in Islam's Scripture* [Princeton, NJ: Princeton University Press, 2001], p. 49.)

32. This formulation was the argument by Imam Al-Ashʿarī, the ardent defender of the "uncreated Qurʾan" school. On God's *sifat*, or "attributes," he wrote: "One should not say that they are He, nor other than He, nor not He, nor not other than He." For both this quote and a meticulous evaluation of how this view can build a bridge between Islamic and Christian theologies, see: Joseph L. Cumming, "Ṣifāt al-Dhāt in Al-Ashʿarī's Doctrine of God and Possible Christian Parallels," 2012, www.josephcumming.com. Accessed on May 14, 2016.

33. The argument that the Qurʾan accepts the divinity with its Word theology was revived in the modern era by Ibrahim Luqa, an Egyptian Coptic priest, in his 1938 work, *Al-Masihiyya fi I-Islam*, or "Christianity in Islam." The book, after its third printing in 1967, was banned by Egyptian authorities. In it Luqa persuasively argued that the Qurʾan depicts a suprahuman Messiah, but less convincing is his conclusion that this amounts to the affirmation of the Messiah's divinity. See Ivor Mark Beaumont, *Christology in Dialogue with Muslims: A Critical Analysis of Christian Presentations of Christ for Muslims from the Ninth and Twentieth Centuries* (Milton Keynes, UK: Regnum, 2005), pp. 123–125.

34. Ayoub's remark is from "The Word of God in Islam," *Greek Orthodox Theological Review* 31, nos. 1–2 (1986): 73.

35. Qurʾan 4:171–72, Bewley translation.

36. Leirvik, *Images of Jesus Christ in Islam*, pp. 89–90.

37. All quotes, along with other supportive information, are from Richard N. Longenecker, *The Christology of Early Jewish Christianity* (Naperville, IL: Alec R. Allenson, 1970), pp. 26–32.

38. The Epistle to the Hebrews has traditionally been attributed to Paul, but most scholars believe that it must be written by a later follower of Paul, a writer with an excellent command of Greek and a good knowledge of Judaism. The text seems to be a warning to fellow Christians who could "lapse" to Judaism, indicative of the Gentile-Jewish tension in the early Church. More interestingly, the author takes great pains to show why Christ, "Son of God," is superior to the angels, which can be seen as a rebuttal to an angelomorphic christology. (See: Michael Goulder, "Hebrews and the Ebionites," *New Testament Studies* 49, no. 03 [July 2003]: 393–406.) In Goulder's words, the author of the epistle does not "give seven scriptural proofs of the inferiority of angels for no good reason. The opposition against which he is writing is Jewish-Christian; and the earliest witness we have of Jewish Christians' Christology, Irenaeus, tells us that they thought Jesus was a man possessed by a heavenly power, an angel" (p. 405).

39. John Hick, "A Pluralistic View," in *Four Views on Salvation in a Pluralistic World* (Grand Rapids, MI: Zondervan Books, 2010), p. 58.

40. Mark 6:3. It is interesting that in the Gospel of Matthew, the same passage

appears slightly differently: *"Is not this the carpenter's son? Is not His mother called Mary, and His brothers, James and Joseph and Simon and Judas?"* (13:55, emphasis added). One could speculate that perhaps the expression "Son of Mary" found in the earlier Gospel of Mark got adjusted in Matthew, due to possible questions the expression could have triggered in the sense of implying an unknown biological father to Jesus.

41. Qur'an 23:91, Bewley translation.

42. Qur'an 19:88–93, Bewley translation with Arabic words anglicized.

43. David Thomas and Alexander Mallett (eds.), *Christian-Muslim Relations: A Bibliographical History, Volume 4, 1200–1350* (Leiden, the Netherlands: Brill, 2012), p. 528.

44. See Rod Cardoza, "New Paths in Muslim-Christian Dialog: Understanding Islam from the Light of Earliest Jewish Christianity," *The Muslim World* 103, no. 4 (October 2013): pp. 458–461.

45. Neal Robinson, *Christ in Islam and Christianity* (Albany: State University of New York Press, 1991), p. 48.

46. The al-Razi quote is taken indirectly from Mahmud Mustafa Ayoub, "Jesus the Son of God: A Study of the Terms Ibn and Walad in the Qur'an and the Tafsīr Tradition," in *Christian-Muslim Encounters*, ed. Y. Y. Haddad and W. Z. Haddad (Gainesville: University Press of Florida, 1995), p. 124. Besides al-Razi, the Mu'tazilite theologian Ibrahim al Nazzam (d. AH 231/AD 845), too, wrote that God might have called Jesus "Son" to indicate his spiritual adoption. He argued that this was no different from God's calling Abraham his "Friend." Robinson, *Christ in Islam and Christianity*, p. 48.

47. Razi quoted by Ayoub, "Jesus the Son of God."

48. Matthew 12:18.

49. Qur'an 43:59, Bewley translation. Only the word *slave* is replaced with *servant*, which I see as a more accurate word.

50. The Qur'anic appearances of Holy Spirit in relation to Jesus are in 2:87, 2:253, and 5:110.

51. Qur'an 16:102, Bewley translation, although Bewley prefers to translate "Holy Spirit" rather as "Purest Ruh."

52. Sidney H. Griffith, *Encyclopaedia of the Qur'an*, vol. 2 (Leiden, the Netherlands: Brill, 2001–2006), s.v. "Holy Spirit," p. 443.

53. The Razi quote is taken from Ayoub, *The House of 'Imran*, p. 177.

54. Qur'an 4:171, Bewley translation with Arabic words anglicized.

55. Qur'an 5:73, Bewley translation with Arabic words anglicized.

56. David Thomas, *Encyclopaedia of the Qur'an*, vol. 3, s.v. "Trinity," p. 369.

57. Qur'an 112:1. This is the first verse of the short chapter "Al-Ikhlas," or "Sincerity," which is often recited during daily prayers.

58. Kaufmann Kohler and Samuel Krauss, "Trinity," *Jewish Encyclopedia*, vol. 12 (New York: Funk and Wagnalls, 1906), p. 260.

59. The *Clementine Homilies*, homily 16, chapter 15, "Christ Not God, But the Son of God," in Philip Schaff (ed.), *Ante-Nicene Fathers: The Twelve Patriarchs, Excerpts and Epistles, the Clementia, Apocrypha, Decretals, Memoirs of Edessa and Syriac Documents, Remains of the First Age* (Grand Rapids, Ml: Christian Classics Ethereal Library, 1885), p. 1121. Fully available at: https://archive.org.

60. The claims seems to have been made by Gregory of Nyssa, a defender of the Orthodox trinitarian position against Arianism and other "heresies." See Michael Cover, *Lifting the Veil: 2 Corinthians 3:7–18 in Light of Jewish Homiletic and Commentary Traditions* (Berlin: Walter de Gruyter, 2015), p. 300.

61. See Maurice Wiles, *Archetypal Heresy: Arianism through the Centuries* (Oxford: Clarendon Press, 1996).

62. Jaume de Marcos Andreu, "Servet and Islam," p. 14, available at: https://www.academia.edu/8730845/Michael_Servetus_and_Islam. Accessed on March 21, 2016.

63. Carter Lindberg, *The European Reformations*, 2nd ed. (Malden, MA: John Wiley, 2010), p. 254.

64. Michael Servetus, *De Trinitatis Erroribus*, 43a. Quoted in Peter Hughes, "Servetus and Islam: In His Life," in *Servetus: Our 16th Century Contemporary* (Boston: International Association for Religious Freedom, 2011), p. 12.

65. Peter Hughes, "Servetus and Islam: In His Life," p. 11.

66. Servetus, *De Trinitatis Erroribus*.

67. Jaume de Marcos Andreu, "Servetus and Islam: In His Writings," in *Servetus: Our 16th Century Contemporary* (Boston: International Association for Religious Freedom, 2011), p. 25.

68. Martin Mulsow, "Socinianism, Islam, and the Radical Uses of Arabic Scholarship," *Al-Qantara: Revista de Estudios Árabes* 31, no. 2 (July–December 2010): 557.

69. Hugh Pope, "Socinianism," *The Catholic Encyclopedia*, vol. 14 (New York: Robert Appleton Company, 1912), www.newadvent.org/cathen/14113a.htm. Accessed on May 25, 2016.

70. Mulsow, "Socinianism, Islam, and the Radical Uses of Arabic Scholarship," p. 557.

71. Nicholas Terpstra, *Religious Refugees in the Early Modern World: An Alternative History of the Reformation* (Cambridge, UK: Cambridge University Press, 2015), pp. 154–156.

72. Ibid., p. 559.

73. Denise Spellberg, *Thomas Jefferson's Qur'an: Islam and the Founders* (New York: Alfred A. Knopf, 2013), p. 80.

74. Ibid. For the influence of Islam on Enlightenment thinkers, also see: Ziad Elmarsafy, *The Enlightenment Qur'an: The Politics of Translation and the Construction of Islam* (Oxford, UK: Oneworld Publications, 2009).

75. Stubbe's book is freely available today on archive.org. For a good evaluation of the book, along with other important contemporary views on Islam, see Humberto Garcia, *Islam and the English Enlightenment, 1670–1840* (Baltimore, MD: Johns Hopkins University Press, 2012), pp. 5–9, 30–59.

76. Garcia, *Islam and the English Enlightenment, 1670–1840*, p. 160.

77. Ibid., pp. 159–161.

78. Ibid., pp. 166–167.

79. Although some prominent early Seventh-Day Adventists are known to be "Arian," the church later moved to accept a trinitarian theology. See Elmer Wiebe, *Who Is the Adventist Jesus?* (Maitland, FL: Xulon Press, 2005), pp. 141–143. In fact, "Until near the turn of the twentieth century, Seventh-day Adventist literature was almost unanimous in opposing the eternal deity of Jesus and the personhood of the Holy Spirit." (Merlin D. Burt, "History of Seventh-day Adventist Views on the Trinity," *Journal of the Adventist Theological Society* 17, no. 1 [Spring 2006]: 126). Personal thanks to Jerald Whitehouse for pointing out this diversity of opinion within the Seventh-Day Adventist Church on the Trinity.

80. George Wilkins, *The Trial of the Unitarians, For a Libel on the Christian Religion* (London: Printed for Longman, Rees, Orme, Brown, and Green, 1830), p. 3. The book is fully available at: https://archive.org/details/trialofunitarian-00wilk, thanks to the digitizing sponsorship of Princeton Theological Seminary Library. Accessed on July 14, 2016.

81. Ibid., p. 3.

82. Ibid., pp. 3–4.

CHAPTER EIGHT

1. Hadith narrated in Al-Qurtubi, *Al-Tadhkira fi Ahwal al-Mawta wa al-Akhira* ["The Reminder of the Situations of the Dead and the Afterlife"], 2 vols. (Beirut: Dar al-Kutub al-'Ilmiyya, 1985), p. 774. Quoted here from Zeki Sarıtoprak, *Islam's Jesus* (Gainesville: University Press of Florida, 2014), p. 157.

2. Qur'an 84:1–6, Haleem translation.

3. Qur'an 36:52, Bewley translation.

4. "The World's Muslims: Unity and Diversity," Pew Research Center, 2012, p. 66. The full text available at: http://www.pewforum.org/files/2012/08/the-worlds-muslims-full-report.pdf. Accessed on May 30, 2016.

5. Qur'an 4:157, 158.

6. Qur'an 3:55, author's translation.

7. According to the thirteenth-century Persian exegete of the Qur'an, al-Baidawi, "I will take you your death" could have five different meanings: "Achieve the whole of thy term and tarry till thy appointed end," or "take thee from the earth," or "take thee to myself sleeping," or "destroy in thee the lusts which

hinder ascent to the world of spirits," or "some say that God let him die for seven hours and then raised him to heaven." Geoffrey Parrinder, *Jesus in the Qur'an* (London: Oneworld Publications, 2013), chapter 11.

8. The Qur'an verse taken as evidence of Jesus' being alive with the angels is the one we referred to while suggesting an "angelomorphic Christology." It reads: "The Messiah would never disdain to be a servant to God nor would the angels near to Him," Qur'an 4:171–172, Bewley translation. Zeki Sarıtoprak sums up the traditional Islamic view on this as follows: "It is believed that Jesus ascended to the realm of angels in heaven, or *sama'*, the Arabic word for heaven. Sama' in classical Islamic theology is understood as the location in the physical realm to which Jesus ascended. However, it can be understood as a part of the unseen world, as indicated in the story of the Prophet's ascension, the *Mi'raj*. The majority of Qur'anic commentators believe that Jesus ascended bodily and spiritually and that the body of Jesus had an angelic quality. If this is the case, the dimension in which Jesus lives is different than the dimension in which human beings live. Therefore, he does not need food or drink to survive, similar to angels, who are, according to Islamic theology, creatures of God made of light and do not need to eat and drink; praising God is their sustenance." Sarıtoprak, *Islam's Jesus*, p. 20.

9. Qur'an 19:33, Bewley translation.

10. Qur'an 43:61. Traditional authorities such as al-Zamakhshari (d. 1144), al-Razi (d. 1209), and al-Suyuti (d. 1505) are all of the opinion that this verse is a textual proof for the eschatological descent of Jesus. See Sarıtoprak, *Islam's Jesus*, p. 29.

11. Qur'an 4:159, Bewley translation.

12. This story about al-Hajjaj is narrated in *Tafsir al-Qummi*, an exegesis of the Qur'an by Ali Ibn Ibrahim Qomi, a tenth-century Shiite scholar. The quotation here is taken from Neal Robinson, *Christ in Islam and Christianity* (Albany: State University of New York Press, 1991), pp. 168–169, with the adaptation of "him" into "them."

13. Ibid.

14. Hadith narrated by Abu Huraira, *Sahih Bukhari*, vol. 3, book 34, no. 425.

15. With minor variations, this hadith is repeated in *Sahih Bukhari*, vol. 3, book 34, no. 425; *Sahih Bukhari*, vol. 4, book 55, no. 652; and *Sunan Abu Dawud*, book 37, no. 4310.

16. Hadith in *Sunan Abu Dawud*, book 37, no. 4310.

17. Muslim bin al-Hajjaj, "Al-Fitan," in *Al-Sahih Muslim* 110; taken here from Sarıtoprak, *Islam's Jesus*, p. 68.

18. R. Hillenbrand, *Encyclopaedia of Islam*, vol. 6 (Leiden, the Netherlands: Brill, 2001–2006), s.v. "Manara," p. 362.

19. This sermon is available on YouTube at https://www.youtube.com/watch?v =0LuywigIstE. Accessed on May 28, 2016. Also see Michael Crowley, "Khorasan:

Behind the Mysterious Name of the Newest Terrorist Threat," *Time*, September 25, 2014.

20. "Isis Believes Jesus Will Come to Their Aid; Journalist," Infowars.com, February 19, 2015; summary of Graeme Wood's comments on CNN. Also see the longer article by Graeme Wood in *Atlantic*, "What ISIS Really Wants" (March 2015).

21. A few of the most extreme crimes of ISIS have been condemned even by al-Qaeda. See "Even al-Qaeda Condemn Murder of Jordanian Pilot as 'Deviant,'" *Daily Mail*, February 4, 2015. Also see "Hamas, Islamic Jihad Condemn Paris Attacks," *Times of Israel*, November 14, 2015.

22. See Sarıtoprak, *Islam's Jesus*, p. 115.

23. Ibid., p. 117.

24. Ibid.

25. Ibid.

26. Ibid., p. 118.

27. Ibid., p. 119.

28. Ibid., p. 120.

29. Said Nursi, *Şualar* (Istanbul: Yeni Asya Neşriyat, 1994), pp. 467 and 512.

30. Thomas Banchoff, *Religious Pluralism, Globalization, and World Politics* (Oxford, UK: Oxford University Press, 2008), pp. 235–236. Also see Thomas Michel, "Muslim-Christian Dialogue and Cooperation in the Thought of Bediuzzaman Said Nursi," *Muslim World* 89, nos. 3–4 (October 1999): 325–335.

31. "Nostra Aetate: Declaration on the Relation of the Church to Non-Christian Religions," Proclaimed by his Holiness Pope Paul VI, October 28, 1965, http://www.vatican.va/archive/hist_councils/ii_vatican_council/documents/vat-ii_decl_19651028_nostra-aetate_en.html

CHAPTER NINE

1. This is a part of verse 57:16, as translated by Abdullah Yusufali.

2. Youssef M. Abraham, "Outside View: Muddy Boots in the Mosque," United Press International, November 18, 2004.

3. Arnold J. Toynbee, *Civilization on Trial* (Oxford, UK: Oxford University Press, 1948), p. 187. All quotes are from the same chapter in this book, "Islam, the West, and the Future."

4. Ibid., p. 188.

5. Ibid., pp. 192, 194.

6. Ibid., p. 199.

7. Ibid., p. 201.

8. Ibid., p. 200.

9. Ibid., p. 210.

10. Ibid., p. 189.

11. Or sometimes the pharaoh is equated with the contemporary "world system." As a case in point, Muslim writer Aisha Stacey argues: "Egypt at the time was the known world's superpower. The ultimate power rested in the hands of very few. Pharaoh and his trusted ministers directed matters as if lives of the population were of little or no consequence. The political situation was in some ways similar to the political world of the 21st century. In a time when the young people of the world are used as cannon fodder for the political and military games of the most powerful, the story of Moses is particularly pertinent." Stacey, "The Story of Moses" (part 1 of 12), IslamReligion.com, May 12, 2013. Accessed on June 2, 2016.

12. In the words of Seyyed Hossein Nasr, "Centuries of confrontation with the Christian West followed by a period of intense missionary activity, which still continues in certain regions of the Islamic world in new forms, have created among some contemporary Muslims an aversion not only to Christianity but, in the case of some of the modernised classes, even to the Islamic conception of Christ and Mary." Nasr, in *Images of Jesus Christ in Islam*, 2nd ed., ed. Oddbjørn Leirvik (London: A. and C. Black, 2010), pp. 2–3.

13. For Job in the Qur'an, see 38:41–44. For Elijah, see 6:85, 37:123 and 130. For Elisha and Ezekiel, see 38:48.

14. Qur'an 10:94.

15. Hidayet Aydar, "Isra'iliyat as an Intercultural Knowledge Bridge and Reflections on the Ottoman Folk Culture," *Journal of Academic Social Science Studies* 6, no. 8 (October 2013): 98.

16. John C. Reeves, ed., *Bible and Quran: Essays in Scriptural Intertextuality* (Boston: Brill, 2004), p. 160.

17. See Simon A. Wood, *Christian Criticisms, Islamic Proofs: Rashid Rida's Modernist Defence of Islam* (London: Oneworld Publications, 2012), pp. 13–14.

18. Muhammad Abduh, *Tafsir al-Manar*, vol. 3 (Cairo: Dar-al Manar, 1954), p. 343. Quoted in Chawkat Georges Moucarry, *Faith to Faith: Christianity & Islam in Dialogue* (Leicester, UK: Inter-Varsity, 2001), p. 65.

19. This paraphrase of al-Aqqad's view on Jesus comes from F. Peter Ford, " 'Abbas Mahmud al-'Aqqad's *The Genius of Christ*: An Innovative Muslim Approach to Jesus," in *Jesus in Twentieth-Century Literature, Art, and Movies*, ed. Paul C. Burns (New York: Continuum, 2007), pp. 189–190.

20. The comment on Abduh, that he envisioned "a Jesus-centered renewal of Islamic law and Muslims' behaviors," comes from Sarıtoprak, *Islam's Jesus*, p. 117.

21. Luke 17:21. This translation is from the King James Bible. The phrase "within you" has been translated in more modern versions such as the New International Version or the New American Standard Bible as "in your midst." I used the King James version because it has been quite powerful in establishing the Western Christian understanding of a spiritual kingdom.

22. This is from a commentary on Luke 21 by Joseph Benson, *Commentary of the*

Old and New Testaments (New York: T. Carlton & J. Porter, 1857). Fully available on http://biblehub.com.

23. John 19:15.

24. "The Re-establishment of the Khilafah Is an Obligation upon All Muslims," editorial, www.khilafah.com, June 24, 2007. This website advocates the views of Hizb ut-Tahrir, "a political party whose ideology is Islam."

25. For a good evaluation of the Caliphate and other political concepts in Islam and the discussions about them, see Asma Afsaruddin, *Contemporary Issues in Islam* (Edinburgh: Edinburgh University Press, 2015), pp. 54–85.

26. The only Qur'anic verse that seems to use the title "caliph" for the leadership of a human being rather than humanity as a whole is 38:26, which speaks to (King) David, and says: "O David! We did indeed make thee a vicegerent on earth: so judge thou between men in truth." Yet there is common agreement among the modern commentators and translators that this verse concerns David alone and that "the Qur'an does not give clear guidance on the position of the Caliph as the supreme leader of the ummah." Sean Oliver-Dee, *The Caliphate Question: The British Government and Islamic Governance* (Lanham, UK: Lexington Books, 2009), p. 16.

27. Qur'an 2:30–33, Bewley translation with Arabic words anglicized.

28. Qur'an 6:165, Bewley translation with Arabic words anglicized.

29. Qur'an 35:39, Bewley translation with Arabic words anglicized.

30. "During the Umayyad period, the exegetes made no connection between the Qur'anic term khalifa and the politico-religious reality of the institution of the caliphate. This tendency began to change about the middle of the second/eighth century when a more comprehensive interpretation started to appear." It was scholars such as Tabari who "created a complete merger between the Qur'anic khalifa and the head of the Islamic caliphate." Wadad Kadi, *Encyclopaedia of the Qur'an* vol. 1 (Leiden, the Netherlands: Brill, 2001–2006), s.v. "Caliph," pp. 277–278.

31. Luke 20:46–47.

32. Luke 18:9–14.

33. John 8:7.

34. Mark 2:27.

35. This horrible pattern has been reported in various instances in Nigeria, Somalia, and Afganistan, especially under the rule of extremist groups such as al-Shabab or the Taliban, or extrajudicially in the tribal areas of Pakistan. For an overview of such incidents, see Justice for Iran, "Mapping Stoning in Muslim Contexts," February 2012, http://www.wluml.org/sites/wluml.org/files/Mapping%20Stoning%20in%20Muslim%20Contexts_Final.pdf.

36. Qur'an 24:4, Bewley translation.

37. Matthew 23:23–24.

38. Al-Shatibi, *Kitab al-Muwafaqat*, I, 5, line 14. Quoted here from Fazlurrahman, *Islam* (Chicago: University of Chicago Press, 1966), p. 115.

39. Andreas Gotzmann and Christian Wiese, *Modern Judaism and Historical Consciousness: Identities, Encounters, Perspectives* (Leiden, the Netherlands: Brill, 2007), pp. 17–18.

40. Ibid., p. 18.

41. Matthew B. Hoffman, *From Rebel to Rabbi: Reclaiming Jesus and the Making of Modern Jewish Culture* (Stanford, CA: Stanford University Press, 2007), p. 15.

42. Taken from the translation in *Images of Jesus Christ in Islam*, p. 197.

INDEX